THE BOOK OF THE ·22

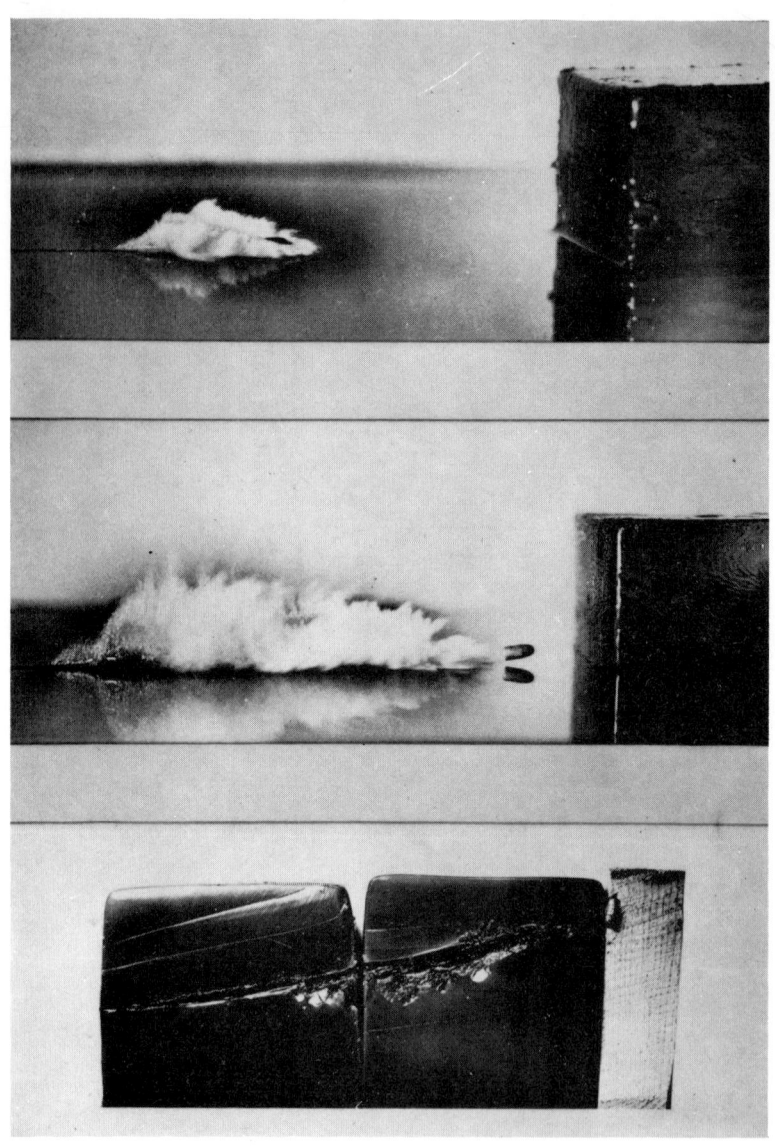

Ricochet from ·22 Long rifle

The Book of the ·22

by
RICHARD ARNOLD

With 64 pages of plates and many textual illustrations

KAYE & WARD
LONDON

First published by
Nicholas Kaye Ltd
1962

Revised edition published by
Kaye & Ward Ltd
1972

Copyright © 1962 Nicholas Kaye Ltd
Revised edition Copyright © 1972 Kaye & Ward Ltd

All Rights Reserved. No part of this publication may be reproduced, stored in a retrieval system, or transmitted, in any form or by any means, electronic, mechanical, photocopying, recording or otherwise, without the prior permission of the Copyright owner.

ISBN 0 7182 0911 7

All enquiries and requests relevant to this title should be sent to the publisher. Kaye & Ward Ltd, 21 New Street, London EC2M 4NT, and not to the printer.

Printed in England by
Fletcher & Son Ltd, Norwich

TO
TRUDY AND DAVID

BY THE SAME AUTHOR

Automatic and Repeating Shotguns
The Shooter's Handbook (revised edition)
Modern Sea Angling
The Complete Sea Angler

AUTHOR'S NOTE

The advent of metrication in this country has meant the disappearance of a lot of our heritage in terms of measurement. I do not know what the future of the ·22 calibre firearm is going to be—are we going to have to substitute a metric dimension? I hope not. The ·22 stands in a unique position; whether known as the 'point two-two', 'two-twenty' or 'point twenty-two', it is probably the best-loved of all rifle calibres. Thank heaven the Western World has not gone metric, and the ·22 will carry on as before. As for myself, though I have accepted metrication and indeed have endeavoured in my recent edition of *The Shooter's Handbook* to cater for the transition period, I am determined not to call the ·22 by any other name—Shakespeare and his rose be damned!

Saint Ives, RICHARD ARNOLD
Huntingdonshire

ACKNOWLEDGMENTS

The author desires to express his thanks to the following for their very kind co-operation in the provision of information and permission to reproduce material and illustrations:

Colt's Patent Fire Arm Manufacturing Co.; Dardick Corporation; Ithaca Gun Co.; Marlin Firearms Co.; O. F. Mossberg and Sons, Inc.; Noble Manufacturing Co. Inc.; Remington Arms Co.; Savage Arms Corporation; Smith & Wesson Inc.; Sturm, Ruger & Co.; Winchester Repeating Arms Co.; Williams Gun Sight Co.; Maynard P. Buehler Inc.; Lyman Gun Sight Co.; and W. R. Weaver Co., all of the United States of America. To Valmet Oy, of Finland; to Waffenfabrik Husqvarna of Sweden; to The Trade Delegation of the U.S.S.R. in Great Britain for their kind co-operation in allowing me to inspect and handle their weapons as well as provision of technical information; to The Metals Division of Imperial Chemical Industries Ltd, and to Webley & Scott Ltd of Great Britain; to Messrs. Le Personne & Co. Ltd., London; Salter and Varge Ltd., London; Parker-Hale Ltd., Birmingham; and finally to Messrs Thomas Bland & Son (Gunmakers) Ltd, of London, W.C.1 and in particular Mr W. Caseley, their managing director, for his invaluable assistance and co-operation.

CONTENTS

Author's Note		7
Acknowledgments		8
List of Illustrations		11
List of Tables		17
CHAPTER 1	Historical Outline	23
2	Modern Developments	46
3	Types of ·22 Rifle	71
4	The Shooting Positions	79
5	The ·22 Pistol	110
6	Of Groups and Grouping	129
7	Sights	142
8	Target Shooting	176
9	Sporting Shooting	197
10	Ammunition	209
11	Firearms Certificates	225
12	Air Rifles and Pistols	246
INDEX:		253

ILLUSTRATIONS

Plates

    Ricochet from ·22 Long rifle   *frontispiece*

I The Finnish 'Lion' and Finnish 'Lion Junior' match rifle and precision target rifle

II Remington bolt-action rifle, 'Matchmaster' rifle and Mossberg rifle

III Remington 'Rangemaster' and Winchester 'Olympic'

IV Dardick 'Tround' ammunition, pistol and the Dardick action feed

V Dardick rifle pistol, shown ready for action and showing the magazine and 'Tround' ammunition

VI The Marlin Model 100 (American single-shot), Stevens Model 15Y and Remington Model 514

VII Remington 'Targetmaster', the 'Coltsman' and Mossberg Model 320K

VIII 'Coltsman' with Colt telescope sight, the 'Colteer' and the Valmet 'Era'

IX Marlin Model 81-DL, Model 81C and Savage Model 5

X Marlin Model 81-DL, Stevens Model 86 and Remington 'Sportsmaster' 512A

XI Mossberg Model 346A, Marlin Model 81C and the 'Scoremaster' Remington

XII Mossberg 340B, 342K, and 340K

XIII Mossberg ·22 WRF Magnum, the Husqvarna box magazine Model 1622 and Marlin Model 80C

XIV Marlin Model 101, 80DL and 346B

XV De luxe Mossberg 'Chucksters'

XVI Stevens Model 15, Savage Model 340 and Stevens Model 84

XVII Marlin Model 80-C, Savage Model 110, and Savage Model 4 de luxe

XVIII Marlin Model 80 DL, Models 80 DL and 101 with 'scope sights

XIX A study in penetration

XX Wood penetration

XXI	A ·22 bullet approaches a flat stone surface, strikes it and ricochets
XXII	Impact on simulated human or animal tissue, with ·22 L.R. solid and hollow-point bullets, with a ·22 Magnum and with a ·22 Hornet
XXIII	A ·22 bullet passing through a plank; hitting a can of beer
XXIV	A ·22 bullet passing through an electric light bulb and through a block of wood
XXV	Remington 'Fieldmaster' Model 572, lightweight model and Savage Survival Gun
XXVI	Savage Model 29, Model 21, and Marlin semi-automatic Model 99
XXVII	Marlin 'Super Automatic' Model 98, with Micro-Vue $4 \times$ 'scope and Savage Model 6 de luxe
XXVIII	Stevens Model 87, Remington Nylon 66 ·22 autoloader and Remington 'Speedmaster'
XXIX	Remington 550, Ithaca X-5 and Ithaca clip magazine ·22 repeater
XXX	Action of Ithaca auto-loader, Mossberg auto-loader 350K and 351K
XXXI	Mossberg 352K, Marlin 89-C, Stevens 85-K and Marlin 89-C
XXXII	Mossberg 400 with iron sights, and exposed action view, action closed and with Mossberg 4M4 ($4 \times$)
XXXIII	Marlin ·22 Magnum Model 57-M, 'Levermatic' Model 57 and 'Golden 39-A'
XXXIV	Marlin 'Golden 39-A Mountie', Model 56-L with $4 \times$ 'scope, 39-A' 'Mountie' and 'Golden 39-A'
XXXV	Webley and Scott ·22 single-shot pistol, ·22 target revolver and Savage Model 101 single-shot pistol
XXXVI	Ruger 'Bearcat' Model BC-4, 'Single Six' and Colt 'Frontier Scout'
XXXVII	Smith & Wesson 'Airweight', ·22 'Combat Masterpiece', 1953 Model 22/32 target
XXXVIII	Ruger (RST-4), Mark I ·22 L.R. target pistol, Standard automatic and Colt 'Huntsman' ·22 L.R.

ILLUSTRATIONS

XXXIX Colt 'Woodsman' short and long barrel, ·22 L.R. 'Match Target', Smith & Wesson Match model
XL Smith & Wesson ·22 Match pistol with recoil reducer, 4 × Weaverscope, 4 × Weaverscope on Buehler pistol mounts and Marlin Micro-Vue 4 × telescope sight
XLI Mossberg Model 4M4, Coltmaster 2·5 × telescope sight, Mossberg 2M4 and Coltmaster Junior 4 × 'scope sight
XLII Lead alloy wire for rim-fire bullets, extruded in hydraulic press, is fed into the bullet-making machine
XLIII ICI rolls its own brass for the cartridge case. Priming
XLIV Putting the 'fire' into the 'rim'
XLV The primed cases passing to the loading machine and cases and bullets meet in the bulleting machine
XLVI The canneluring machine makes final adjustments and final inspection
XLVII Measuring the bullet's velocity and every batch being tested
XLVIII B.S.A. Supersport rifle and German Walther
XLIX German Walther in ·22 Hornet calibre and BRNO Czech bolt action
L German 'Krico' and Finnish 'Sako'
LI Austrian 'Tyrol'
LII Browning self-loader Model 'B' and Browning slide-action repeater
LIII Mossberg 'Targo' spring-trap IA; base plate and aluminium, pistol-shaped frame
LIV Mossberg 'Targo' shotguns—Model 320 TR, single-shot, and Model 340 TR, 7-shot
LV Walther KKM 'Matchmaster' ·22 L.R. target rifle
LVI B.S.A. 'Century' and 'International' target rifles
LVII B.S.A. Martini action
LVIII F.N. Mauser sporting rifle—·22 Swift calibre; and B.S.A. short-action, centre-fire ·22 rifle
LIX Action of B.S.A. 'Majestic' rifle
LX Parker-Hale 'International' sight and Model 16 aperture sight

LXI   Parker-Hale 'Sportarget' receiver sight and Model 16E
LXII Parker-Hale 18 'Neta' peepsight and 'Quickloader'
LXIII Hammerli 'Olympia' target pistol, Hi-Standard 'Duramatic' field pistol and 'Supermatic Tournament' 10-shot autoloader
LXIV Hi-Standard 'Double Nine' ·22 revolver and snub-barrel 'Sentinel' revolver; Iver Johnson 'Trailsman 66' ·22 revolver

ILLUSTRATIONS

Line Drawings — *Page*

1. *LYMAN* 'All-American' 2·5 × telescope sight; the 4 × model; the 6 × model; the 10 × model; the 'Super Targetspot' high magnification model . 143
2. *LYMAN* 3-point mount for 'Super-Targetspot'; sunshade; 'All-American Tru-Lock' telescope sight mounts 145
3. Telescope sights—'Ajack' 2·5 × 70; 4 × 90; 'Ruediger' 2·5 ×; Nickel 'Supralyte' 2·5 × 52; Nickel 'Supra E' 4 × 81 147
4. *WILLIAMS* 'On the Range' telescope sight mounts . 149
5. *WILLIAMS* mount rings for telescope sights . . 151
6. *WILLIAMS* 'Quick-Convertible' telescope sight mounts; side mount with 'Foolproof' receiver sight on Remington 'Gamemaster'; 'Ace-in-the-Hole' peepsight 153
7. *LYMAN* Model 57 receiver sight; model 66 . . 155
8. *LYMAN* Tang sights 1a and 2a; model 55 receiver sight; model 53; model 48 159
9. *LYMAN* front and middle sights . . . 161
10. *REDFIELD SERIES*: 70 receiver sight; 102 hunting sight; ramp 173

LIST OF TABLES

		Page
1	Sporting Telescope Sights (U.S.A.)	157
2	Target Telescope Sights (U.S.A.)	158
3	Ballistics of ·22 Magnum Rim-fire Cartridge for 24-inch barrels	216
4	Average Ballistics of British (I.C.I.) ·22 Rim-fire Ammunition—I: Short and Medium Ranges; II: Long Ranges	220
5	Drop in Inches—British Rim-fire ·22 Ammunition	221
6	Average Ballistics of Winchester ·22 Rim-fire Ammunition	221
7	Average Ballistics of Winchester and Western Super Speed and Super X ·22 Centre-fire Ammunition	221
8	Mid-range Trajectory (Average) Winchester and Western ·22 Centre-fire Ammunition	222
9	Average Ballistics of Remington Rim-fire ·22 Ammunition	222
10	Average Ballistics of Remington Centre-fire ·22 Ammunition	223
11	Average Mid-range Trajectory of Remington Centre-fire ·22 Rifle Ammunition	223
12	Average Ballistics of Giulio Fiocchi (Italian) ·22 Rim-fire Ammunition	224
13	Average Ballistics of Norma Centre-fire ·22 Ammunition	224

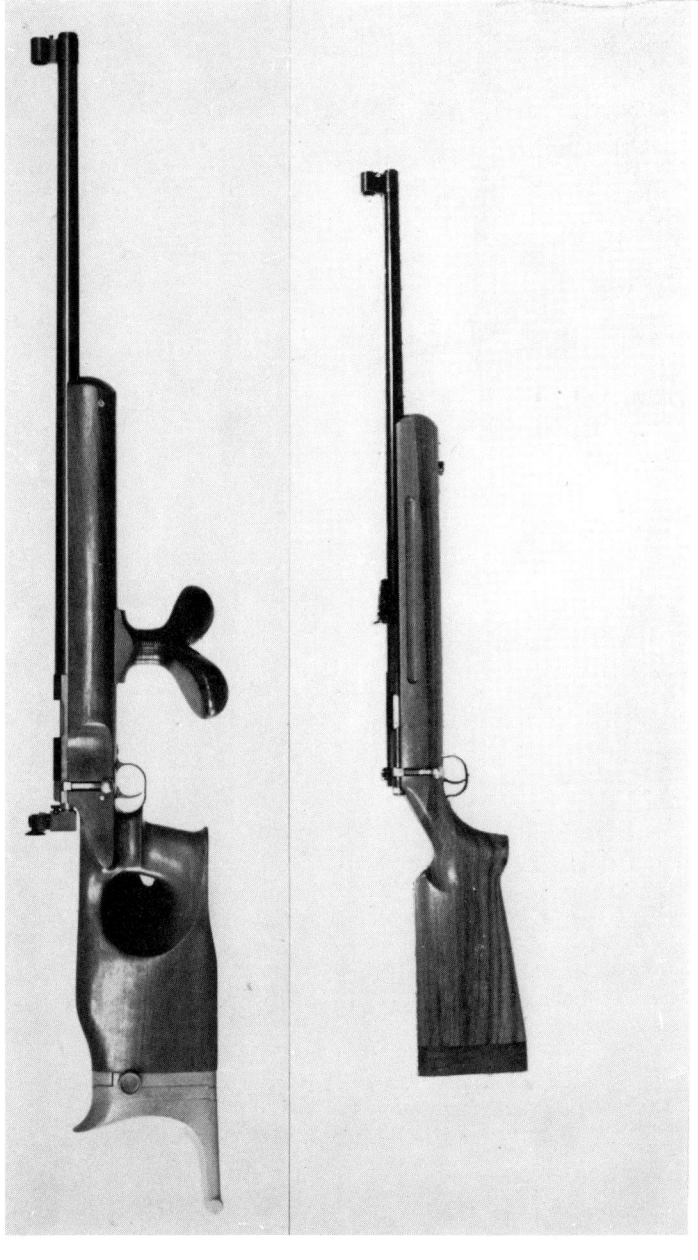

PLATE I

Top—A typical European 'Match' rifle, the Finnish 'Lion'. *Bottom*—The Finnish 'Lion Junior', precision target rifle

PLATE II

Top—Remington bolt-action target rifle, Model 521T. *Centre*—Remington 'Matchmaster' target rifle, Model 513T. *Bottom*—Mossberg

PLATE III

Top—Remington Model 40X 'Rangemaster' target rifle. *Bottom*—The famous Winchester free match rifle, the 'Olympic'

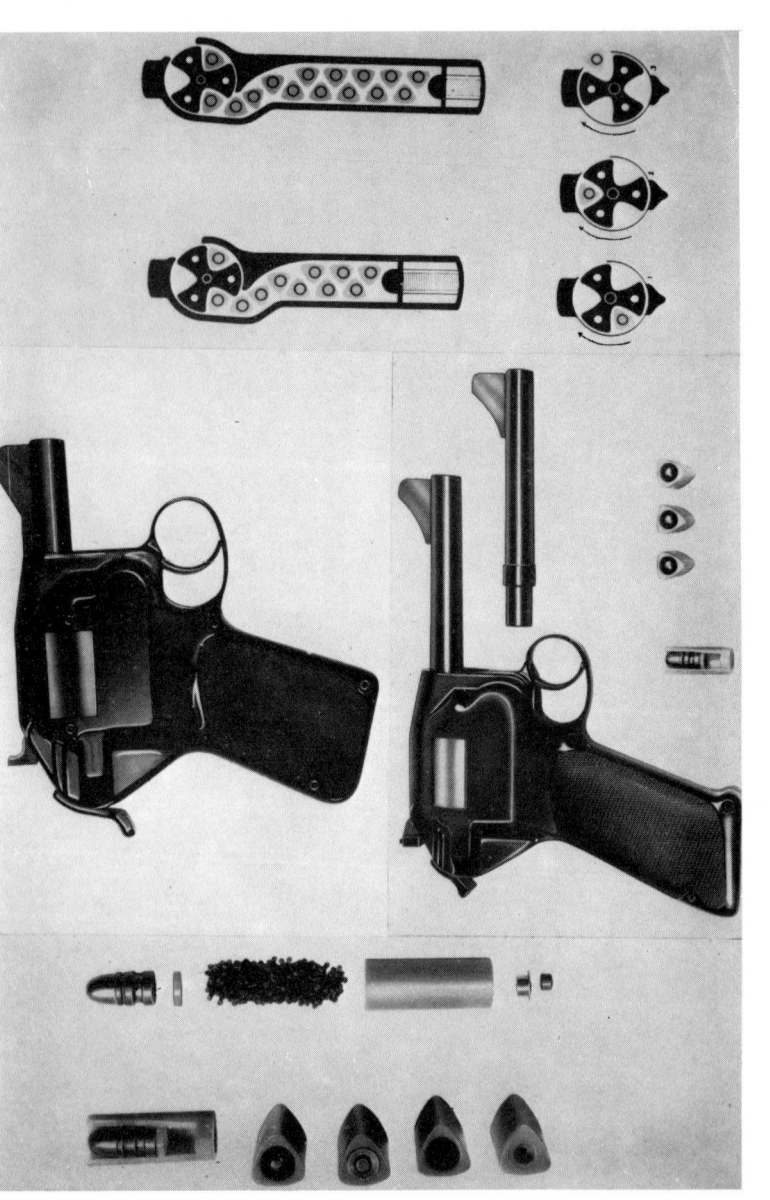

PLATE IV

Left—Dardick 'Tround' ammunition. *Top centre*—The Dardick pistol. *Bottom centre*—The amazing Dardick pistol with interchangeable barrels: this photograph shows the 'Tround' ammunition. *Right*—Showing how the Dardick action

CHAPTER ONE

HISTORICAL OUTLINE

PROBABLY the most popular calibre of all small arms in the world today, certainly the most important from the standpoint of initial training in the use of rifled weapons, the ·22 inch has a fascinating history.

The backwoods of the North American Continent, the rowdy, garish bars and brothels of the mid-nineteenth century Wild West, the mountains of the Tyrol, and the glittering, cultured salons of an eclectic European Society of the same period, have all played an important part in the development of this popular arm. Inevitably, the cartridge proved to be the most important unit in this story, and it is the story of the development of the ·22 cartridge, rather than the weapon itself, which is so fascinating.

From a tiny BB cap, the cartridge developed into two main divisions: the rim-fire and the centre-fire. Of the two, the rim-fire is the true ·22-calibre cartridge, as the centre-fire is, strictly speaking, a large-calibre cartridge which has been 'necked down' to take a ·22-calibre bullet.

But though the story of the ·22 begins with the development of the rim-fire cartridge, to obtain a clear picture of its origins we have to take a look back into the history of firearms.

From the very beginning, firearms, whether military or sporting, were large in calibre. Even the development of new methods of ignition, wheel-lock, snap-haunce, flint-lock, and percussion, did not bring about any noticeable reduction in the calibre or bore of the weapon. Handguns of 20-bore and over were the usual size, while military weapons up to 8-bore were not uncommon. This can readily be appreciated as necessary when one considers the conditions under which the weapons were used. First, the propellent, gunpowder—or as we now call it, 'black powder'—was fairly crude and not very powerful. Secondly, military weapons were not equipped with proper sights, and were used for mass volleys, aimed in the general direction of an enemy so that accuracy was not over-important. Thirdly, the fouling of the barrels when black powder was used caused further inaccuracies. Fourthly, a heavy ball was necessary to deal with an enemy who might well be wearing some form of armour or padded, leathern jacket.

In the sporting world, however, more attention was devoted to achieving accuracy, and this, in turn, meant improvements in sighting and loading.

The early stages of development of firearms follow a fairly regular pattern. A new idea was brought out and adopted by the sportsman first; the military heads, in all countries, invariably held on to obsolete pieces as long as possible. Thus it was that the sportsman, or hunter, really originated the small-bore rifle.

Hunters in the Tyrol in the early eighteenth century used small-calibre weapons. These small-calibres would seem large bores to modern eyes, but, in comparison with the 10-bore and 12-bore weapons commonly in use, rifles and smooth-bores firing balls of twenty and more to the pound are the true ancestors of the modern ·22 rifle.

From the Tyrol these weapons were gradually introduced into North America and a remarkable development occurred there. As any student of geography readily appreciates, North America may be said to consist of forests and plains. The plainsman, hunting big game, shooting at ranges of 100 yards and over, required a large-calibre gun to deal a mortal blow and to fly to its target without undue deflection through strong winds. For him the European hunting piece was ideal.

The backwoodsman, hunting non-dangerous game in thickly wooded regions, where the range was seldom above 70–80 yards, frequently much less, seeking small deer, turkey and similar game, often had to travel in the wilds with his 'caravan' on his own back. The impedimenta of lead for balls, powder, flints, patches and so on when undertaking an excursion after game would be considerable if a large-bore weapon were used. The hunter, therefore, began to use smaller calibre weapons, firing small bullets, and therefore, less weight of lead to carry. The quantity of powder required was also less.

The plainsman relied upon a heavy powder charge and a large ball with its terrific shocking power to make up for his defects in accuracy. The backwoodsman wanted to be able to use his weapon accurately and *quickly*. In the thick forests he was not likely to get much time to estimate ranges before the game escaped. In order, therefore, to obtain as flat a trajectory as possible, and thereby know the sighting of his weapon to, say, 100 paces, he increased the powder charge while reducing the size of the bullet. Thus, he foreshadowed the development of the modern high-velocity small-bore cartridge.

But this weapon, later developed into the famous Kentucky or Pennsylvanian rifle, was amazingly accurate, and many references have been made to this in its 100 years of popularity from 1725 to 1825, probably the most famous being General George Hanger's passage in his book *To All Sportsmen* in which he described how he narrowly escaped being shot by an American rifleman.

The Kentucky rifle, though, contrary to popular ideas, was not nearly as small in calibre as the ·22. As against the large-calibre plains and military weapons of ·80 inch, the Kentucky varied from ·30 up to as much as ·70, the average bore being about ·40. It must be remembered that the backwoodsman, though armed to deal with small game, nevertheless had to have sufficient stopping power in his weapon to deal with marauding Redskins if he wished to keep his scalp.

The smaller calibre had, however, proved itself and contributed in no small measure to the defeat of the British forces in the American War of Independence. The next stage in the development of the small-bore was the introduction of the percussion system and the invention of the percussion cap. This was followed, about 1840, by the most important factor in the history of the ·22—*the invention and development of the rim-fire cartridge.*

In the middle of the nineteenth century, when the rim-fire was introduced, cartridges were no novelty. Early in the previous century French soldiers had used paper containers which held a powder charge only, from which we get the word 'cartridge paper'. Ball was carried separately. It was only a matter of time before ball and powder, or shot charge and powder, were combined in the same case, though the actual introduction of the *cartouche*, or cartridge as it was later termed, into the weapon, was either via the muzzle or by some form of breech-loading.

The early cartridges were fired by percussion caps, mounted on to nipples, which were detonated in the normal manner of muzzle-loaders. But with improvements in the percussion principle the cap was rapidly incorporated in the cartridge itself. An early effort was the needle-fire gun, designed by M. Pauly, a Swiss—though the system is often, erroneously, called the 'Prussian' needle-fire system. In this the case was metal, a great advance on the old style, and the charge was ignited by means of a long firing-pin which was driven through the base of the cartridge, passing through the charge and wads, to strike the fulminate which was located in the base of the bullet. The long firing-pin or needle was prone to damage, and there was always a serious gas leakage through the needle channel in the cartridge.

Another step was the development of the pin-fire system—which, though not altogether safe, was more effective than the needle-fire.

Then came the rim-fire. This was the first really moisture-proof cartridge, which provided an efficient gas check and at the same time contained all three major items of primer, powder and bullet in the same case. Before the rim-fire, all other cartridges had to depend upon some form of percussion ignition separate from the cartridge case, either by pellet, tube or tape primer.

Take a rim-fire cartridge in your hand and examine it closely. The modern specimen you examine is little different (apart from powder) from the original design of over 100 years ago.

In France, M. Flobert developed a small rim-fire cartridge known as BB (bullet breech) caps. This was about 1840. The original purpose of the BB cap was to allow the enthusiast to practise indoors, with both rifle and pistol, and weapons firing BB caps are sometimes called 'saloon' guns or pistols, derived from the French *salon*. On the Continent, such guns are still referred to as 'Flobert'. There has been little or no change in the basic construction of this cartridge. The body is punched out of sheet copper and then drawn into a tube. The rim is then added and filled with a primer. The original primer, fully corrosive and rather unstable, was pure fulminate of mercury. Ignition of the charge is effected by trapping the rim between the face of the barrel and the firing pin or hammer.

The original BB caps did not contain a powder charge—the bullet was propelled by the detonation of the primer alone.

On the Continent the description 'Flobert' is met with in Proof Regulations. In Belgium, for example, all *rim-fire* (not centre-fire) ·22s are classified as 'Armes Floberts' and must carry special proof marks. In Germany, also, ·22 rim-fire BB capped guns, or 5·6 mm. shot loads, are referred to in proof regulations as 'Flobert'. Normal type ·22 weapons, e.g. short, long and long rifle, are exempt from this description and come under the terms of *Kleinkaliberbüchse*, or, loosely, small-bore arms.

It was not very long before the BB cap was improved and this by a firm of American gunmakers in order to circumvent the patents held by another!

In America, Horace Smith and Daniel Wesson founded a partnership in 1852 in Norwich, Connecticut: ultimately to become world-famous as Smith and Wesson of handgun fame. Some sixteen years earlier, four years before M. Flobert had invented his rim-fire cartridge, Colonel Samuel Colt had brought out his famous revolver and so thoroughly did he cover his patent that it was virtually impossible for anyone to make a revolving firearm, handgun or carbine, legally. Naturally many gunmakers were anxious to make a repeating weapon which would not infringe Colt's patents, and Smith and Wesson began to develop a system invented by a Mr Jennings.

In this system the ammunition (consisting of a hollow lead bullet with a fulminate primer propelling charge) was carried in a tube magazine under the barrel and fed into the chamber by a trigger guard lever, but the cartridge was inefficient and doomed the weapon. In despair and contemplating having to wait until Colt's patent expired, Smith and Wesson took up the ·22 rim-fire. They planned to use this calibre in a weapon with a *bored-through* cylinder. Strangely enough, Colt had never thought of this contingency: all his weapons were loaded from the front of the chamber which was solid at the rear. However, in 1855 Rollin White had forestalled Smith and Wesson and secured a patent on the bored-through cylinder. A deal was concluded between the parties and two years later, in 1857, Smith and Wesson made their first ·22 rim-fire repeating revolver, using all metal cartridges. This ammunition was an improvement on Flobert's BB caps and was virtually the modern ·22 short.

The modern match rifle shot, using a precision-built arm, with accurate ammunition, would never recognize the ancestor of his weapon if he saw Smith and Wesson's original ·22 revolver. It was a seven-shot model, the rifled barrel contained five grooves (in the original model three grooves) and was built on a rounded brass frame. The barrel was short—$3\frac{1}{8}$ inches, and was octagonal. Loading was effected by tipping up the barrel, which was hinged on top of the frame. The overall length of this arm was a mere seven inches.

Three years later Smith and Wesson patented the rim-fire cartridge, and for about ten years they held undisputed control of the metallic cartridge field.

It must not be thought that the rim-fire cartridge was confined to the ·22 calibre. The ·32 calibre was popular, and B. Tyler Henry adapted the original small calibre and brought out the ·44 Henry cartridge, the *first* of all Winchester rim-fire cartridges.

The original ·22 Smith and Wesson cartridge shot a 30-grain bullet, propelled by a 3-grain black powder charge. Both the ·22 and ·32, as built by Smith and Wesson, were in demand by officers during the American Civil War, chiefly on account of their small size and ease in loading. Their stopping power was not great, but it must be remembered that in those days a man shot in the stomach by even so small a bullet was likely to die of gas gangrene in a few hours.

The little ·22 was soon in great demand as a personal defence weapon, in pepper-box, in derringer, in single-shot, and revolver form. Some were extremely tiny weapons, to be concealed in a lady's muff or purse. Probably one of the most notorious ·22 revolvers was the 'Ladysmith' model produced by Smith and Wesson. This was designed especially for the protection of lady cyclists! The weapon was very popular and made wide sales until

HISTORICAL OUTLINE

Joseph Wesson, Daniel's son and successor on his death, who was extremely high-principled, found out the sordid truth! The little ·22 'Ladysmith' was also known as the 'prostitute's favourite' owing to the small space it occupied in a handbag or stocking top and was in great demand by those ladies. Joseph Wesson ceased manufacturing the weapon rather than have such people buy them.

In the meantime, however, Flobert's rifles were being improved upon and appeared in several forms.

Though Flobert had, by his invention of the rim-fire cartridge, paved the way for the development of the modern metallic ammunition and made a great contribution towards the development of the rifle, none the less his own rifles were not particularly good.

The first Flobert rifles were chambered for the ·22 BB cap. Now the BB cap was not a very powerful cartridge as the sole propellent was the primer; even the later CB cap, which incorporated a small powder charge in the case, was little better. It has been calculated that the muzzle velocity of the BB cap is about 780 feet per second, and the round ·22-calibre ball weighs 20 grains. Compare this with the muzzle velocity of the standard ·177-inch *air rifle* slug which is in the region of 550–600 feet per second, and the modern *short* ·22 rim-fire cartridge which has a muzzle velocity of 925 feet per second. The lack of practical value of the BB cap and its poor ballistics is fairly obvious.

Flobert's first rifles were not particularly strong in the breech, and after a few shots had been fired, the fouling in the barrel caused by the black powder used in those days was sometimes enough to create sufficient pressure, even with the comparatively 'feeble' BB caps, to blow open the breech block. The defect in the system is apparent when it is realized that the *hammer* served to hold the breech block in position and there was no other locking device. It is interesting to note, however, that Flobert's rifles, with their rotating block action, were the forerunners of the Remington action. Subsequent rifles designed by Flobert gradually appeared with stronger actions and his target model, chambered for the ·22 long rim-fire, was popular on the Continent, in the United Kingdom and the United States.

The last quarter of the nineteenth century, so far as the history of small-bore firearms is concerned, was a curious one. Shooting was very popular in Europe amongst the upper classes of society and it was not uncommon for shooting matches to be held with Flobert type rifles and pistols in the drawing-room. On the other hand, North America abounded in small game and the small-game hunter was rather loathe to use large-calibre ball on woodchucks, squirrels, and the like. Most game shooting in the United Kingdom was done with either shotguns, or, for deerstalking, with a large-calibre rifle. But even in the British Isles there was a growing demand for a small-calibre rifle for small- and medium-game shooting, and the extremely short rook-shooting season in the English counties was also a factor for the development, in England at any rate, of the sporting small-bore rifle.

The masses, as some economists or social historians would term them, as opposed to the professional hunter and the leisured sportsman, were interested in rifles only from the point of view of the professional soldier, or in the shooting gallery.

The shooting gallery was generally a hall equipped with a very short range, to which the general public could repair and, after paying a small fee, shoot with small-bore rifles at targets, clay pipes, balls thrown into the air on fountains and so on; rather like the shooting booth or gallery found in the present-day fairgrounds and pleasure beaches, and even in the modern pin-table saloons, the haunts of the less law-abiding types of Central London and modern seaside resorts. There were also shooting galleries which specialized in genuine shooting instruction, but the term 'gallery' is nowadays synonymous with the fairground.

Probably the most famous gallery rifle was the Winchester Model 1890. This rifle has probably been handled by more shooters throughout the world than any other. It was a Browning invention and was built in the familiar 'pump' or 'trombone' action. Discontinued in 1937, Winchester made no fewer than 849,000 of this model and it is still in wide use today. It was chambered for the ·22 short, long, and long-rifle ammunition.

During this same period the ·22 rifle was adapted for many different purposes. About 1858 Remington brought out a rifle cane. This was similar in appearance to the modern ·410 walking-stick gun and though this is rather suspect as a poaching weapon, the rifle cane was invented purely for defensive purposes. It was chambered for the ·22 short case, though some models were also chambered for the ·32 short rim-fire. Strangely enough, this model continued in production until just before World War I. About ten years later one of the first Stevens rifles was introduced. This was known as the 'Pocket Rifle' and was really developed from the pistol, as it had a barrel of only ten inches in length and utilized a detachable skeleton stock. Three years later, in 1872, Stevens improved on the pocket model and introduced their 'Bicycle' rifle. It is really amazing, when making researches into firearms history, how often the word 'bicycle' appears when related to firearms!

It is also surprising how often references to the fair sex appear in firearm history. When Flobert invented the rim-fire cartridge he was responsible for the introduction of shooting to women. Women had been shots before then, of course, but from a rather Amazon standpoint. In 1886, Stevens introduced a 'Ladies' Rifle', in ·22 calibre, and these continued in production in varying forms for about ten years. Indeed, at that time, it would seem that if a woman purchased a rifle she was respectable, but if she purchased a handgun she was less likely to be so!

By the 1880s and 1890s, the rim-fire cartridge was established in three main sizes, the ·22 short, the ·22 long, and the ·22 long rifle. But apart from a few enthusiasts, it was mostly looked down upon as a 'toy' weapon. It was displacing the elastic or steel spring crossbow used in the British Isles and on the Continent for small-game shooting, but the ammunition was rather low in velocity, high in trajectory, and the small-calibre barrels extremely prone to fouling from the black powder then in use.

American manufacturers, principally Maynard, Winchester and Stevens had begun to use centre-fire cartridges in ·22 calibre and were reaching velocities in the region of 2,000 foot seconds, but something else was needed to develop further the ·22 calibre firearms from either a gallery toy or a small personal defence weapon into a really useful weapon. That development lay in the propellent field, and the next important step in the evolution of the ·22 was the introduction of smokeless powder.

While the ·22 rim-fire rifle was developing, a number of small-bore sporting guns were being manufactured for small-game shooting in Europe. These were known variously as 'pea rifles', in reference to the appearance of the bullet, or 'rook' rifles. Cartridges used were centre-fire and rather short and stubby, in fact, similar to handgun cartridges in appearance. Chief amongst these may be mentioned the ·297/·250 'Rook Rifle' and the same calibre 'Morris Short'. Comparing the muzzle velocity of the 'Morris Short' at 875 foot seconds and the 'Rook Rifle' model at 1,100 foot seconds against the modern I.C.I. ·22 Long Rifle High Velocity of 1,400 foot seconds we can see what great improvements have been made in the ballistics of ·22 ammunition. One of the factors in the disappearance of the larger calibre 'rook' rifles was the cheapness of the ·22 rim-fire ammunition, as well as the greater accuracy of the latter.

The small-calibre 'rook' rifles—the term is used in a general sense to include all the small-game centre-fire weapons—were generally constructed in single-shot weapons. The action used was invariably the snap-action, similar to modern shotguns, and though many weapons were hammer guns, the more expensive were hammerless. I have seen several models in 'rook' calibre built exactly like double-barrel big-game or 'express' rifles, and the cost must have been pretty fabulous.

The ·22 rim-fire rifle, however, appeared in many different forms. The falling block action, the rising block, the bolt action, even self-loaders, and so on, were gradually developed and in many cases before the new actions were applied to the large-calibre arms. The development of each type of action seems to have been adopted territorially rather than logically. Thus, the falling block action was popular in North America, the bolt action in Europe, the rising block (of which the Martini action is the most famous) in the United Kingdom.

The Martini action, so popular at the present day in Britain, and appearing on the finest examples of British small-bore match rifles, the B.S.A., was invented by a Swiss and based on the famous Peabody action. It was adopted in 1869 by the British Army for use with the Henry Rifle, giving rise to the famous Martini-Henry, but was abandoned as a military weapon because

HISTORICAL OUTLINE

successive military actions through the world had shown the need for repeating arms. It was replaced by the Lee-Enfield in due course.

Though the falling block action is looked upon as an American idea, one of the finest types was the Farquharson action, the invention of a Scotsman. Small-calibre weapons, medium-game rifles, and even big-game rifles were successfully built with this action and amongst the famous gunsmiths using it were Holland and Holland, Westley Richards, and Webley and Scott. In America today, the modified Farquharson is greatly used, particularly in the high-pressure ·22 rifles using 'varmint' and 'wildcat' cartridges.

Bolt actions became universally popular, especially from the military point of view, and were readily adopted by the manufacturers of ·22 rifles; most single-shot ·22 rifles in the U.S.A. today, as well as on the continent of Europe, are of bolt-action style. Martini style of action is the favourite choice only of Great Britain and for this type of gun, principally single-shot target shooting, it seems the wisest choice.

It was with the introduction of repeating arms that the ·22 really forged ahead. Winchester used what was basically a Browning invention in their 1890 slide-action ·22 repeater, following this up in 1903 with what was virtually the first successful automatic ·22 to use the ·22 Winchester auto-rim-fire cartridge.

The year after Winchester launched their famous model '1890', the Marlin Firearms Company introduced their model '1891'. This was one of the most famous repeating rifles ever manufactured. The magazine held twenty-five short cases or twenty long. The action was side ejection underlever; an action which is extremely popular today in the United States for even large-game rifles.

The ·22 rifle was developing towards perfection in tube magazines, whereas the large-calibre rifles, used for military purposes, were graduating towards box magazines, only France using a tubular magazine. The Spencer rifle, with the tube magazine in the butt, was the one tube magazine which has never been adopted by any country for military purposes, yet for the ·22 rifle it was very effective.

Up to the last decade of the nineteenth century there was a big gap between the calibres. The ·22 was progressing in a spectacular way, in the target field, in the sporting field, and as a weapon for defence. *The reduction from large-calibre military weapons was probably the outcome of the results of the little ·22.* Be that as it may, at Thun, in Switzerland, in 1883 Major Rubin introduced the ·295 military rifle. A few years later Great Britain adopted the ·303 and in a short time the military calibres of ·450 and ·500 were reduced to more reasonable dimensions; Greece, Holland, Italy, Japan and Portugal adopting the ·256 Mannlicher.

In 1883 the 'Morris' tube of ·22 inch-calibre was introduced for short-range rifle practice. This was a ·22 rifle barrel which could be fitted inside the barrel of standard service arms, the forerunner of the modern 'adaptor', and it was indirectly responsible for a sharp increase in the popularity of the ·22.

There were, however, the inevitable snags.

Popular though the ·22 rifle and pistol were becoming, nevertheless, even on small game, unless a direct hit was scored on a vital organ, the animal could live to escape and die miserably later. As a defensive weapon, with improvements in medical science in cleaning and healing wounds, it was not much of a man-stopper, being merely a threat with a sharp sting to it. Enthusiastic sportsmen in the United States, as well as in Europe (though here the credit rightfully belongs to the Americans), began to look around for ways to increase the velocity of their rifles, yet at the same time retain the smallness of calibre. One of the snags of the ·22 in 'built up' areas was the tendency of the bullets to ricochet when deflected—a danger to third parties or domestic stock. The enthusiasts wanted to develop a projectile which would disintegrate rather than ricochet and began to experiment with what is now known as 'wildcat' ammunition; the term wildcat not, of course, referring to the feline of that type, but to pioneer experimenting in much the same way that oil prospectors sink a series of 'wildcat' drills when searching their territory.

One of the first experimenters in the United States was A. O.

HISTORICAL OUTLINE

Niedner who, about 1888, tried to speed up the ·22 Winchester centre-fire cartridge. This was a black powder cartridge, firing a 46-grain bullet, and with a muzzle velocity of 1,540 foot seconds. It had a mid-range trajectory over 200 yards of not less than 13·5 inches. This cartridge was the ancestor of the modern ·22 Hornet which develops a muzzle velocity of 2,500 foot seconds and has a mid-range trajectory at 200 yards of four inches!

Niedner, however, with only black powder at his disposal, was unable to effect the improvements he desired, though at a later stage he was to play a vital part in the development of high-speed cartridges when new powders were available.

The first high-velocity cartridge in this calibre was developed about five or six years later, in 1894, by Reuben Harwood after nine years' intense experimentation. Using a 60-grain bullet, the cartridge was made from a 25/20 Maynard case necked down to ·22 calibre. Subsequent variations of the cartridge used bullets varying from 48 grains to 75 grains and with the former, using du Pont No. 1 Smokeless Powder, Harwood claimed a velocity of 2,000 foot seconds, an improvement of some 500 foot seconds over previous designs, and with this he claimed remarkable accuracy at up to 200 yards. He called this cartridge the Harwood 'Hornet'. Ruben Harwood, together with L. Lewis, experimented to arouse interest and show in a practical way that, though they had only black powder at their disposal, it was possible to achieve high velocity and flat trajectories with the small ·22-calibre weapons.

The only trouble, at that period, was that there were no rifles built to handle these cartridges; the ammunition was in advance of its time and new, stronger weapons had to be made.

During the first decade of the twentieth century high-pressure smokeless powders became available and the high-velocity cartridges came into their own. The experiments of Reuben Harwood, Linwood, Lewis and Niedner began to pay off, and, profiting by their researches, an American lawyer, Charles Newton, an amateur ballistics enthusiast, began to use smokeless powder in high-velocity ·22 and other calibre cartridges.

In the winter of 1905–6, Newton developed the first ·22 high-power *rifle* and the results of his experiments showed that the new combination of rifle and cartridge was efficient against larger animals than the woodchucks he intended to use it against. He brought out the ·22 Savage Hi-Power, to be used in combination with the Savage Arms Company Featherweight Rifle. This was known as the 'Imp' cartridge and was put on the market about 1911.

The original of this cartridge was a 25/25 Stevens straight case which Newton necked down to ·22 calibre. He continued to experiment, changing the original cases and loads, reaching a velocity of 2,500 foot seconds which, high though it seemed, was, in Newton's opinion, well below the practical velocity he could attain. He soon realized that the short, light bullet lost velocity very rapidly and ultimately by using a longer bullet with a greater weight, reached velocities of up to 3,100 foot seconds. This resulted in the ·22 Newton cartridge.

The ·22 Savage Hi-Power used a 70-grain bullet—the ·22 Newton used one of 90 grains.

In 1912 Savage adopted Newton's ideas: yet no less than nineteen more years were to pass before another high-velocity ·22 cartridge was commercially manufactured when the ·22 'Hornet' was introduced by Winchester.

In addition to his development of the high-velocity cartridge, Newton experimented with different systems of rifling, including improvements upon the famous oval system first used by Charles Lancaster about 1830. Incidentally, this system was in use by Charles Lancaster's successors (Stephen Grant and Joseph Lang of London) until the outbreak of World War I. Results of many experiments which Newton carried out showed that the oval bore retained its accuracy far longer than the conventional rifling and gave a reduction in pressure over the land-and-groove system through reduction in friction. In this oval bore, Newton saw great possibility for high-velocity arms.

The position in England was rather gloomy at this period.

Most British sportsmen were using American rifles for ·22 work. Probably the most popular models in use in England about the period Newton was developing his first high-velocity cartridge, were the Stevens 'Ideal' and the Winchester. Both were falling block actions, with under-levers and hammers.

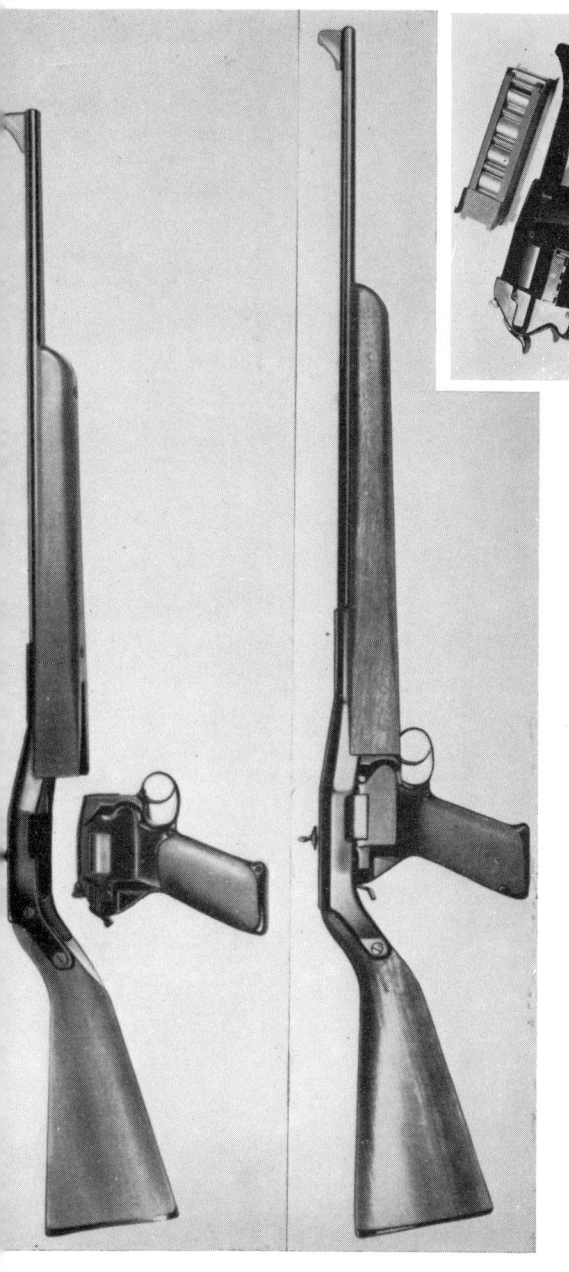

PLATE V

Top—The Dardick combination rifle pistol, showing how the pistol action fits into the rifle. *Centre*—The Dardick combination rifle/pistol complete and ready for action. *Bottom*—Dardick pistol, magazine, and 'Tround' ammunition

PLATE VI

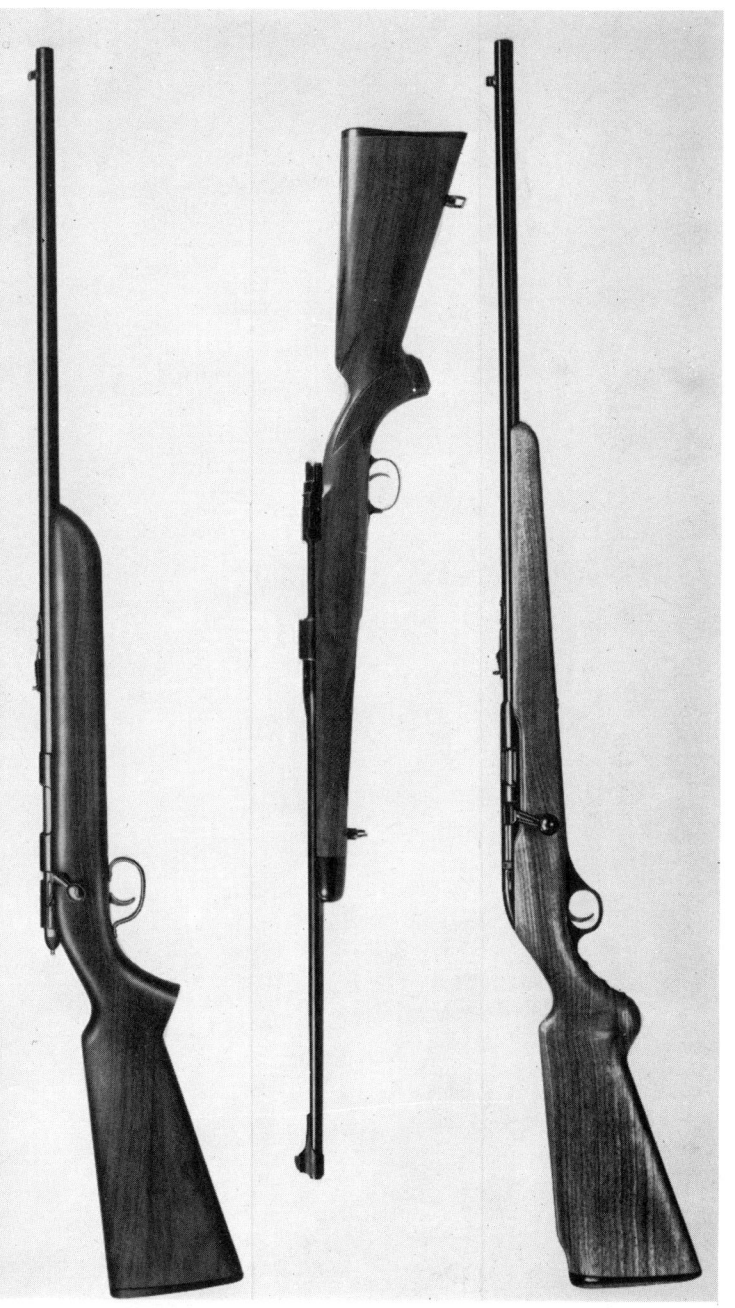

PLATE VII

Top—The Remington 'Targetmaster' single-shot, Model 510A. *Centre*—The 'Coltsman'—standard model. *Bottom*—Mossberg single-shot Model 320K

PLATE VIII

HISTORICAL OUTLINE

It took a war to develop the ·22 in Great Britain!

In 1902 the unhappy episode of the Boer War was over: the chief lesson the British military leaders learned, and which today the British authorities seem to have forgotten, was how powerful a force even a few *expert* riflemen could be. The marksmanship of the Boer farmers was of a very high order and the casualties they inflicted were enormous. But the lesson was learned and the Commander-in-Chief, Lord Roberts, conceived the brilliant notion of developing the *civilian* shooting in the United Kingdom and making the British into a 'nation of riflemen'. From the end of the Boer War until 1910 there was a great boom in civilian shooting in England, principally with the miniature rifle. The military training of the British rifleman underwent a great change and so well was the lesson learned that in 1914 the advancing Germans who came up against the small, but highly trained, British Army, thought they were armed with machine-guns for so deadly was the rapidity of their accurate firing.

The ·297/·230 Morris tube had been the principal training small-bore arm, but it was woefully inefficient. At 100 yards the drop in inches of this cartridge was 15·5, and at 200 yards no less than 70 inches! Compare this with the modern ·22 Long Rifle High Velocity Cartridge which, at 100 yards, has a drop of 11·2 inches, and at 200 yards of 52 inches. The ·22 Hornet has a drop of 3·4 inches at 100 yards, and 16·5 inches at 200 yards. So great has been the progress in ·22 ammunition.

There were no comparable cartridges in ·22 calibre on the market at that time. The Americans led the field, though a very popular ·22 rim-fire cartridge in Europe, and Great Britain, was the Rhenish Westphalian. In 1910, however, the Americans, through the Union Metallic Cartridge Company, took the lead in Great Britain, and were soon followed by Winchester. At the same time there were numerous experiments taking place in the shape of bullet noses, pointed versus blunt, and the variation in the amount of twist in rifle barrels.

Greener adapted the Service Martini-Henry and fitted a ·22 barrel, naming it the 'Converted Martini', following this up with the first genuine British target model built specially, with the Martini action, for ·22 target rifles.

About the same time the British War Office developed the ·22 War Office Miniature Rifle. This was a perfect replica of the standard Lee-Enfield, with the typical bolt action, WD sights, protecting wings, and bayonet fittings. I used one of these rifles for many years and found it good for sporting shooting though rather on the light side for target work.

But that was the only attempt that the British War Office ever made to produce a *special* ·22 rifle for service training. In the United States, however, the special ·22 military rifle is an essential part of military shooting, and with the introduction of the floating chamber, they are able to use the cheaper ·22 ammunition and at the same time simulate the recoil of the Springfield Service arm.

The Russians also use a specially designed ·22 Service arm for training troops and their standard of marksmanship is very high indeed.

Since 1945, the development of the high-velocity cartridge, principally in 'wildcat' form, has been speeded up in America: in Britain, however, concentration has been upon the rifle rather than the cartridge, owing to the severe restrictions of the Firearms Act, 1937 and the jaundiced eye of authority which is strongly against 'wildcat' experimenters. Probably, no matter what other models are compared with it, the British Martini action target rifle, as built by the B.S.A. concern, is the nearest perfect target rifle in use anywhere in the world today.

A new development was the introduction in 1950 by the Remington concern of their '222' cartridge. This, if one discounts the later 6-millimetre cartridges, is the most up-to-date small calibre high-velocity cartridge available to the general public today. It is a rimless case, centre-fire cartridge and has a velocity of 3,200 foot seconds yet only makes half the noise of the ·22 Swift. Though the Remington Model 722 rifle was chambered for it, European manufacturers soon took it to heart and it was found to give excellent results in the Finnish 'Sako', which is also produced for the ·22 Hornet.

From a survey of the progress made in ·22 weapons and ammunition, having regard to the deterioration of the rifle in warfare, in this connexion it must be remembered that we are shooting with rifles at 200 to 300 yards in modern battles, just as musketeers and fusiliers of old used to do when engaging their foes—whereas with our modern military arms we should be able to engage the enemy with rifles at over 1,000 yards. In the light of this close-range shooting the modern high-velocity ·22-calibre rifles would seem to have military possibilities. The drawbacks are not so obvious. Paradoxically, the high-velocity cartridges are more likely to be deflected off course by wind than the slower ones: secondly, warfare is supposed to be conducted 'humanely' and the terrific shocking power and destructive tissue effect of the high-velocity ammunition as used in high-velocity ·22 cartridges would result in charges of barbarism against the user, contravening the laws of civilized warfare. Which, in view of Hiroshima and Nagasaki, and the napalm bombs, seems pretty hypocritical.

We have seen the development in recent years of precision-built target and sporting ·22 rifles, and witnessed the great strides made in the manufacture of suitable ammunition. Velocities of 4,000 foot seconds are no longer looked upon with awe; they have been attained and there is little doubt that higher velocities will be experimented with. But these ultra-high-velocity cartridges will present new problems and may very well result in basic changes in firearms as we understand them today.

Ultra-high-velocity cartridges will not necessarily improve the accuracy of the shooting—the old muzzle-loaders and early black-powder cartridge users were able to give good accounts of themselves and many early cartridges were fully as good, at short ranges, as modern ones.

The use of these high-velocity cartridges will affect, more than anything else, the rifling of the barrel. Newton experimented with Lancaster's oval borings, and there might well lie the future of high-velocity weapons. The terrific pressure and heat generated by high-velocity cartridges exercise immense wear and tear on conventional metals and standard types of rifling, and there is little doubt that new developments will take place in the action of the firearms as well.

But that lies in the future. For some considerable time the standard ·22 rifle and its ammunition, particularly in the rim-fire category, will be the mainstay of the small-bore rifleman for target and sporting shooting at small game and vermin.

Alongside the development of the ·22 rifle and its ammunition there have been inventions, some excellent, some useful, some downright impractical, relating to the ·22 as a training arm, as an ancillary weapon, or as an accessory to it.

Two remarkable developments stand out: one perfected in the United States and one in Great Britain.

The first, the *floating chamber* principle, was the invention of Marshall Williams, who devised it whilst serving a sentence in a United States penitentiary for an offence during the days of Prohibition. For some time the American forces had been using the Colt ·45 semi-automatic pistol for training their personnel, but the cost of ammunition presented problems. The use of a ·22 pistol, built like the ·45, did not solve the problem. Smaller calibre ammunition made it more economic but without the buck of a heavy pistol in recoil, the use of a ·22 did not assist much in preparing a nervous recruit to handle the heavier handgun. Williams devised the floating chamber in which the gas produced from the fired cartridge of a ·22 was allowed to escape at the front of the chamber. This gas thrust against the area of the cartridge base plus the considerably larger area of the chamber front. The backward action of the gases was therefore considerably increased, the thrust of the weapon in recoil greater in consequence. The net result was that a ·22 pistol was built giving the same recoil as the larger ·45.

The next step was the incorporation of the floating chamber using the ·22 long rifle cartridge into the Browning machine-gun. In addition to building floating ·22 chambers for many semi-automatic rifles, Williams designed the short-stroke piston for the Garand automatic carbine, but that is outside the scope of a brief historical survey of the ·22.

Improvements have been made on the original Morris tube invention—·22-calibre adaptors have been made to insert into the barrels of shotguns, whilst Parker-Hale Ltd of Birmingham brought out a really first-class adaptor for the Webley and Scott ·455 calibre service revolver. This, though it did not incorporate any floating chamber principle to increase recoil, was none the less a great aid in training the pistolmen in shooting. It was made in two patterns, as a single-shot adaptor, in which the cylinder was

HISTORICAL OUTLINE

removed from the pistol so that it was fired in skeleton form, or complete with a special cylinder chambered for the ·22 rim-fire cartridge. This adaptor was also manufactured for the ·38-calibre Enfield Service Revolver.

These adaptors are still in use today and used fairly extensively. They do not affect the accuracy of the revolvers and are guaranteed to shoot into a ¾-inch group at 20 yards, which is better than the handler can claim.

The most remarkable development was, however, the principle, derived from the Morris Tube, by Mr A. T. C. Hale in introducing the system which he called 'Parker-rifling'. In this, worn barrels are bored out and a new rifled tube is inserted. Nor is this confined to worn barrels, for many larger bores, such as ·303 service rifles, can be converted to ·22 rifles by this process. It is an economical way of making a first-class sporting arm from an obsolete military one. It is not suitable for military cartridges, nor for high-power sporting cartridges, though Parker-rifling is suitable for the ·22 Hornet. It seems strange that many a useless high-power, large-calibre weapon should become a small ·22-calibre arm capable of extremely accurate shooting, yet there it is.

Commonplace the ·22 may be, yet its history is colourful and proud: whatever the future may hold in the development of firearms and ammunition, the little ·22 occupies an important position in the history of firearms as a whole. Large-bore riflemen may hold it in contempt, but most successful riflemen start with this weapon, while for military purposes its utility in training has been proved time and time again.

From the standpoint of the ordinary shooter, the ·22-calibre rifle is the most important in the world and there is a lot to be said for their attitude. Perhaps, speaking of Great Britain alone with its growing numbers of riflemen, one could parody the old song and say: 'Four thousand rifle clubs can't be wrong!'

CHAPTER TWO

MODERN DEVELOPMENTS

THE middle of the nineteenth century was a period of great development in the story of firearms. The middle of the twentieth century is equally important as a period of intense development in the ·22 calibre weapons. It is significant also that these developments must inevitably find themselves incorporated in the field of large-calibre weapons. And in addition to achievements in the development of arms and ammunition, there occurred a remarkable trend towards the manufacture of ·22 rifles and handguns by gunmakers who had either hitherto ignored this field altogether or who had withdrawn from it for some considerable time.

The first development of any importance concerns the problems which have arisen through the employment of high-speed ammunition. The intense heat developed, the terrific pressures, coupled with the speed of rotation of the projectile in the bore, have reached the stage where new metals have to be contemplated in the manufacture of high-speed rifle barrels and actions.

The greater the speed of the bullet, the greater the friction in the bore of the rifle, and this in turn leads to greater wear, even to distortion of both projectile and barrel. To combat this problem, manufacturers, principally in the United States of America, have resorted to one of the early forms of rifling, that of *micro-grooving*. This was known as early as the sixteenth century, and is best described by contrasting it with conventional rifling. In the latter, the grooves are deep and the lands, the raised portions, are heavy and cut deeply into the bullet.

Micro-grooved rifling, on the other hand, consists of several shallow grooves and the bullet is not cut so deeply. There is a further advantage in micro-grooving, in that leading and fouling are reduced to a minimum coupled with a reduction in gas leakage.

MODERN DEVELOPMENTS

Micro-grooving has received an impetus from the American firm of The Marlin Firearms Co., of New Haven, Connecticut. They introduced Marlin 'Micro-groove' rifling in both ·22 and larger-sized calibres, and even go so far as to build big-game rifles incorporating this principle. In 1953, after many years of careful research work and intensive testing, Marlin announced that their engineers had perfected the 'Micro-groove' rifle barrel. Based on results of trials carried out in general firing at 100 feet and 100 yards, the new system of rifling showed a substantial net gain in accuracy improvement as compared with conventional barrels. At the time Marlin announced the availability of the Micro-groove rifling in ·22-calibre weapons, it had already made pilot tests of this system with high-power cartridges and exhaustive tests with high-velocity centre-fire ammunition were carried on throughout 1954.

I have stated that the principles of micro-grooving are not new, but the method of making it has undergone a radical change. The accepted methods of cutting rifling have been built around the principle of *removing* metal from the inside of the barrel by successive cuts until the desired depth of grooves has been achieved.

The Marlin concern developed another method in which no metal is removed.

They force a tool through the bore of the barrel on the swedging principle, producing a highly burnished interior. The shallow grooves are sixteen in number, compared with conventional two-, four- or six-groove rifling, and Marlin claim that not only does this method of rifling result in greater accuracy, through the projectile retaining a true original shape, but the bullet fired through those barrels is less affected by muzzle blast. Furthermore, erosion is substantially reduced. In a two-year trial and test period the micro-grooved rifles gave 15 per cent closer groups than the conventionally rifled match rifles. Hence it follows that with the present trend towards higher velocity ammunition, the micro-groove rifle is a very practical proposition for the future.

The next major development—quite startling and unconventional, yet one which gun enthusiasts have been forecasting for years—was neither in the rifling nor in the ammunition but in the structural substances of the rifle. Again, the ·22-calibre was the chosen medium.

In 1959, Remington announced the introduction of their autoloading ·22 rifle built of steel and *nylon*. The stock is manufactured from this material, and what is also of note, is the fact that the *receiver* is also built from this substance. The stock is also one piece from butt to tip of fore-end. Barrel, breechblock and locks, of course, are machined from steel, but the rest of the weapon in which they operate is nylon.

Prior to introducing this rifle, Remington had experimented with various designs and as a result of intensive sales research they concluded that any new-style ·22 rifle would have to satisfy the following requirements.

(*a*) Its style and functional performance must be superior to anything else available,

(*b*) It must be capable of withstanding any amount of abuse and ill-treatment,

(*c*) The weight, as a sporting arm should be less than 5 lb., and

(*d*) The price had to be competitive.

The old story of trial, experiment and re-design entered the picture. But with each model built two ever-present problems presented themselves. Firstly, the present stock manufacturing equipment was unsuitable to effect the styling desired and secondly, production and performance were affected by machining cuts which produce 'tolerances'. The wear and tear of machine tools, jigs, dies, cutters, etc., ultimately brings about not merely tolerances, but an accumulation of tolerances.

As a result the designers and engineers decided that some other system of manufacture would have to be commenced and the following specifications were submitted to du Pont, the discoverers of nylon:

1. A material must be found which would produce a rifle stock and receiver in one unit.

2. Such a material must be capable of being formed into any desired shape.

3. High tensile, flexural and impact strength were essential.

4. It must have a high resistance to abrasion.

5. It must not be affected by extremes of heat or cold and if set on fire must be self-extinguishing.

PLATE IX

Top—Marlin Model 81-DL: a 25-shot tubular magazine repeater with Micro-Vue 4× telescope sight. *Centre*—Marlin Model 81C with Micro-Vue telescope sight. *Bottom*—Savage Model 5 de luxe

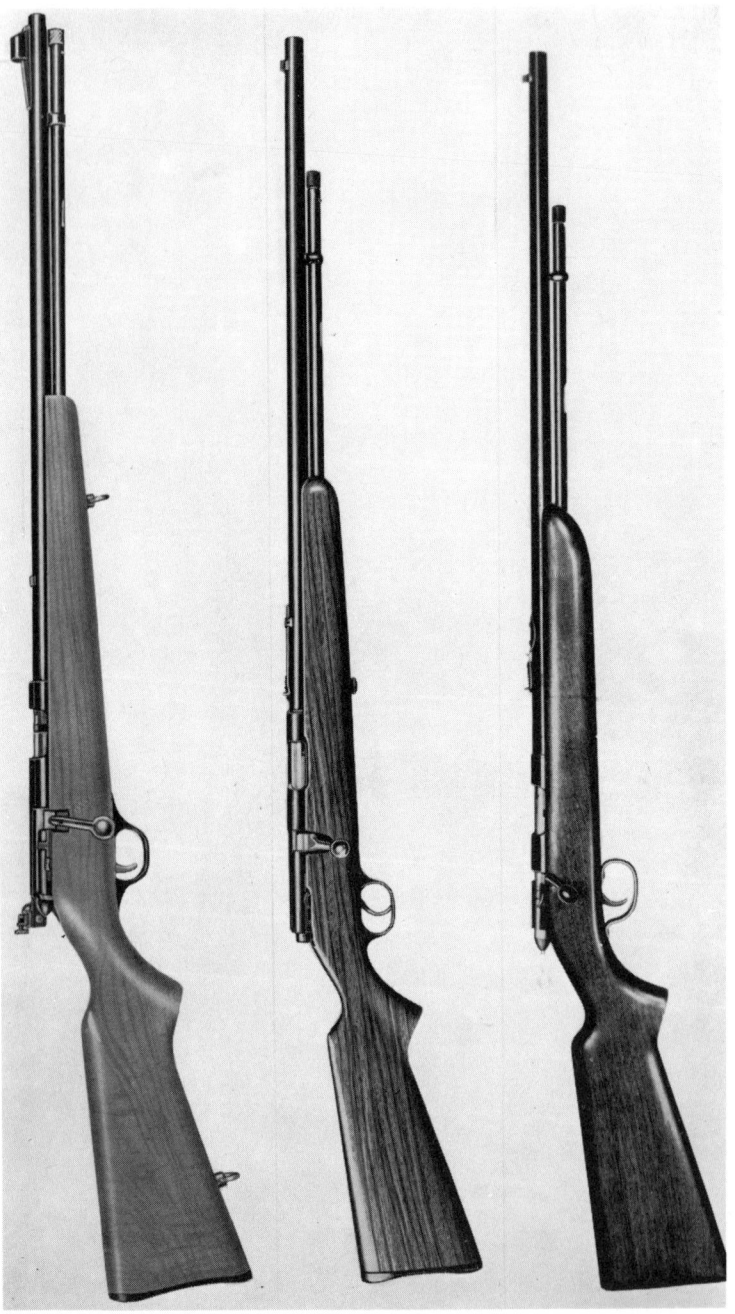

PLATE X

Top—Marlin Model 81-DL. *Centre*—Stevens Model 86. *Bottom*—Remington Model 512A—'Sportmaster'

PLATE XI

Top—Mossberg Model 346K. *Centre*—Marlin Model 81C. *Bottom*—The 'Scoremaster', a Remington Model—type 511A

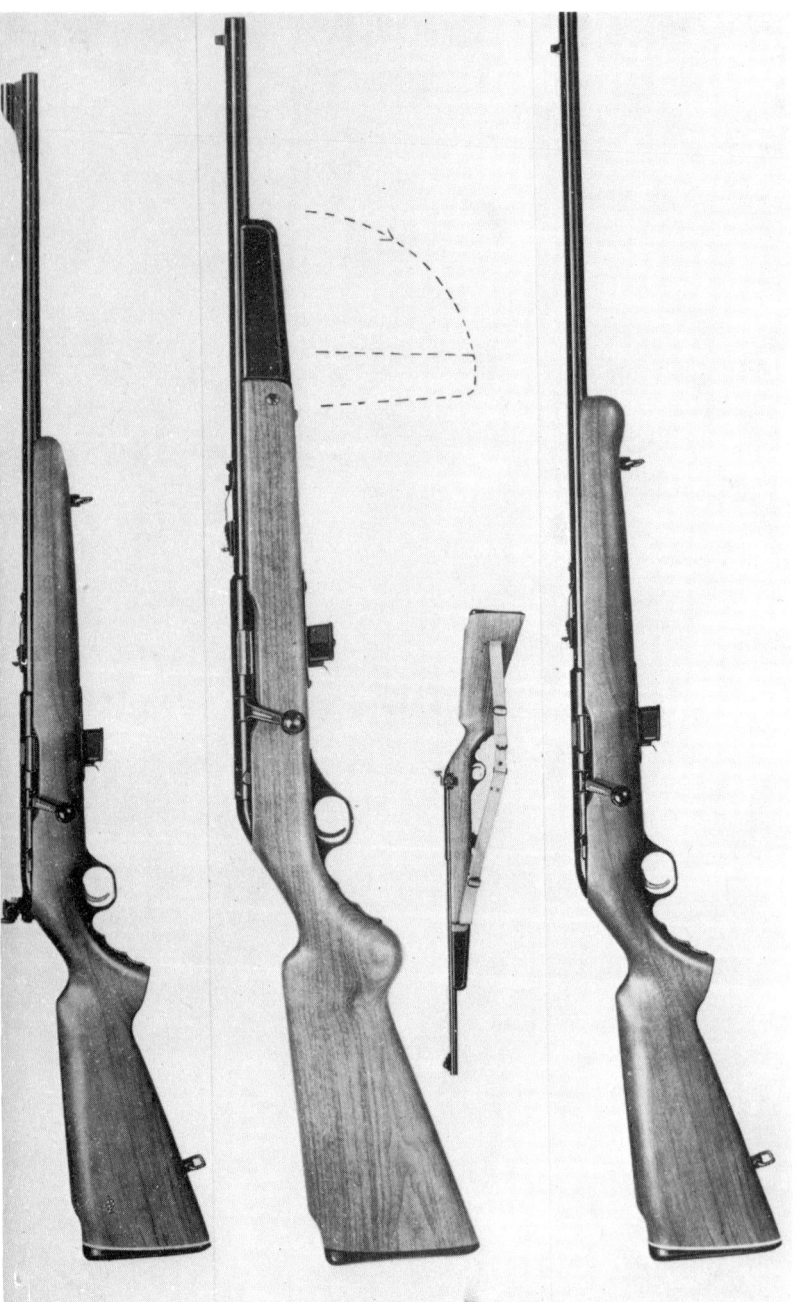

PLATE XII

Top—The Model 340B Mossberg. *Centre*—Mossberg 342K. *Bottom*—Mossberg 340K

PLATE XIII

Top—The new Mossberg ·22 WRF Magnum, the 'Chuckster', also showing Mossberg C-LECT-POWER Model 1A25 2·5×. *Centre*—From Sweden's Royal Arms Factory, the Husqvarna box magazine Model 1622 bolt-action repeater. *Bottom*—Marlin Model 80C and Micro-Vue telescope sight.

PLATE XIV

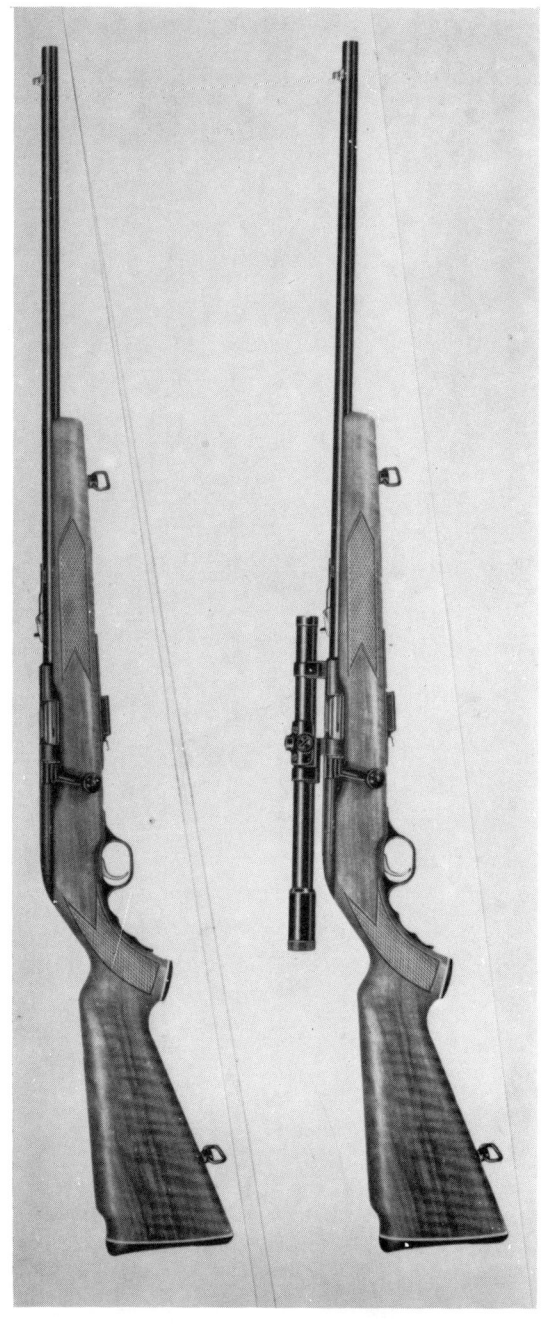

PLATE XV
De luxe Mossberg 'Chucksters' with (*top*) iron sights and (*below*) telescope sight

PLATE XVI

MODERN DEVELOPMENTS

6. It had to be light in weight.
7. It had to have no corrosive effect on metals.
8. It must resist attacks by oils, solvents, fungus, acids, alkalis, insects, and rodents.
9. It should have an easily repairable finish.
10. It had to be self-lubricating.
11. It had to be capable of holding permanent colours.

In a few months the du Pont chemicals department recommended their product Nylon ZYTEL-101, a substance better known as structural nylon.

Almost immediately a prototype was machined out of solid nylon and underwent a firing test of 75,000 rounds—from which, needless to state, it emerged satisfactorily. A set of moulds, from which the stocks were ultimately to come, was built and the stocks began to appear. The stock is moulded in two halves and joined down the middle. Furthermore, so accurate is the moulding, with no 'tolerances', that the complete stock and receivers are identical and they act as gauges against which the steel bolt, for example, is tested. If the steel parts do not fit the receiver, then it is the steel part which is at fault!

When the stock comes from the moulds it is coloured through and completely finished. The conventional colours are outstyled: 'Mohawk Brown' and 'Seneca Green' are the hues in which it is produced. Complete moulding time for a stock including checkering work on grip and fore-end, slots and cuts for the insertion of the barrel, bolt and trigger, is approximately sixty seconds!

However, before placing the rifle on the market, the Remington testers got to work and the things they did to that model typify a gun-lover's nightmare. Rifles were run over by heavy lorries, flung from top-storey windows, frozen down to below 40° and over 250°. They were acid-treated, submerged in oils, buried in dust, dirt and mud, and sunk into water. They were subjected to all types of solvents and under all these trials and tribulations the stock neither warped, failed nor prevented the weapon from firing. After exhaustive shooting tests it was found that the steel parts showed measurable wear, something which the nylon did not. According to the manufacturers, no lubrication is necessary as the material is self-lubricating, all that is necessary being a wipe-over to collect bullet lubricant from the face of the bolt and to wipe over the steel exteriors with an oily rag to prevent rusting.

As there is no distortion of the stock and fore-end, it follows that there is no interference with the barrel which is bedded at the fore-end and solidly at the chamber end.

Following on the startling news from Remington and their new nylon rifle came news of another amazing development: this time in the handgun field, firstly with a larger calibre arm but in which the ·22 calibre also plays its part.

This was the introduction by the Dardick Corporation of Hamden, Connecticut of a new type of arm featuring open-chamber construction and *triangular, plastic-cased* ammunition.

The Dardick project was designed to use ·38-calibre cartridges built from a plastic material called 'Fortiflex' but had also evolved into three basic models for ·38-calibre cartridges with replaceable ·22-calibre barrels; furthermore it could be instantly converted into a lightweight rifle!—accomplished by removing the pistol barrel from the frame and inserting the basic mechanism into a rifle-stock and barrel assembly.

But what is the 'Open Chamber' system?

This system has also been termed the 'Split Chamber' system and has been sought by designers and manufacturers of arms for almost 100 years. Briefly, it consists of a gun system in which there is no longitudinal insertion or extraction of ammunition into or out of a gun chamber. Loading of ammunition in the 'Open Chamber' system is done by indexing a round in front of the barrel by lateral motion only, thereby eliminating reciprocating parts such as breech bolts, slides and so forth.

Of necessity, in order to accomplish lateral loading in the conventional firearm, the chamber has to be split longitudinally into a minimum of two sections which separate to receive the ammunition and then close—to form a supporting chamber. In other words, the wall of the chamber has to have a circumferential discontinuity.

Attempts by gun designers throughout the world to utilize the split-chamber systems of various types all resulted in failure on account of the longitudinal rupturing of the cartridge case at the joint formed by the chamber sections. In each and every one of these instances the cartridge cases had conventional circular cross sections.

Experiments by Dardick revealed that such rupturing of the cases was due to the fact that the split-chamber sections (being elements of beam structures) underwent far greater deflections than a conventional chamber, which forms a continuous wall round the ammunition. Used in conventional weapons, circular cartridge cases have normal wall thickness and cannot tolerate such a magnitude of deflection. They fail because of the excessive tensile stresses they undergo at the unsupported sections along the joints in the split chamber.

Mr David Dardick was the first to bring about the feasibility of the split-chamber system with high-pressure ammunition by using a *non-circular* cartridge case section. He based his thesis on the structural principle that in any tube of non-circular section which is subjected to internal pressure, the pressure tends to reduce the tube to a circular cross section. Extensive firing tests proved that a cartridge case, built in non-circular form, would not rupture in spite of considerable deflection of the split-chamber wall sections.

Dardick's open-chamber system utilizes a rotary cylinder which contains triangularly shaped, open, longitudinal recesses. The cylinder is mounted into a frame which also carries the barrel and ammunition is loaded laterally into the recesses in the cylinder.

When the cylinder is rotated into the firing position the ammunition is brought into alignment with the barrel and in this position the fixed receiver section covers the exposed side of the triangularly shaped cartridge case. After firing, the cylinder continues its rotation, ejects the fired case and brings the next cartridge round to the firing position.

The triangularly shaped cartridge case contains what are basically the conventional components of primer, powder charge and bullet. Here again plastics enter the picture. A batch of cartridges was made of extruded aluminium but it did not provide the right answer and after extensive tests with other materials it was established that a rigid or linear polyethylene such as 'Fortiflex', produced by the Celanese Corporation of America, could be formed into a three-sided cartridge case as it had the required toughness and resistance to heat, combined with the proper modulus of elasticity. Fortiflex is completely stable between 50° below and 150° above zero, is over 50 per cent lighter than brass, and provides a better gas seal than conventional metal cartridges.

This results in more uniform velocities; that is, better ballistics. A further advantage is that of economy: the plastic cartridge cases are much more economical than metallic ones and there is a further advantage in that plastics, being 'non-strategic' materials are much less likely to be scarce than metals in a period of emergency.

The open-chamber principle also makes it possible to develop military weapons of significantly lighter weight and higher rates of fire as well as greater reliability and simplicity.

The first open-chamber system manufactured by the Dardick Corporation was a continuous feed, double-action handgun in 11, 15 and 20-shot magazine capacity. This weapon incorporated into one all the advantages of both conventional revolver and semi-automatic pistol. The chances of malfunctioning are greatly decreased in this system whilst at the same time the fire power is considerably increased. The weapons can be converted rapidly from ·38 to ·22 calibre and instantaneously into a ·22 rifle. This is unique in arms design.

Dardick called their triangular ammunition 'trounds' and these are adaptable to a great variety of powder loads and bullet weights. Inside each 'tround' is a tiny polyethylene disc which divides powder from bullet and which successfully prevents the escape of gas past the bullet before it is solidly engaged in the barrel rifling. All calibres of trounds are the same outside dimensions in their casings.

Then the first half of the twentieth century closed with startling news from Winchester when they set the American firearms industry about its heels with the announcement of a new *magnum* ·22 rim-fire cartridge.

This cartridge was developed by the Western-Winchester

MODERN DEVELOPMENTS

Division of the Olin Mathieson Chemical Corporation, but when they introduced the cartridge Winchester had not then built a rifle for it! Generously, the Winchester people offered this new cartridge to the gun trade in the United States and manufacturers were quick off the mark in adopting it. There has been, in the past and present, considerable criticism of the ·22 long rifle rim-fire cartridge as a hunting cartridge. Between the ·22 Long Rifle rim-fire and the ·22 centre-fire Hornet is a considerable gap. For purposes of comparison consider the High Velocity ·22 Long Rifle with its 40-grain bullet which has a muzzle velocity of 1,400 feet per second and energy of 174 foot pounds, against the ·22 Hornet with its 45-grain bullet, a muzzle velocity of 2,500 foot seconds and energy at the muzzle of 625 foot pounds.

Marlin were very quick to announce that their lever action Model 57-M, micro-grooved rifle was chambered for the new cartridge. O. F. Mossberg were almost as quick: they announced two new rifles, Models 620K and 640K, and named the 'Chuckster' specially built for this new ammunition. The 620K is a single-shot bolt action rifle and the 640K a 5-shot bolt action repeater. Savage announced, in turn, that their famous Model 24 combination rifle shotgun, with a ·22 barrel superposed over a ·410 shotgun barrel and which had hitherto been chambered for the ·22 long rifle cartridge, would also be available in ·22 Magnum chambering. This arm was issued as the survival arm for the U.S. Army bomber crews during World War II and is now proving a very popular sporting arm in the United Kingdom as well as North America.

Enthusiasm for the new cartridge was not, however, confined to the rifle manufacturers. The six-gun makers were soon busy with it: Colt, Ruger, and Smith & Wesson all came out, almost immediately, with handguns chambered and re-barrelled for the new load. Colts, for instance, chambered three models, two handguns and one rifle, the Frontier Scout (all-blue version), the Buntline Scout and their Colteer 1-22 single-shot rifle. They also planned to chamber their Officers' Model Match for this load in 1960.

This ·22 Magnum differs from the normal ·22 cartridge in two respects. Firstly, a substantial increase in muzzle velocity and energy, secondly the ammunition incorporates a special *jacketed* hollow-point bullet. The bullet is 40 grain and projected at a muzzle velocity of 2,000 feet per second.

The Magnum ·22 is not Winchester's first attempt to improve on the ·22 rim-fire. Way back in ·22 history they brought out a special ·22 Extra Long Cartridge. This had a case somewhat longer than the standard Long Rifle ·22 rifle and was, originally, built only for special Winchester guns, though Mossberg, Stevens, Maynard, and others did chamber rifles for it. The ·22 Extra Long utilized a lead bullet of 40 grains but it only had a muzzle velocity of 1,030 foot seconds in a 28-inch barrel.

Comparable ballistic figures are set out on page 216.

For the man who does not like ballistical tables, which though interesting to some are confusing to others, instead of reading the figures if one states that the ·22 Magnum has the muzzle energy exceeding that of a ·38 Smith & Wesson cartridge and packs more energy, wallop and velocity at 100 yards than the ·22 Long Rifle High Velocity develops at the muzzle, a clear picture of its potentialities can be obtained.

Developments in guns, actions, and cartridges do not complete the picture, however. The combination of better ammunition and weapons meant that 'possible' scores in target shooting were becoming fairly commonplace and rifle associations and sports governing bodies throughout the world revised drastically their competitive target values as well as size of targets.

Meanwhile the number of riflemen throughout the world continued to grow and with this growth the ·22-calibre arms took the lead. The close of the first half of this century saw some exciting things in the story of the ·22 rifle, for in the United States one manufacturer, who had hitherto confined all activities to high-grade shotguns, suddenly announced his entry into the rifle field, and with a ·22-calibre arm at that. This was the advent of the Ithaca autoloading 'Lightning' rifle. Then Colts, who had not manufactured shoulder arms for several decades, came into the picture with their Colteer and Coltsman Rifles, again in ·22 calibre. Way back in the middle of the nineteenth century Colt did manufacture a rifle, which spurred the Winchester concern into action to manufacture pistols. Came a showdown when the Winchester representatives visited the Colt factory and displayed the guns they

MODERN DEVELOPMENTS

proposed to market, resulting in withdrawal of the Colt rifle and abandonment of the Winchester pistol!

To crown all, Savage Arms Corporation, who make ·22 rifles on a large scale, announced in 1959 their introduction of a handgun, their first handgun for years—called the Savage Model 101 Pistol. This was another new arm in ·22 calibre.

Russia has been a mysterious land for many decades, and many and strange have been the rumours about its aircraft, its technical developments and its arms. But continuous successes of Russian, and Russian-influenced riflemen in international competitions has shown not only how thoroughly the Russians tackle the shooting game, but also exhibited the high quality of their firearms. It has been my pleasure to handle, and inspect freely, Russian arms and I have been delighted with their handling and appearance. Their quality is good, their appearance sometimes a little unorthodox, as in the case of their 'Record' upside-down match pistol in ·22 calibre, but their effectiveness cannot be denied.

The automatic target pistol from Russia, known as the 'Record' and to which I have just referred, caused a furore in shooting circles when it made its appearance in international shooting matches. The furore was brought about by, firstly, the striking appearance of the pistol, known subsequently as the 'upside down model', and, secondly, by its success.

The barrel was located in the lower part of the receiver on the same level as the trigger, whilst the sights were carried on a bar parallel with and above the barrel, and level with the top of the pistol grip. The pistol thus had the appearance of a hack-saw. The barrel was locked by the bolt body and recoil spring. A micrometer screw adjustment was incorporated into the sight at the rear and both sights were detachable. The magazine, which housed five rounds, was installed above the barrel in the upper part of the receiver and the cartridges were fed automatically into the chamber when the slide was shifted to the extreme forward position. Both trigger pull and creep had adjusting screws, and the hand rest was also adjustable. Despite its unconventional appearance, this handgun was specifically designed for rapid fire shooting at disappearing targets.

From America came, in late 1959, news of a new departure for

American manufacturers, and once again the spotlight was on the ·22-calibre firearm.

One of Winchester's best-known rifles was their celebrated single-shooter, using the falling block action. Of the many models of single-shooters, Winchester are justly proud of their 'Schuetzen' model which, discontinued during the early years of World War I, was the last real American free-type rifle.

Since 1916 American marksmen have not had an American free-type rifle available for their use in international matches, until the announcement in late 1959 that Winchester had developed a special match rifle for American marksmen.

The Schuetzen was a special variation of the Winchester Model Single Shot, which devolved directly from John Moses Browning's first rifle, covered by Patent of 2 October 1879, and begun in the Browning Brothers' store in Ogden. They sold their patent to Winchester late in 1882. The type of action was built on the old Sharp's breechblock and lever, and is familiar to all firearms enthusiasts.

In March 1897 the Schuetzen appeared for the first time in the Winchester catalogues and was described as having an octagonal 30-inch barrel with fancy walnut pistol grip, fully checkered stock, Schuetzen pattern stock with cheekpiece, Schuetzen buttplate (Helm pattern), and also incorporated such features as a heavy barrel, double-set trigger, palm rest, mid-range vernier peep and wind-gauge sights.

The Schuetzen continued to be offered, with variations in stock and form, until the 1914 catalogue was issued, and appears to have ceased production by 1916. In its final form it was a take-down rifle.

During recent years the American rifleman felt the necessity for the development of a special American match rifle for American marksmen, and no one was more conscious of this necessity than the Winchester concern. In 1956 they conducted experiments with a free-rifle model. Winchester utilized a standard receiver and bolt assembly of their Model 70-bolt-action job. An improved version incorporated a rectangular receiver into the design but continued to use the Model 70 bolt. After many painstaking tests and experiments the new Winchester 'American

PLATE XVII
Top—Marlin Model 80C. *Centre*—Savage Model 110. *Bottom*—Savage Model 4 de luxe

PLATE XVIII

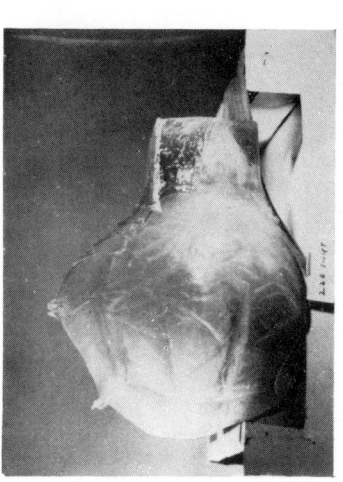

PLATE XIX

A study in penetration

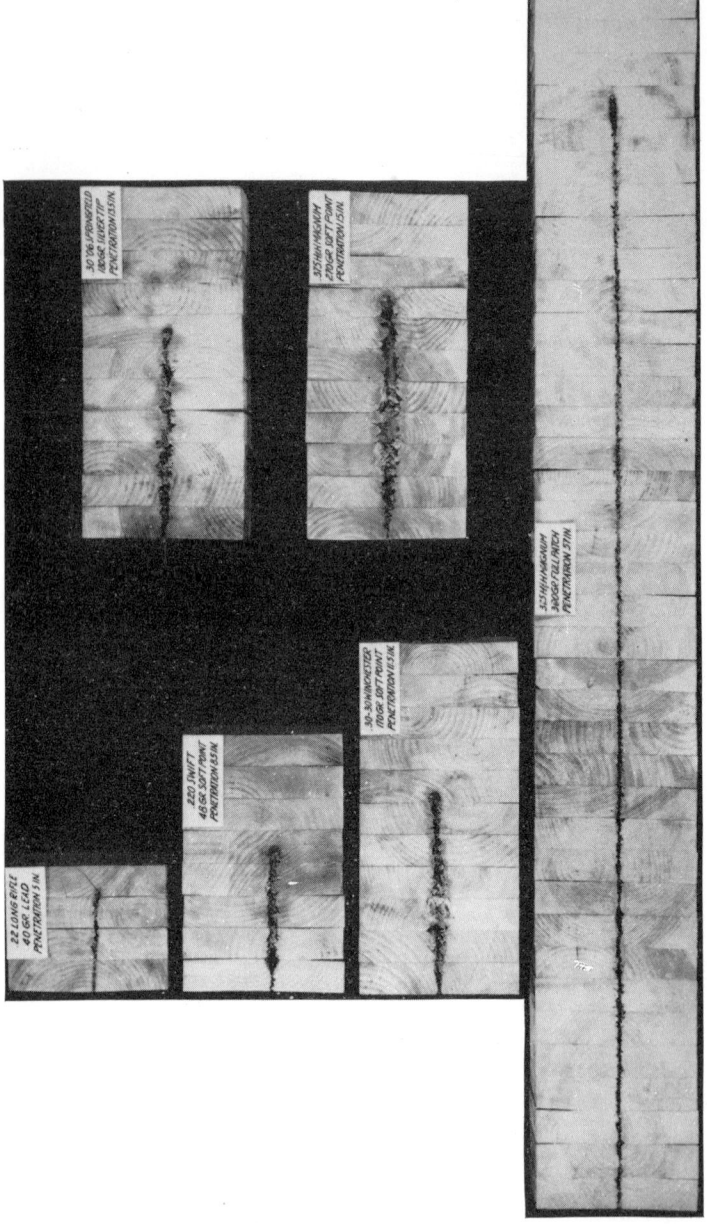

PLATE XX

Wood penetration, contrasting ·22 ammunition with larger calibre ammunition

MODERN DEVELOPMENTS

Olympic' free-style rifle was developed, as a single-shot rifle that had neither safety nor ejecting mechanism.

The rectangular receiver, coupled with the free floating qualities of the barrel ensured maximum accuracy. A further feature of this gun was a double-set trigger. Naturally, the gun was built in ·22 calibre, chambered for ·22 Long Rifle ammunition.

Unusually, for an American firearm, Winchester decided against mass production of this gun. Small public demand for such a rifle, coupled with the relatively high cost of production, would, they felt, result in only small quantities being available, built to special order.

The American Army co-operated with Winchester in the production of this rifle and the United States Army Advanced Marksmanship Unit at Fort Benning, Georgia, was associated with it through all the experiments. Tests were also conducted with this rifle in 7·62 millimetre NATO calibre.

Whilst I have emphasized this return to a match rifle by an American concern as being of importance the question must be posed—what practical results followed the experiments?

This is a natural enough question because Europeans have been well-equipped with match rifles. But from the American standpoint an important aspect lay in the fact that from lessons learned in the development of this rifle, American sporting firearms will undoubtedly be influenced and improved upon.

Incidentally, testing of the rifle produced many ten-shot targets (centre to centre) at 200 yards which ranged from 1–1½ inches extreme spread. When Lieutenant V. F. Wright of the United States Army Advanced Marksmanship Unit took first place in prone and kneeling positions in the 37th World Championships held in Moscow in 1958, he was using a Winchester free-rifle action. His kneeling score, with this rifle, was a tie with the world's record.

There is today a greater and more intense interest in international match shooting with the rifle. Turning back the pages of history to the Creedmoor matches and other international contests of times past, the rifles used attracted more attention than the shooters. This new development by Winchester should add greater interest to the sphere of international shooting; after all, a national team, using weapons produced by that country, is a more attractive proposition than teams using arms from another source. The incentive to beat the other fellow is greater and the will to win considerably increased, and it is with those sentiments that Winchester's match rifle was welcomed into the ranks of the free-type rifle. From the sociological standpoint the spectacle of, say, a Finlander using a British rifle, firing Russian ammunition, and with sights supplied from Spain might be symbolical of a perfect world, but the excitement of a team of say, Finlanders, using Finnish rifles and Finnish ammunition, shooting neck-and-neck against, say, a British team with British rifles and ammunition, would be hard to beat.

Such then is the story of the little ·22 rifle and its ammunition: a fascinating story, built up of many contrasts, and a story which is still incomplete because the pattern of development is speeding up and improvements come hard and fast. In certain quarters some writers, whose 'authority' must be suspect have written glibly that the ·22 rim-fire ammunition is not suitable as a sporting arm for 'it wounds more than it kills'. One such writer even went so far as to suggest in a British sporting paper published in England (though he, himself, lived in Canada) that the ·22 rim-fire should be completely banned from sporting shooting. The Winchester Magnum ·22 has given the lie to such impractical and loose talk: whilst the general body of conscientious hunters have for years found, that at suitable ranges and against suitable targets, especially when coupled with telescope sights, the normal ·22 rim-fire has given excellent results.

With continued growth of interest in target shooting there is also, inevitably, an interest in sporting shooting and this should ensure for the little ·22 a future every bit as interesting as its past. The enthusiast will ignore those demands for a ban on certain types of firearms set up by a very small minority, for they will remember that such criticisms and squeals do not emanate from the ranks of gun designers or improvers of ammunition, only from theory and the muddled thinking of the 'armchair ballistician' and 'chaise-longue sportsman'. In the story of firearms it has ever been that those who have criticized the most have done the least to improve or design a satisfactory substitute.

CHAPTER THREE

TYPES OF ·22 RIFLE

I AM very fortunate in that shooting and firearms are not only my hobby, but also my livelihood as well. Surrounded as I am during working and leisure hours by all kinds and conditions of firearms, none the less I find myself mystified by many requests from people for 'a ·22 rifle' and their bewildered reaction when this vague request is countered by asking, 'For what purpose is it required?'

Now there are many different aspects of ·22 rifle shooting. Breaking it down into two main groups, there are target shooting and sporting shooting. But again, target shooting breaks down again into club shooting at short ranges on indoor ranges, chiefly from the prone position; shooting in the positional shooting competitions of standing, kneeling and so forth; and free shooting. Each type of target shooting requires a different form of rifle. Field or sporting shooting, again, demands different types of rifle for its different facets. Pest shooting around and about the farm may only require a light single-shot rifle, the vermin hunter may require a repeating rifle, either auto-loader or manually operated, whilst the small-game shooter will find himself requiring either a centre-fire ·22-calibre rifle, or one chambered for the ·22 rim-fire Magnum.

Again, there is the use of the shot cartridge in the miniature trap shooting so popular in the United States and which, one day, I hope will also be popular in Great Britain.

Let us take target shooting first.

The target shooting rifle must be extremely accurate. It must also have a heavy barrel, be quick in its lock action, and of almost perfect construction. The rifle and its ammunition used in target shooting competitions must fulfil certain requirements: it must, for example, have a maximum calibre of ·22 of an inch, it must fire a bullet not exceeding 40 grains in weight, and, unless used in 'free' competitions, must have a trigger test of 3 lb. minimum. There is no limit on the weight of a target rifle but it is required to be of a pattern which will load single shots and must only be used as a single loader. A 'free' rifle, on the other hand, must not have a greater calibre than 5·6 mm. or ·22 in. Its weight must not exceed 8 kgs.

Most target shooters abroad use the bolt-action for target shooting but British shooters find that their favourite is the falling-block 'Martini' action as manufactured by the B.S.A. concern who have, indeed, brought this type of action almost to perfection.

Typical target rifles are the B.S.A. Martini 'International' Model, available in both right-hand and left-hand models and on which Messrs B.S.A. Ltd are actually working an improvement at the moment this book is going to press; the Winchester Model 52C, Remington's 40X, the celebrated Finnish Lion, the Anschutz Models 54 in Match and Super Match, the Czechoslovakian Model 4, the French 'Federal', the Hammerli 'Olympia' Model and many others. All, except the B.S.A., employ a bolt-action.

The price of these high-grade, precision-shooting instruments, which are almost works of art, are very high indeed and will cost the would-be target shooter in the region of £100. After which he requires other accessories such as spotting scope, shooting clothing, and so on.

The field sportsman, however, has a much wider choice of rifle. He may choose any variety of action he pleases—lever action, as in the Mossberg 'Palomino', or the various Marlin Models such as the 'Levermatic', 'Golden 39A' or perhaps the Noble Model 275: he may prefer an auto-loader repeater such as the Browning, the Harrington & Richardson Model 800, the Marlin Model 99, Mossberg 351-K; or the Savage & Stevens Models 6 or 87 respectively, the Winchester Models 55, 77; or the famous Remington Nylon 66 or its cheaper standard model 550. The Czechoslovakian BRNO in auto-loading form, or the German 'Krico', and the Italian 'Jaeger' are very popular amongst European hunters.

He may, for personal reasons, prefer the slide-action type of repeater. Mossberg, Savage & Stevens, Winchester and Noble,

TYPES OF ·22 RIFLE

as well as the F. N. 'Browning' are popular sporting models, but he will probably choose for field work, on account of its dependability, the bolt-action. In Great Britain the B.S.A. rifle both in rim-fire and centre-fire is a wise and popular choice, though Manufrance of St Etienne produce excellent sporting bolt-action rifles, with the Czech BRNO, the German 'Krico', Schonaeur, Finnish 'Valmet Oy' and the Swedish 'Husqvarna' giving them a good run for their money. American sportsmen may choose from a variety of models built by Winchester, Remington, Savage, Mossberg, Marlin, Harrington & Richardson, and others, whilst the Canadian 'Cooey' is growing in popularity, not only on the western side of the Atlantic but in Great Britain and in other parts of the world, being a dependable little gun, and not very expensive to purchase.

Meanwhile a new name has crept into the ranks of arms manufacturers for both target and hunting rifles and pistols. The U.S.S.R. today produces some of the finest sporting and precision target weapons it has been my good fortune to examine. And with the trade agreements between Great Britain and the Soviet Union these arms are available to British sportsmen. They are by no means cheap but their excellent quality of workmanship and their efficiency as shooting irons has been well established in international matches.

It is the boast of the Russians that their best-quality firearms are not mass-produced, but hand-made in the strictest traditions of gunmaking. My examination and handling of Russian arms bears this out. In addition to sporting and match rifles and pistols the USSR also manufacture a variety of combination rifle/shotguns, including those with barrels rifled for ·22 centre and rim-fire ammunition. Typical Russian arms are the 'Streda' single-shot target rifle and their MTS-5 over-and-under combination sporting rifle.

The 'Streda' really is a magnificent-looking job with a good record of successes in the international match shooting field. It has a solid, heavy barrel which is locked to the receiver by means of lugs and grooves. The action is of the Russian sliding-bolt type. The foresight, with hood, is removable and is supplied complete with a set of ring and rectangular elements of various sizes. The aperture rear sight is provided with detachable sight elements. Adjustment of the rear sight is via micrometer screws giving a graduation value of ·044 mm.

The orthopaedic, specially shaped walnut or beech stock incorporates pistol grip, cheek-piece and a right-hand thumb rest, and the stock is fixed at a considerable angle to the right relative to the centre line of the barrel bore. The purpose of this off-setting is to render the rifle more convenient for firing from all positions. The heavy fore-end, which carries a swivel, has a palm rest, whilst the rear butt face carries a shaped heel-plate of Swiss style. Heel-plate, palm rest, swivel and length of the butt are all adjustable.

I think that the Russians, by providing such a full set of components, accessories and so forth with their firearms have taken a great step forward. The usual term 'optional extras' often means that the object purchased is inadequate in the first instance. The Russians, however, are ahead here, and in their camera field, for example, they invariably supply virtually everything required. The Japanese, too, supply their motor cars complete. In firearms, as in other fields, the 'optional extras', which are virtually necessities, often conceal a true price and the purchaser ends up spending considerably more than he first thought, or even desired.

In the combination gun field the Russians manufacture a great range similar to the Stevens Model 24 and the German 'Drilling' type. For example, they build a model MTS-5 in which the upper barrel is chambered for ·22 ammunition, whilst the lower barrel is chambered for a larger rifle cartridge. The MTS-30 is a Drilling type with two upper 20-bore barrels with a third, lower, barrel in ·22 calibre (or larger).

But, whether hunting or target shooting, it pays us to look at the different types of action in use.

The *lever-action* is a typical American idea. It is faster than the bolt-action and so permits the sportsman rapid firing if the need should arise but though popular with American hunters it is a difficult tool to use when in the prone position and does not give as good a group at long ranges as the bolt-action. The most famous lever-actions are the under-levers, in which the action of drawing the lever downwards draws back the breech-bolt, ejects the fired round and cocks the hammer. The raising of the lever then carries the breech-block forward, feeds the next round to be fired into the chamber and locks the block.

One never sees heavy match or target rifles built with this action, but for hunting shooting models turned out by Winchester, Marlin, Noble and Mossberg are as well known in Europe as in America.

The *slide-action*, again, though popular in hunting circles, is not found amongst serious target shooters. It is also called the pump-action and, old-style, trombone action. The fore-arm of the rifle is movable and operates the breech-block. Pulling the sliding-forearm to the rear, opens the breech-block and carries it back, ejects the spent case; whilst the forward movement carries the next round into the chamber, brings the breech-block forward and locks the action. Most slide-action rifles carry a tubular magazine under the barrel, but the Mossberg concern manufacture a slide-action repeater with a clip-type magazine. As a hunting rifle it is almost as quick in action as an auto-loader.

The *bolt-action* is probably the most popular of all, being found in both target and sporting weapons. It may be of two types: self-cocking, in which the action is cocked when the bolt is pushed forward and locked; or non-cocking, in which the action, when closed, is safe, and the striker has to be set before firing. This is generally found in the cheaper, single-shot ·22 rifles used for 'plinking' and for training the young.

Most Continental rifles are built around the Mauser bolt-action, whilst the centre-fire rifle, though popular in other actions, is by far and away most popular in the bolt-action style.

There is a peculiar bolt-action rifle manufactured by Manufrance of St Etienne in which three ·22 tubes are carried together. The bolt holds three firing pins and the three barrels are discharged simultaneously. The idea behind this weapon is to give the hunter a better chance of hitting his game, as three bullets, not one, are directed against it. An immediate reaction is, 'Unsporting, why not use a scatter-gun?'—but the second reaction, by many sportsmen, is, 'Why not? If it means that the animal or bird, vermin or game, is more likely to be killed instantaneously through the use of this gun, then by all means let us use it. Clean killing is more important than purism.'

Of rising block actions, the B.S.A. range of target and sporting rifles is probably the most famous. This is a very dependable, quick, and simple action founded on the basis of the old Peabody patent, modified by Martini and adopted by Great Britain with the Henry rifling in the famous Martini-Henry military firearm.

Certainly the Martini action has no rival as a single loader, whilst a bolt-action, properly built, can stand up to a tremendous amount of hard work and abuse which would put a semi-automatic or other repeater out of action completely.

Of repeating arms in the semi-automatic category—the long-recoil system is the most favoured, though gas-operated rifles and shotguns have their advocates.

There is, however, no general purpose rifle which is suitable for both hunting shooting and target shooting. Whilst one may use, with success, a heavy match rifle in the sporting field, the lightweight, more easily handled sporting firearm is absolutely useless as a competition rifle.

Furthermore, though rifles are produced in thousands, every rifleman differs a little in stature or physical proportions for no two are alike. It is a mistake for the rifleman to accept a rifle *as built* either for sporting shooting or target shooting if he is going to get the best out of his abilities. The 'custom' gun, built by experts for shotgunning, is no mere fad. Guns have to be tailored to the sportsman for they are a very personal matter. This does not mean that one cannot shoot with an off-the-peg rifle or shotgun—one can and probably quite well—but for the very finest shooting, rifle and rifleman must match and balance together as one unit. The rifleman should, therefore, have the weapon carefully adjusted to himself for length of arm, breadth of shoulders, size of hand, length of neck, so that it handles naturally as if it were part of himself, as if it were, indeed, an extra arm.

For example, let us consider some differences in stature and their effects on dimensions of a rifle.

A person with short arms requires a rifle with a much shorter stock than a person with long arms. A small person (unless fairly heavily built) or an elderly or very young shooter will also probably find that it is necessary to have a lighter rifle than a heavier built or stronger rifleman. It is not only the arm which has to be taken into consideration when selecting the right length of stock: the length of the shooter's neck is important. If a stock is built too short the rifleman is going to have an uncomfortable time, firstly because he won't be able to grasp it properly, his trigger hand will be uncomfortable; secondly the aperture sight, base of the receiver, or even the stock itself is liable to deal him unnecessary punishment, chiefly in the region of the nose when the rifle recoils. The grip of the stock must be comfortable, neither too thick, nor too curved. The fore-end, too, must be of such a length that the rifleman can assume a good position, and broad enough to afford a comfortable hand-hold, and at the same time avoid too much bulk or excessive weight.

A rifleman with an arm length of, say, 28 inches, should have a stock with dimensions from butt to trigger of about $12\frac{3}{4}$ inches, and from trigger to hand-stop of about 13 inches. A shooter with an arm length of, say, 32 inches, requires a butt-to-trigger measurement of at least 14 inches, probably as much as 15, and the trigger-to-hand-stop length of from $14\frac{1}{2}$ to 16 or more inches. It is easy to make a preliminary check of the butt-stock length by bending the trigger arm at the elbow at right-angles, then placing the butt against the upper arm near the inside of the elbow. This should result in the right side of the butt stock and the right forearm resting alongside each other and, if the butt-stock is the right length, the rifleman should be able to use his trigger finger normally on the trigger.

Finally, rifles on the market vary from the downright cheap to the ultra expensive. There is only one counsel to offer: buy the very best you can afford. Avoid cheap, very cheap rifles at all costs. In cheap rifles many things are liable to happen. The metal is simply not good enough in the barrel to stand up to the firing of a lot of ammunition and it wears out rapidly—one cannot, of course, really expect it to do otherwise. The woodwork is liable to warping and cracks, and this affects, not only the safety of the weapon, but its grouping and potential accuracy. The actions are liable to undue wear and looseness and the headspace, in a bolt-action of the cheap category, is liable to excessive growth at an undue speed.

Buy the best you can—it's wisest, safest and, in the long run, the most economical.

Of sights, metallic and optical, slings, and other equipment of the rifle we shall deal in a later chapter.

CHAPTER FOUR

THE SHOOTING POSITIONS

FOR the rifleman there are a number of different positions from which he can shoot at both target and in hunting. These are all basically the same, except that the hunter is allowed more latitude in the actual method he adopts, not being circumscribed by competition rules designed to give all shooters an equal chance.

Perhaps the favourite of all shooting positions used by riflemen in Great Britain, and one in which they always do so well in competitions both national and international, is the prone position. This has been largely brought about by the fact that in Great Britain, as nowhere else in the world, the accent has been on indoor ·22 ranges, mostly at twenty-five yards' range. On the Continent, and in the United States, the club rifleman goes in much more for open-air range work, at longer ranges, and is much more versatile in his choice of shooting position. So much so that whereas today British shooters take high scores in the prone position, they do not do nearly so well in the standing and kneeling competitions.

The prone position as adopted by the target rifleman is based very much on the military position. It has the advantage that it provides the steadiest of all shooting platforms and is ideal for the beginner.

Let us consider the prone position, firstly, from the standpoint of the target rifleman. And, in conjunction with the prone position, memorize the following salient rules which are the elements of successful rifle shooting.

The rifle should be held comfortably, the right hand holding the rifle by the small of the butt. It does not matter where the thumb of the right hand is placed, some like to close this round the 'hand' of the stock, others like to hold it along the right side of the stock. So long as the rifleman is grasping the weapon comfortably, and securely, that is all that matters.

The fore-end of the rifle should rest across the palm of the left hand which is near the upper sling swivel. As nearly as possible the left elbow should be *under* the rifle, ensuring good triangulation. The left hand being well forward, and the left elbow under the rifle are the foundations upon which good and accurate shooting are built: this does not apply to target shooting in the off-hand position with the palm-rest. Release of the trigger is effected through the second joint of the index finger of the right hand. If the rifleman has only a small hand, or is built with short arms, the first joint may be used. It is immaterial that the index finger be used if the rifleman finds, as some do, that it is preferable to use the second finger. Provided the rifleman is happy about it and he is able to let off the trigger correctly there is nothing against this practice.

Now to return to the prone position.

The Army march their recruits to the firing point and there line them up facing the target and then, before assuming the prone position, turn them half-right. This is the very fundamental of taking up any shooting position and it is impossible to assume a shooting position easily without its application.

It follows therefore that the first maxim in assuming the prone position is *not to lie down facing the target*. On the Continent, where in many clubs the riflemen shoot from a raked or sloping platform, they are apt to shoot from a position more directly facing the target, but probably their lower scores in this position show how cramped it is. The physical requirements of the prone position are such that the rifleman should lie with his body at an angle of about 45 degrees to the line of aim. Through this the rifle points effortlessly and naturally towards the target. The legs should be spread out comfortably with the inside of the feet, if possible the heels (having regard to physical peculiarities of the individual), flat to the ground. In actual fact, on most indoor British ·22 ranges this means that the shooter is taking up much too much room and the position has to be modified slightly. Some riflemen like to draw the right knee forward, others to stretch their legs out straight behind them, feet together, and toes on the ground. By and large, however, for steadiest shooting the

THE SHOOTING POSITIONS

spreadeagled legs is the best position. Captain Horatio Ross, one of Britain's finest riflemen of the late nineteenth century, used a very uncomfortable-looking prone position for shooting; his right knee was bent, the inside of the foot flat on the ground, whilst his left knee was on the ground and the left foot rested on its toe. Furthermore, he shot at the target in a more direct position, rather after the modern Continental manner. In spite of this, or because of this, he won many important rifle matches, even in his late sixties, at ranges, with full-bore rifles, of up to 1,000 yards.

The spine should be straight and the elbows well under the body so that the chest is raised off the ground. The cheek should be pressed firmly against the stock of the rifle and, without any strain whatever, the eye should be as near the action as possible. The fore-end should be grasped firmly with the rifle hard against the heel of the hand and the grasp round the small of the butt should be firm. The rifle should be *pulled* well into the shoulder by the right hand. There is another school, however, which insists that the small-bore rifle may be held lightly, not loosely, and performances by experts adopting this rule certainly justify their use of it.

The essence of the hold, in the target prone position, is that the hands are the fixed positions on which the rifle rests. If the rifleman finds that he is holding the muzzle too high, he moves the left hand back to lower it. If he finds he is holding too low, then he pushes the left hand further forward. Under no circumstances should he attempt to raise or lower the muzzle by moving the fore-end about on the fingers of the left hand. The mechanics of this alteration of sight line are simple. Alter the elevation of the rifle by altering the slope of the left forearm, but not by moving the left elbow.

With accumulation of experience, and practice, it is possible gradually to lower the position of the body by extending the position of the arms, giving a steadier shooting position. But never vary the hold which must remain the same for all shots. Variations in holding alter the aim: tightness or looseness of hold do the same thing: variations in holding also tire the muscles unnecessarily and the result becomes reflected in the score sheets, ending up in indifferent, even downright bad shooting. As for the hard, firm hold, or a looser hold, the effect of a very tight hold is to increase muzzle lift and, unless the shooter adopts the relaxing butt-down technique between shots, it becomes rather tiring. However, good scores are made by marksmen using very tight holds and it appears to be a case of what one is used to or has confidence in.

It is when shooting from the prone position that the rifleman learns to appreciate the correct breathing technique. When the target is correctly aligned with the sights and the rifle is fired the shooter must, at that moment, be holding his breath. This is done *after* exhaling, not when the lungs are full. When shooting in the prone position the body is held up by the elbows of both arms, none the less the chest is on the ground. The very action of breathing, with its attendant expansion and contraction of the chest, means that the rifleman is raising and lowering a little with inhalation and exhalation. As a result there is a movement of the foresight up and down. This is overcome, after getting into the aiming position, and before getting into the aim itself, by breathing in, then out, and taking the correct aim. It is imperative that the trigger should not be let off at this stage. A couple more breaths should be taken, and then, on the second exhalation, provided the sighting is still correct, the shot should be let off.

There is a great importance in the correct trigger pull. Faulty trigger work is the cause of more wasted shots, and bad temper, which again leads to wasted shots, than anything else. The whole object of a correct trigger release is to ensure that the cartridge is fired without incurring any disturbance in the aim. Incidentally, though the phrase 'trigger pull' is used, one should never actually pull a trigger. One may squeeze a trigger, press it, release it, or let it off, but on no account must this involve any pulling motion. The squeeze, for that is the correct way to release a trigger, is to be deliberate, confident, and constant.

The movement of the trigger finger must never in any way communicate movement to the hand. This is so because the slightest movement of the hand will move the rifle, and the simple mechanics of the lever will prove that this results in a larger disturbance at the muzzle of the rifle, in turn diverging the flight of the bullet from its intended path.

THE SHOOTING POSITIONS

Although the whole procedure takes place in a fraction of a second, the mechanics of firing a rifle are rather complex. First of all the eye signals to the brain that it is time to release the trigger, the brain sends down a message to the controlling nerves and muscles and the trigger finger reacts. When the trigger is released, a striker or firing pin travels forward and strikes the primer in the base of the cartridge which detonates and ignites the powder charge. The burning, rapidly expanding gases from the powder charge can only travel in one direction, against the base of the bullet, and this they do, along the barrel, towards the muzzle and on its way towards the target. All this is done in an infinitesimal fraction of time but even so, the slightest waver at the muzzle during this time will be sufficient to spoil the score.

To take an example to its limits. Suppose the rifleman had a barrel which actually touched the target. If the rearmost portion of this weapon were moved so that at a point about three feet from the end it was one-eighth of an inch out of line it would readily be seen how far out of true the tip would be. This can be experimented with on paper. Take a straight edge a yard in length and draw a line along it. Assume that the three feet of the straight edge, for the purpose of this example, represents thirty yards in distance. Using an imaginary fulcrum on one end of the straight edge, about four inches from that end, move it one thirty-second of an inch out of line. Now take a pencil and extend the new angle and then draw a line to connect the two free ends. That final line would represent the distance that the bullet would have moved off target if the straight edge had represented the line of aim.

It will be seen therefore how important it is for the tyro to concentrate on the *exact* trigger pressure needed to fire the rifle. By constant practice, and by this only, one should arrive at the point where one can take up the slack of the trigger to the position where the slightest additional pressure will cause it to fire. With every heartbeat of the rifleman, the muzzle will waver slightly (this being most noticeable if a telescope sight is used) and at the exact moment the sights come on target, apply the slight additional pressure required to ease the trigger off.

It is very tiring to remain in the shooting position, even in the prone position, for a string of ten shots. To overcome this one must adopt what has been termed the butt-down technique, which enables the marksman to rest between shots and yet have the rifle available for instant, correct aim. After the shot has been fired, open the breech and then draw the right elbow back. Draw the right hand back along the butt until the thumb is behind the butt plate. At the same time the butt is lowered so that the toe of it rests on the hand. From this position raise the butt back into position again until the thumb is between butt plate and shoulder, then gently shift the shoulder towards the butt, lower the thumb and press the cheek against the side of the butt. Lay the right hand flat on the ground and push it forward so that it comes opposite the left elbow. In this position the rifleman may rest for a few seconds. To reload, close the breech and get back into the trigger release position is simple and there is no disturbance of aim. The whole purpose of this very simple technique is to allow the rifleman to relax, and nothing is more vital to accurate marksmanship.

The competition shooter will find that he has to observe certain fundamental rules laid down by the International Shooting Union and these cover two types of prone shooting position, the 'regular' prone position, and the 'free' position. The latter is defined as any position with the shooter lying either forwards or on his back with only one restriction, namely, that the rifle must be held by the shooter solely and must not touch the ground nor any form of artificial support. The 'regular' prone position, however, is a different kettle of fish.

Regulations for the prone position are that the shooter must lie down forwards with the upper part of the body supported by the elbows and that the rifle must be supported by the hands of the shooter only and held against the shoulder and cheek. A sling is allowed for the left arm. The underside of the left wrist joint of the left hand must be at least 15 centimetres above the ground or the rug, but there is a special dispensation for very small competitors. The right arm or hand must not touch the left arm, sleeve, or the sling; nor must the rifle touch either the sling or

THE SHOOTING POSITIONS

the sleeve of the left arm behind the grip of the left hand.

Though the prone position is the steadiest of all shooting positions, none the less this is the one position in which it is easiest to tilt the sights to one side, or 'cant' the rifle. Now if the rifle is canted to either side the bullet will be directed to the side and at the same time be thrown low on the target. A post or blade foresight does make it easier for the beginner to detect, and avoid, this fault but if he is using a ring type of foresight it may not be immediately apparent—unless, of course, the disc is mounted on to a post.

In field shooting the sportsman does not have to be so careful about the use of a sling or observing the niceties of the regulations governing target shooting. His aim is to get into a comfortable shooting position, take advantage of whatever cover or concealment he can, and get off his shot as accurately as possible.

However, whether field shooting or target shooting, the greatest amount of time spent in practise with dry snapping is essential coupled with acquiring the knack of relaxed breathing. Breathing space is used by the vulgar to denote either a fraction of time, or a time in which to regroup. To the rifleman it is much more, it means taking your time, relaxing, not holding one's breath, avoiding all tension. The relaxed shooter is the happy one and a happy shooter is the successful one.

There is a further position which is used by both the hunter and the long-range full-bore target shooter. This is also a prone position but in which the sportsman lies on his back. Unlike other shooting positions the marksman takes up a position by lying on his back practically in line with the target. It is a very useful sporting shooting position and is easily rolled into from the sitting position and gives a very steady shooting platform. Moreover, it may be used to take shots which the prone forward position would find most uncomfortable and from which kneeling or standing positions would be almost impossible, such as shooting down a steep hillside.

Usually the shooter lies on his back with the left foot flat on the ground and the lower part of the leg in an almost vertical position. He turns the right leg sideways, with the back of the right calf, just above the ankle, crossed over the front of the left instep. The butt is pulled back into the right shoulder and grasped in the normal way by the right hand. The left arm may be crossed over the chest and the buttplate held in the left hand, inserting the latter between shoulder and butt, or the left hand may be used to support the back of the head. The fore-end of the rifle rests on the inside of the right leg.

In this position the rearsight of a normal rifle would be too far away from the shooter's eye, so it must be mounted as far rearward as possible on the butt and fairly high. One word of caution. Great care must be exercised so that the muzzle of the rifle is clear of the shooter's legs, otherwise a self-inflicted gunshot wound may result.

An alternative method is to lie half-back, actually on the right hip and side with the left leg crossed over the right knee. The rifle is rested over the left knee and the butt held into the right shoulder with the left hand on the fore-end.

Off-hand Shooting

OFF-HAND shooting may be described as shooting with a rifle from the standing position. It sounds simple enough, but, like most simple things, it proves to be rather complex when examined thoroughly. The standing position means that the shooter is shooting against additional handicaps: the shooting platform is by no means as steady as when in the prone position, and the period when the sights can be correctly aligned on the target is much shorter. Furthermore, different techniques, even different forms of rifle, are required for varying circumstances under which off-hand shooting is taken.

The military rifleman shooting from a standing position adopts a special stance, with a bent left arm carried well away from the body: the sportsman shooting at stationary game may adopt a similar stance, or he may bring the left hand back to a position just in front of the trigger-guard, rest the rifle on the finger tips and bring the elbow as close to the body as possible. If shooting at moving game the tendency is for the left arm to be extended up the fore-end of the rifle and the stance of the shotgunner imitated.

The rifleman, shooting in competition in the standing position,

PLATE XXI

Top—A ·22 bullet approaches a flat stone surface at an angle. *Centre*—It strikes the top of the stone and runs, spinning across its surface—then *Bottom*—ricochets off with its original flight course changed, yawing at an unpredictable angle of flight

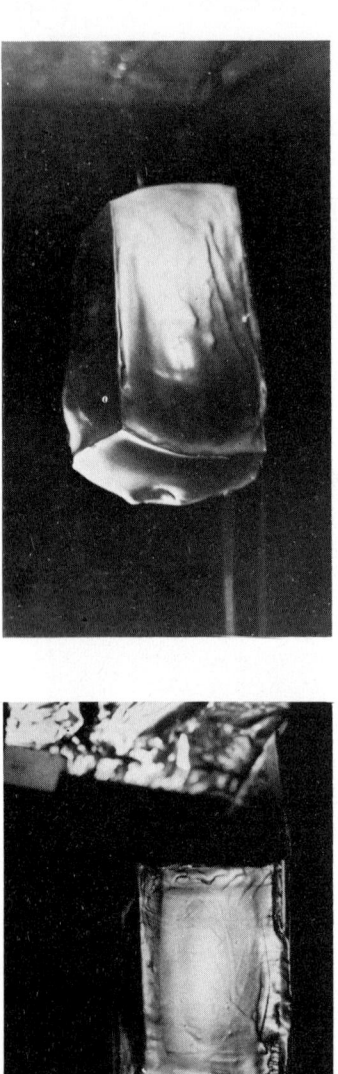
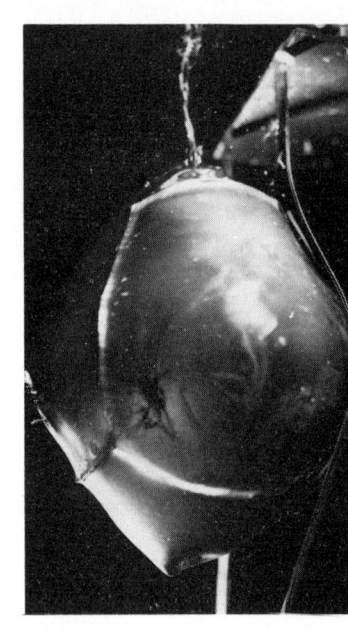
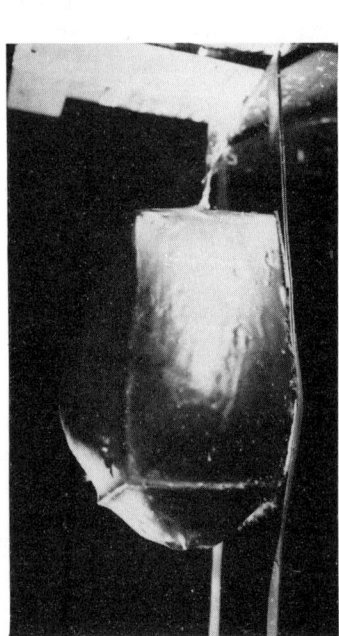

PLATE XXII

Top left—Effect of impact on a block of gelatine, simulating human or animal tissue, of a ·22 L.R. solid bullet. *Top right*—Note the greater destructive effect when a ·22 L.R. hollow point bullet is used. *Bottom left*—The ·22 Magnum has greater destructive power

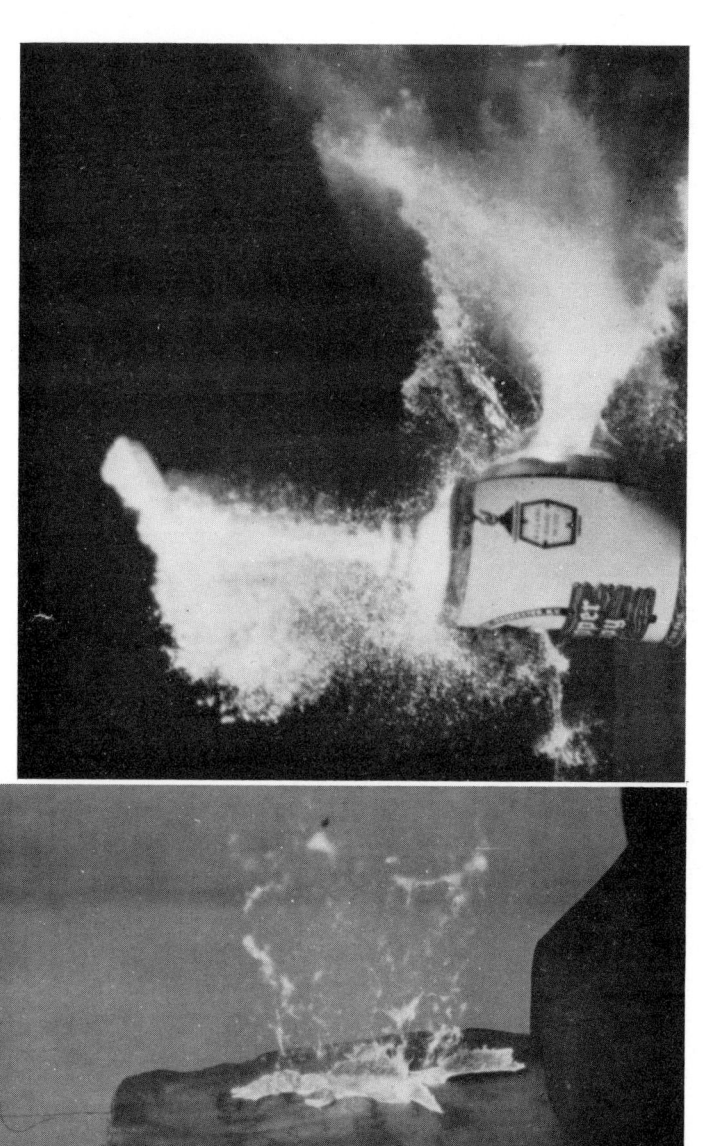

PLATE XXIII

Left—A ·22 bullet passing through a plank. *Right*—A ·22 bullet (L.R.) hitting a full can of beer! Note how the can bursts with the impact. This type of photograph, as well as the preceding ones, effectively demonstrate just exactly what is meant by the terms 'shock power' and 'striking energy'.

PLATE XXIV

Left.—A ·22-calibre L.R. bullet photographed passing through an electric light bulb. *Right.*—A ·22 bullet passing through a

THE SHOOTING POSITIONS

adopts a different hold. The provision of a palm rest, the placing of the elbow into or on the hip, the body well back, is a vastly different stance from the primitive, popular notion of off-hand shooting.

Let us examine the off-hand position in relation to the different aspects of the sport.

In the military stance the body is turned half-round and the feet, spread fairly wide apart, with the knees braced back and the whole body held in a rigid position. The left hand is placed well forward and the rifle is supported by the hollow in the base of the palm, whilst the fingers grasp the weapon firmly. The left elbow is kept directly underneath the rifle, and the right elbow raised so that it is at right angles to the body. This is a relic of volley firing days, though from time to time even the rigid military position has been varied. In a work published by an anonymous author in 1803, entitled *The British Soldier's Guide or Volunteer's Self-Instructor* the standing position is described as follows:

'The rifleman half faces to the right, the butt is placed in the hollow of the right shoulder, the right foot steps back about eighteen inches behind the left, the left knee is bent, the body brought well forward, the left hand without having quitted its hold, supports the rifle close before the lock, the right elbow raised even with the shoulder, the forefinger on the trigger, the head bent, and cheek resting on that of the rifle, the left eye shut, the right taking aim through the sight.'

However, in 1808, only five years later, Colonel Beaufoy published his famous work, *Scloppetaria; or Considerations on the Nature and Use of Rifled Barrel Guns*, and not only described a variant position, but included a plate of a rifleman taking aim in the standing position. Analysis of the picture shows that the left elbow rested on the hip, as in modern off-hand free rifle shooting, but the rifle was supported solely by the thumb and forefinger of the left hand, the other fingers steadying the rifle by pulling on a short sling. The thumb of the left hand supported the rifle from behind the trigger guard. The left elbow was carried close to the body, the feet were spaced about eighteen inches apart.

When, in Great Britain, the National Rifle Association was first formed to ensure permanency of the Volunteer movement, the accent was on military style shooting. And it was the Swiss riflemen who attracted the attentions of reporters and others. There are several colourful descriptions of the Swiss off-hand position of the period, perhaps the most engaging being that published by Dr J. Scoffern in 1860 under the title *The Royal Rifle Match on Wimbledon Common*. Space is insufficient to give it here in full, but there was a similar, though much briefer passage in the *Times* of the day, wherein the reporter stated:

> 'The way these Switzers shoot is something extraordinary. They violate the Hythe maxims absolutely, but nevertheless adopt a system more in accordance with their small-bore heavy rifles. Instead of placing the left hand well forward, as our men are taught to do, holding it firmly with that hand, and using the right hand for little else than to pull the trigger, the Swiss merely rest the barrel upon the left hand, or rather the left fist, planted just in front of the trigger-guard.'

After a short description of the method of loading the rifle, the reporter continued:

> 'Stretching his legs far apart, like the Rhodian Colossus on a smaller scale, the Switzer takes an enormous inspiration. Puffed out like the bull-frog emulous of passing for a bull, the inflated Switzer can no more bend to one side or the other than a hard-rammed sausage. A limited power of vertical movement remains to him, and the Switzer avails himself of it. A boss projecting from the butt-end is tucked between his arm and ribs, both arms are gathered up closely as possible, and the nose—that organ only given to man for ornament, as some affirm—is made subservient to the Switzer's rifle shooting. He uses it as a lateral rest—he steadies his rifle with it. Well, a man so inflated as the subject of our explanation must needs blow his breath off quicker than we can finish our description. You see the muzzle pointed aloft; then, coming downwards to the target almost imperceptibly, you hear a crack and a grunt together—picket and imprisoned breath go off simultaneously.'

The action of drawing the rifle down on to the target contrary to the customary method of bringing the rifle up was a peculiarity

THE SHOOTING POSITIONS

of the Swiss rifleman, as was also the habit of holding breath in the aim. The fact that the Swiss were able to shoot extraordinarily well seems peculiar in view of the handicaps they imposed on themselves, as holding one's breath and a prolonged aim in the standing position are not conducive to good shooting.

The off-hand position as practised in the military style is most unsteady. In high wind the unsteadiness becomes very apparent and owing to the nature of military drill, which necessitates holding the rifle in aim until the command to fire is given, the strain on the nerves and muscles of the soldier becomes almost intolerable. When one takes all this into consideration, and allows for the natural tension and nervous strain imposed on the soldiers concerned, it is no wonder that firing squads do not always do their work cleanly, and that the *coup-de-grâce* administered from the pistol of the officer in charge becomes a necessity.

Of course, shooting from the standing position in the military sphere is a feasible proposition when shooting from a trench or some other fortification or cover. Here the advantage of some support may be taken and, if necessary, a steady, prolonged aim made.

To shoot successfully in the off-hand position, and especially in the military position, requires constant practice. Physical training with the rifle, pump-handling, holding in the aim, dumb-bell drill with the rifle itself, is essential to develop the right muscles. And much good work can be put in shooting 'dry' and, above all, dwelling as short a time as possible on the aim and obtaining, at the same time, maximum trigger control.

From military shooting we turn to field shooting, or hunting with the rifle—here again the sportsman will, if possible shoot off-hand on as few occasions as possible. However, with running game, off-hand shooting is the only really satisfactory method and there are also occasions when off-hand shooting at stationary game or vermin is the only position possible.

For the double rifle, and here, let me add, double rifles *are* built in ·22 calibre (5·6 millimetres on the Continent), the action of the shot-gunner is imitated, and instinctive shooting is the general rule, though carefully sighted and aimed shots in semi-military style may be indulged in. With the single rifle a lot depends on its form and the action in use in the actual position adopted by the shooter.

For good practice at off-hand shooting under field conditions an excellent method is that of using ·22-calibre shot cartridges fired at moving targets. Cans flowing down a stream or in the tideway make excellent practice for this and the short, low power shot cartridges are not likely to do much damage. This enables the would-be hunter to get to know the swing and feel of his weapon in shotgunning style. Continual practice with this type of ammunition, and later ·22 short cartridges with the front sight removed and using an aperture rear-sight and the *hood* of the front-sight only, into which the target is centred is a very fine way of practising off-hand shooting at moving targets. Naturally there is a slight lack of precision compared with target work, but very quickly one becomes accustomed to centring the rifle properly and with practice it is possible to graduate to full charges at properly moving targets and, what is more important, hit them cleanly and accurately with no fuss or bother.

When it comes to match shooting or target shooting in the off-hand position, the situation is somewhat different. The rules and regulations covering off-hand shooting, or shooting from the standing position, as laid down by the International Shooting Union, have also been adopted by the National Small-bore Rifle Association in Great Britain and may be summarized as follows:

1. The competitor must stand on both feet, is not allowed any other support and must not take up a position so close to a wall or dividing screen in such a manner that it is not possible to ascertain whether or not he is actually touching it.

2. The rifle has to be held against the shoulder, the part of the chest nearest to the shoulder, and the cheek.

3. It is permissible for the elbow and upper part of the left arm to rest on the chest and the hip

4. It is forbidden to support the rifle from the chest through the medium of any form of extension or addition to the rifle stock.

5. A sling is allowed unless the rifle is equipped with a palm

THE SHOOTING POSITIONS

rest which the rifleman uses. If he uses the palm rest the use of the sling is prohibited.

6. A palm rest fastened to the fore-stock of the rifle is permitted provided it is forward of the trigger-guard and does not extend for a distance below the barrel in excess of 20 centimetres.

Of course, if the rifleman is left-handed, then the rules relating to right-hand and left-hand are reversed.

Target shooting in the standing position is not very popular, though, fortunately, it is increasingly appearing in competitions because when it comes to international shooting the teams which concentrate on the kneeling and standing positions are able to cancel out the highest scores attained by 'prone' only and 'sitting' only marksmen.

It is a sad fact that in shoots where kneeling and standing positions are shot off in conjunction with the prone position, shooters who are sometimes only a few points down by the time the standing position is reached, sometimes even in front so far as points are concerned, often fall down badly in shooting standing. And in positional shooting it is no use being an expert in two positions and only mediocre in the third. As I have pointed out time and again in articles in shooting papers, it is very difficult to get shooters who are doing well in one position to start learning another: that is simple human nature.

Off-hand shooting in target competitions demands different techniques than shooting off-hand in military courses, or in field shooting. Also, if a shooter is going to get the best out of himself, he requires a special rifle, or, at least, additional equipment for his standard weapon. In free rifle shooting it is permissible to use different rifles, though not to change calibres, and most top-ranking sportsmen throughout the world prefer to use a different rifle for shooting in the standing postion.

Unlike the military arm, different from the sporting arm, the rifle suitable for standing shooting in the target sphere utilizes thumb-hole stocks, palm rests, and hook butt-plates. In military shooting off-hand, the left hand holds the rifle firmly so that the trigger hand, the right hand, is free to manipulate the bolt between shots. In target shooting the trigger arm has only to fulfil the function of letting off the shot, and the left arm is purely a support, not a laborious method of holding the rifle.

The palm-rest should never be grasped tightly with the fingers: its purpose and design is to *rest* on the heel of the palm of the hand, in direct line with the forearm. If no palm-rest is used the rifle should rest lightly on the left hand, some shooters (myself included) preferring to rest the rifle on the tips of the fingers.

Assuming that the rifle can be held steadily enough to take a clear and accurate aim (and it should be possible to hold the position for between forty to sixty seconds, though no longer) the resultant score will depend entirely on the trigger release. Some shooters try to duck out of this by adopting field-shooting habits, by almost snap-shooting, getting off the shot quickly. This is a big mistake. Target shooting in the off-hand position has no similarity whatever to field shooting from the standing position.

The thumb-hole stock, therefore, assumes a position of great importance in the high scores factor. The use of this type of stock almost eliminates the tensions and trigger 'pulling' caused by the conventional type of stock.

The other distinguishing feature of the off-hand rifle is the hook butt-plate. This type of butt was referred to in the description of the 'Switzer' shooting at the first Wimbledon meeting. In Dr Scoffern's description he said:

'... at the end of the stock is a boss, which he tucks between the right arm and right ribs ...'

The purpose of Dr Scoffern's 'boss' and the modern counterpart—the hook butt-plate—in conjunction with the palm rest is to take the weight of the rifle. Elimination of cant is controlled by the upper right arm (or trigger arm) in the hook, and not by the left hand. There is no doubt but that additional steadiness is gained by the use of this device. Also, the hook butt-plate can be used comfortably in the kneeling position.

Both the palm-rest and the hook butt-plate must be securely fixed to the rifle and should not be mere temporary attachments, unless the temporary attachments are very stable. Any movements, looseness, or 'wiggle' in these attachments will be reflected in the

THE SHOOTING POSITIONS

rifleman's scoring.

The rifle used in standing position shooting should have particular attention paid to the trigger, because the main difficulty in shooting standing is the acquisition of a delicate and definite command of the trigger to take advantage of the fraction of time in which the aim is correct.

With regard to the actual shooting position to be adopted we find that it is rare to see off-hand riflemen all adopting the identically same position! In prone shooting, yes; but standing shooting is different. But, whatever variations there may be on the theme, the prime factor is that at all times the shooter must be relaxed. In off-hand shooting the rifleman is more liable to strain than in the other positions, and relaxation is, consequently, of greater importance (if that be possible). In a good position the feet should be about fifteen to eighteen inches apart. It is a mistake to spread the feet too far apart as, especially in the case of older shooters, it brings about extra play on the thigh muscles. The left hip should be pushed forward towards the target (I am dealing with the case of a right-handed rifleman), and the hip-bone should be in a line under the fore-end of the rifle. The left hand, the supporting hand, should be directly under the rifle and the elbow should be supported by the hip bone. Bone on bone is the maxim here. The right arm may be held high, though this is not necessary, and, if a thumb-hole stock is employed, it will be found that the arm will find its own, natural position automatically. There should be no twisting or turning of the body to get into aim on the target, this should be done by moving the feet about, and the position should not be maintained for an undue length of time, certainly not more than sixty seconds.

It follows, as in all forms of shooting, that 'dry' practice must be carried out if anything like decent scoring is going to be achieved. I feel, and I am not alone in this in view of the long talks I have had with all classes of riflemen and from observations on the firing point, that too many shooters, having done indifferently (probably with the wrong *form* of rifle) in off-hand shooting, approach subsequent attempts already defeated. The resultant nervous tension, coupled with the lack of dry practice, means the turning in of poor scores.

One well-known international shot has stated that, in his experience, the standing position 'offers more sport than most forms of shooting since perfection is impossible and you never stop trying to improve.' And that is it, in a nutshell.

But perhaps, even more significant, was the remark of a young target acquaintance of mine who declared, 'When I get a "poss" in the prone I am beginning to take it for nothing out of the ordinary, but when I get 90 in the standing—that's when I feel good.'

The Kneeling Position

THIS is a very popular shooting position for the hunter as it gives a steadier shooting platform than the standing position, though less steady than the prone position, gives a better field of view than the prone position, and yet, from that position, it is easy to stand up. Under some hunting conditions—as, for example, over boggy or marshy ground—the prone position becomes impossible and the kneeling position gives a fairly comfortable shooting stance. It can certainly be assumed than either prone or sitting position with less noise—a very important factor when hunting with the rifle. As the muzzle of the rifle, and the sights, are higher than in either prone or sitting position, the hunter has a better chance of getting a decent view of his quarry if the vegetation is fairly high.

In a hunting kneeling position there are no restrictions on how the rifleman may place his feet or knee, just so long as he is comfortable and steady, that's all that matters, but the target shooter comes up against the rules of the International Shooting Union and has to pay particular attention to them if he does not wish to be disqualified.

Firstly, the rules lay down that the position when adopted must not be so near a support or position that it becomes impossible to determine whether or not the shooter is obtaining any support from it. Support from any other source than the shooter himself is, of course, forbidden. The palm rest, allowed to the off-hand shooter, is not allowed to the kneeler. A sling may be used in that the left arm may be supported in the usual way as in the prone position. A shoulder hook or extension butt is also

PLATE XXV

Top—The Remington 'Fieldmaster' Model 572, slide-action repeater. *Centre*—Remington 'Fieldmaster' Model 572, lightweight model, in 'Buckskin' tan and 'Crow Wing' black. *Bottom*—The famous Savage Survival Gun of World War II—the Model 24 combination rifle/shotgun. The upper barrel is rifled for a ·22-calibre ammunition whilst the lower barrel is bored and chambered for the 3 in. ·410 shotgun cartridge. This is a reversal of European practice where in combination weapons it is generally the lower barrel which is rifled

PLATE XXVI

Top.—Savage Model 29 short slide-action repeater. *Centre.*—Savage Model 219, single-shot, 3-piece take-down, hammerless ·22 rifle.

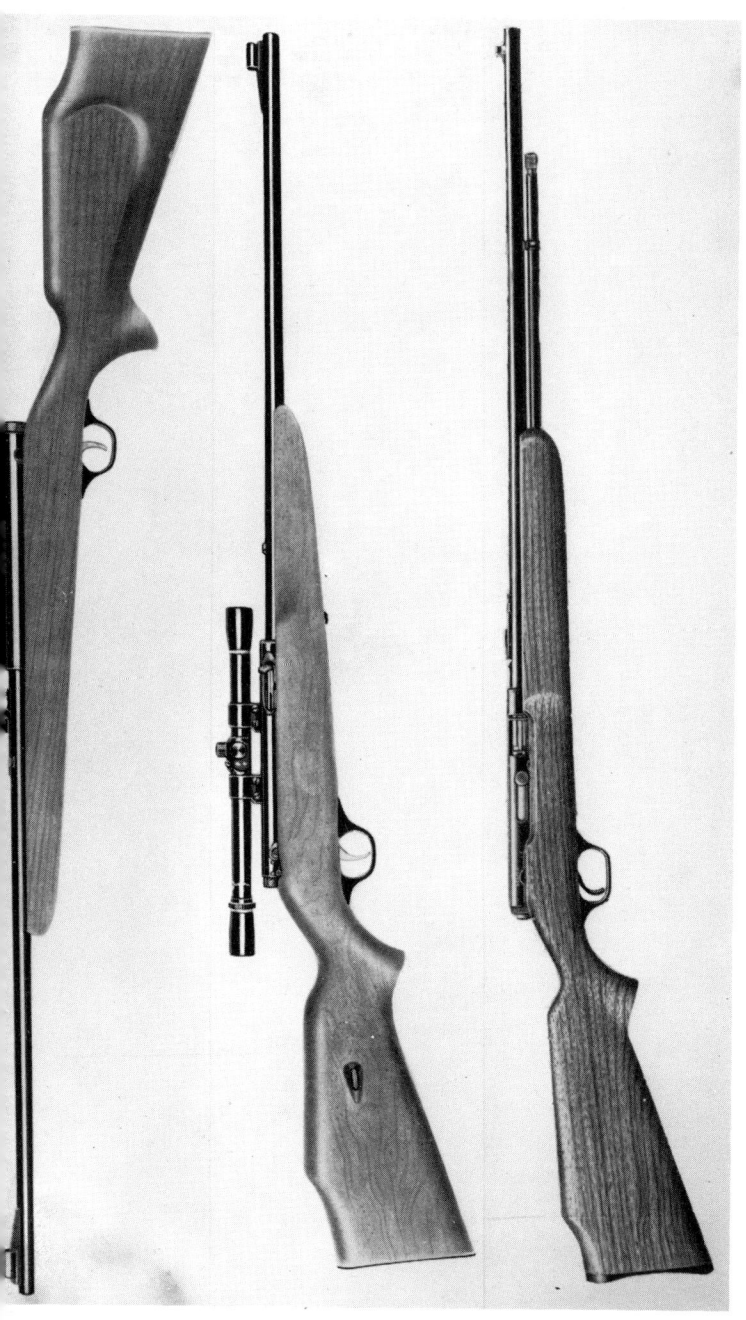

PLATE XXVII

Top—Marlin 'Super Automatic' Model 98, left-hand view. *Centre*—Marlin Model 98 with Micro-Vue 4× 'scope. *Bottom*—Savage Model 6 de luxe

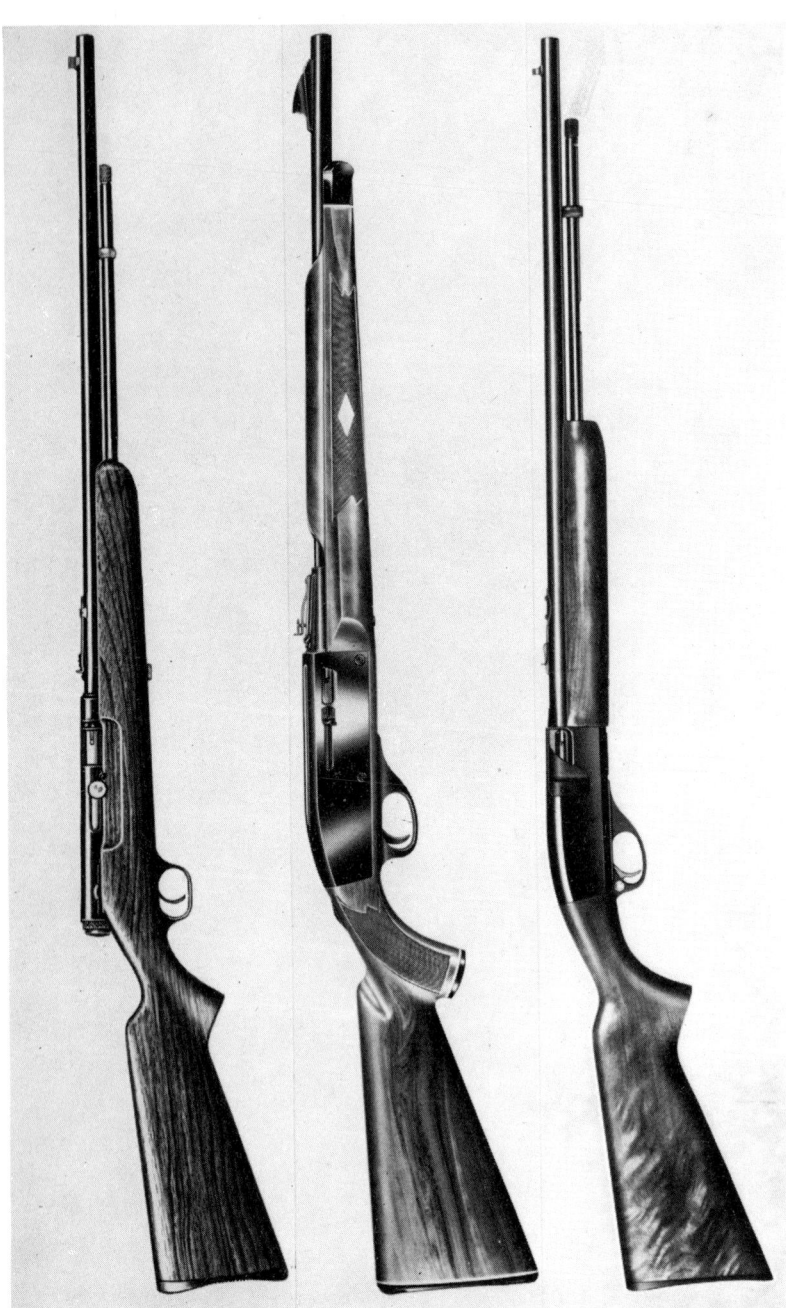

PLATE XXVIII

Top—Stevens Model 87. *Centre*—The revolutionary Remington Nylon 66 ·22 auto-loader in 'Mohawk' Brown and 'Seneca' Green.

PLATE XXIX

Top—Remington Model 550. *Centre*—Ithaca X-5 'Lightning' (tubular magazine model). *Bottom*—Ithaca clip magazine ·22 repeater.

PLATE XXX

Top—Action of Ithaca auto-loader. *Centre*—Mossberg auto-loader, Model 350K. *Bottom*—Mossberg Model 351K

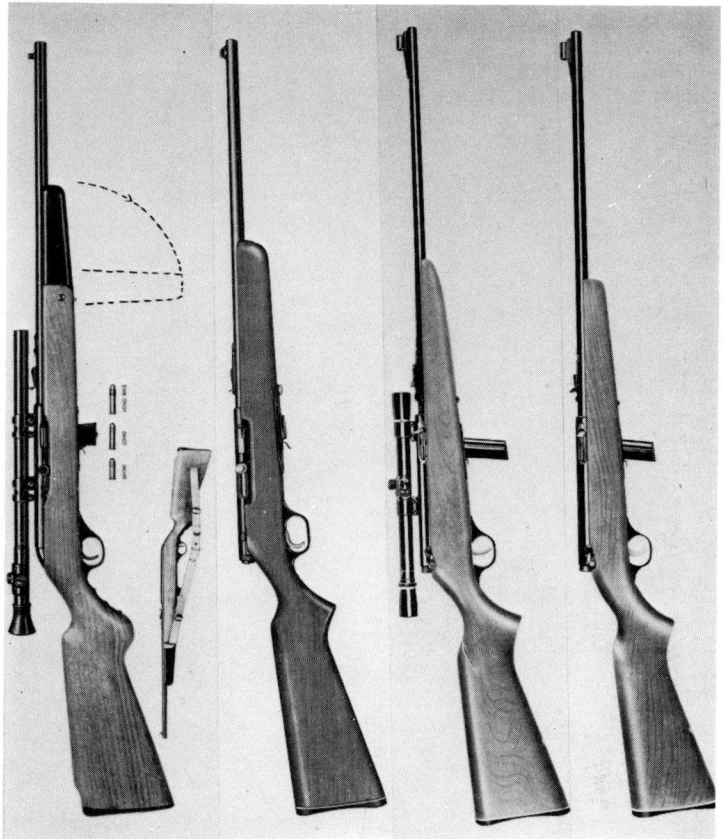

PLATE XXXI

Top—Mossberg Model 352K with hinged fore-end. *Second*—Stevens Model 85-K. *Third* — Marlin Model 89-C with 12-shot clip magazine and Marlin 4 × 'Scope sight. *Bottom* — Marlin Model 89-C with iron sights

PLATE XXXII

Mossberg Model 400 'Palomino' lever action repeater (*top*) standard model with iron sights, (*centre left*) exposed action view. Action open. Note short swing of lever. (*Centre right*) Exposed action view, action closed. The side plate has been removed. (*Bottom*) with Mossberg 4M4 (4×) telescope sight

THE SHOOTING POSITIONS

allowed, but this is problematical because it does not offer the advantages which it offers the off-hand rifleman. The supporting arm has to rest on the knee in such a manner, either before or behind the knee-cap, that it is not more than 10 centimetres (about 4 inches) from the knee-cap. There is a sound reason for this rule as its purpose is to prevent the shooter from resting the whole of the arm on the leg and adopting a semi-prone position. The rules prescribe that only the underside of the left foot, or footwear, may touch the ground but the lower part of the right leg from the knee may touch the ground. This means a bit of latitude for the rifleman in that instead of resting his buttocks on the heel of his right foot, he may twist his foot round and sit on the side of it, provided, of course, that one's ankle is limber enough for it.

In the military position of shooting kneeling, the regulations prescribe that the buttock shall rest on the heel of the foot and this promoted some curious stories of semi-mutinous dismounted cavalrymen who could not see the point of the regulation though they could feel the point of their spurs!

If the right foot is placed in a more or less vertical position, with the toe on the ground and the buttock resting on the heel, it is permitted to place a cushion, approved by the Range authority, under the instep, provided that both knee and toe touch the ground. No solid material is allowed and one is not allowed to use a cushion between buttock and heel of the footwear, though light material, such as a handkerchief, folded, may be used.

When assuming the position the rifleman should lean forward a little to get a good balance when he will find that this is a very steady and comfortable position.

Viewed from the front the left knee, the left hand, and elbow should be directly beneath the fore-end of the rifle whilst the right arm assumes a natural position, in some shooters raised fairly high whilst others carry it fairly closely to the body.

The finest exponents of target shooting from the kneeling position are, undoubtedly, the Russian riflemen. In the 37th World Championships, held at Moscow in 1958, they actually improved on their prone position scores when shooting from the kneeling position.

For sporting shooting the kneeling position is not the best to adopt when the ground is sloping and it is not necessary that the buttock should rest on either the side of the foot or the heel. In fact it is often useful when in the field to shoot kneeling with the body raised off the heel, and elderly sportsmen may find this an advantage. An alternative hunting position is to bend the left knee, throw the body well forward, the left elbow resting on the knee but the right leg is stretched as far rearwards as possible with the knee and foot on the ground. Alternatively, both knees may rest on the ground, in hunting shooting, but this is not a very steady shooting platform and approximates more that of the off-hand position, but may be useful to take advantage of a quick shot from cover which is too low for the standing position and too high for the sitting or prone position.

The Sitting Position

LET us consider the target shooter first. The International Shooting Union Rules describe the Regular Sitting Position as one in which the rifle has to be held as in the kneeling position and the left arm must rest on the knee as in that position. It is permitted for the right elbow to rest on the right knee and the buttocks must be placed either on the ground or the shooting rug.

The sitting position is a very steady one, and was in common use in the early days of the National Rifle Association Competitions at Wimbledon, in fact being much commoner than the prone position which came into use at a later date. But there can be no hard-and-fast rules for the exact position to be taken up as a lot depends upon the physical characteristics of the particular shooter. The essentials are the same, however, in that the body must be turned rather to the right of the target so that the left arm is brought directly under the rifle but it is immaterial whether the feet are crossed, or kept well apart. It was in the sitting position that the sporting rifle competitors shot for the Martin Smith trophy at Wimbledon for many years. In addition to advantages which the sitting position holds over the kneeling position for sporting shooting, other than in wet or boggy conditions when, obviously much more anatomy and clothing are likely to suffer from the damp, it enables the sportsman to deal effectively with a moving target. For most hunting, especially on

THE SHOOTING POSITIONS

sloping ground, though it affords a lower sight level than the kneeling position, it is more convenient than the kneeling pose.

Normally, the sitting position is adopted by sitting down, half-facing to the right of the target, then drawing both knees well up into a comfortable position, with both feet well apart. Some shooters actually prefer to stretch the right leg out a little. Get the left elbow just inside, or just over the knee-cap, and place the right elbow inside the right knee when it will be found that the rifle can be held very steadily. Alternatively, and this is a method which I prefer, especially when sporting shooting, instead of spreading the legs, cross the feet, the left foot over the right.

There are six different shooting positions with the ·22 rifle under International Shooting Rules, namely: the prone position, the free prone position, the kneeling position, sitting position, standing position, and the hunting position. This last lays down that the rifleman must have both arms entirely free from the body. The hunter, using basically all these positions, is permitted to use any support or accessory he wants and any combination of the elements of these positions, he has the advantage of shooting without the rules but the disadvantage that the exact range is not always known or the target clearly seen, perhaps even partly obscured. Yet it is in the kneeling, sitting, and hunting positions that the target shooter can learn most from the field shooter, and it is in dry practice and trigger techniques that the target rifleman shows greater superiority over the average hunter.

CHAPTER FIVE

THE ·22 PISTOL

PISTOLS are generally divided into three categories: single-shot weapons, revolving chamber repeaters, and semi-automatics. It is a common practice today to divide handguns into two classes, pistols and revolvers, but this is incorrect: revolvers *are* pistols.

The single shot weapon is solely a target arm. It is built with a long barrel, often nearly a foot in length, and is well equipped with sights for extremely accurate shooting. Owing to its slow rate of loading, it is suitable only for slow-firing competitions. A typical example of a single-shot target pistol is the Webley model. This has a barrel length of 10 inches, weighs 2 lb. 5 oz. and is equipped with an adjustable rearsight. Single-shot, slow-fire competition pistols have a very light trigger release: some international shooters use triggers so light that a mere touch is sufficient to fire the weapon. Needless to say, this very lightness of the 'set' triggers necessitates special grips which support the whole of the pistoleer's hand with the exception of the trigger finger.

The finest single-shot competition pistol which I have ever handled was a Russian model which followed the best traditions of International and Olympic style. Noted throughout Russia for its high accuracy, the pistol has a very high-precision barrel joined to the frame by two lugs and threading. The barrel bore is locked by means of two locking lugs of the slide and the respective bearing surfaces of the receiver. Barrel length is 290 mm. Front and rear sights are detachable and the positioning of the sighting element in the rear sight is by micrometer screw adjustment. The trigger mechanism with recoil reducer is mounted in the receiver whilst the firing mechanism is installed in the slide. Cocking of the weapon is effected by retracting the slide to the rear. Solely a target model, it was introduced to this country under the title of model

THE ·22 PISTOL

MTS-2. It is so designed that it literally fits the hand like a glove and is so perfectly balanced that one is not conscious of any weight at all. This is a most delightful pistol to handle, and very impressive in appearance and workmanship.

The single-shot target pistol has been expressly designed for precision shooting and has assumed, often, many strange forms. The serious pistoleer in 'free' slow-fire shooting is well advised to have his pistol tailored to suit his individual requirements. In addition to normal sighting, some pistoleers use extended sights, in which the foresight is carried on a rod, or rib, beyond the muzzle itself, for sometimes as much as twelve inches. This assists in more accurate sighting, but makes the weapon harder to hold straight, particularly if there is a gusty side wind on the range, because even a shooting booth can provide queer eddies of wind sufficient to move an extended arm.

For slow-fire timed shots and rapid-fire matches the revolver is a popular arm. They are generally made in either single action, in which the hammer is cocked and then released by the trigger, or double-action in which the pulling back of the trigger raises the hammer and then drops it. The double-action is handicapped by a very heavy trigger pressure required to operate the mechanics of revolving the chamber, raising the hammer, and then releasing it. A single-action trigger pressure varies from 2 to 5 lb.; but a double-action trigger requires a pressure of from 12 to 14 lb. The single action is, therefore, necessary for target shooting; the double-action being essentially a military or police requirement which assists rapid fire at very close ranges, though it does make accurate shooting more difficult.

The revolver suffers from one disadvantage compared with both single-shot and semi-automatic pistols. The bullet has to cross a gap between cylinder and barrel, and the resultant gas leak limits the power of the load. One significant feature of the revolver is that it is rarely fitted with a safety catch; also, of course, the foresight is elevated so that its tip is higher than the backsight, which means that when sighted the muzzle is depressed slightly. This is because the acceleration of the bullet up the barrel forces the weapon back in recoil, but this recoil, owing to the grip of the hand, takes the form of an upward jump. A portion of this recoiling upward jump actually occurs before the bullet has left the muzzle of the pistol and the building of the sights in the manner I have described is to compensate for this.

A feature of target revolvers is the barrel length. Whereas some models for police or military services are built with barrels of 4 inches and under (even 2-inch barrels are not uncommon), the equivalent model, for target work, has a barrel length of not less than 6 inches.

The semi-automatic pistol, erroneously called 'automatic', is a high-precision piece of workmanship, giving a high rate of fire, and may be used in all forms of competition. There are many varieties on the market. The Colt 'Woodsman' and the Colt 'Targetsman' are too well known to require description though the 'Hi-Standard' with 'Stabiliser' barrel, specially designed to reduce recoil and muzzle-jump for the rapid-firing enthusiast, is also enjoying great popularity. A comparatively new name in the firearms world, certainly new since World War II, but one which is growing in popularity is the Ruger model. Continental arms, too, are growing in numbers in the automatic pistol target field. Beretta, of Italy, have a fine model, with barrel weights, muzzle brakes and micro-sights, whilst Walther also have excellent models.

Nearly all modern semi-automatic match pistols incorporate adjustable barrel weights, muzzle brakes, and similar devices in their construction.

Briefly, the single-shot pistol is essentially European in character. The Americans seem to prefer their own semi-automatics and revolvers, however, for even slow-fire competitions. Revolvers are international in character and though the Americans do produce good target revolvers, such as the Smith & Wesson ·22 K 'Masterpiece' and Colt their 'Officer's Match' ·22, the British Webley & Scott Mark IV ·22 target revolver, with 6-inch barrel, is equally as accurate and well-balanced.

For semi-automatics, however, British pistoleers have to look overseas, to the Spanish 'Star' with its $7\frac{1}{4}$-inch barrel, to the various American models, and the International Match pistol made under licence by Hammerli at Lenzburg in Switzerland in

THE ·22 PISTOL

Walther 'Olympic' form, in two lengths of barrel, special target grips, detachable barrel weights and compensator. Not forgetting, of course, that under the trade agreements entered into between the United Kingdom and Soviet Russia the very excellent, and successful, Russian target pistols, including the 'upside-down' model are available to British sportsmen, though they are not cheap.

It follows that ordinary ·22 rifle ammunition is not suitable for pistol work. A revolver, owing to the gas leak between cylinder and barrel (here we are dealing with ·22 weapons, not the large-bore magnums) cannot handle as high a velocity bullet as the single-shot or automatic pistol. On the other hand, the semi-automatic requires ammunition of a consistently high quality otherwise the mechanism may not function correctly, and may jam. A revolver will fire comparatively inferior ammunition much more effectively. High-velocity cartridges are overpowered for use in pistols and an approximate muzzle velocity of 950 f.p.s. is adequate.

It is a mistake to use too high-powered a cartridge. This causes greater recoil, and though this may not be too fatiguing for the shooter in a slow-fire match, in rapid fire it may prove too much for him by delaying his recovery, sighting and trigger-squeeze after each shot. With five shots to get off, accurately, in four seconds, it will be appreciated how important it is that ammunition should not be too powerful. In fact, the Russians prefer to use ·22 short ammunition in their match pistols.

In Great Britain there are very stringent police restrictions concerning firearms and it was with considerable pleasure that I noted some time ago that the National Small-bore Rifle Association were able to announce in their annual report that in spite of such restrictions support for pistol shooting in Great Britain was gaining slowly but surely in popularity. Today there is in England, the British Pistol Club, which not only has set about the task of producing champions and international shots, but also publishes its own magazine.

The growth of pistol shooting in Great Britain does not, however, mean that anyone can go out, purchase a handgun and start shooting. On the contrary, the ownership of handguns is not looked upon entirely with favour by the Home Office, and there is more than a good deal to be said for this attitude. But British pistoleers are better placed than their equivalents in Australia where, in several states, the ·22 pistol is absolutely illegal.

A pistol is very much a personal weapon; it is easily concealed about the person, it may be made extremely small, and if allowed to get into the wrong hands it can constitute a very serious threat to public safety. Though one may read about hold-ups and robberies in which pistols are used: though shotguns have occasionally appeared in criminal cases: it is rarely one hears of rifles or carbines being used by law breakers—in Great Britain at any rate. The very bulk of a carbine or rifle is a deterrent against its use by the criminally-minded, and the provision in the firearms legislations, imposing a minimum barrel length of 24 inches, is a very sound one.

Modern authority merely follows an old precedent in imposing restrictions on the acquisition of pistols for use. King Henry VIII had a statute passed which limited 'handguns' to the 'length of one whole yard, and not under', and the preamble to this enactment stated, *inter alia*, that

> 'Murders, robberies, riots and routs with crossbows, little short handguns, and little haquebuts have become rife, to the great peril of the King's loving subjects . . .'

Apart from the restrictions aimed at preventing evilly disposed persons acquiring and using pistols, it must be remembered that a pistol, owing to its short barrel length, is a more dangerous weapon to third parties than any other firearm: the short barrel length means that a tremendous fire area may be covered by a small swing of the muzzle. But any person who has a genuine desire *and* a valid reason, for using a pistol in competitive shooting under National Small-bore Rifle Association or National Rifle Association rules, should not be refused a permit, providing he satisfies the legal requirements as to capacity; and in the event of a refusal he has the right to appeal to Quarter Sessions.

Pistol shooting today, in the United Kingdom, is practised by something like 1,000 enthusiasts. The N.S.R.A. has approximately

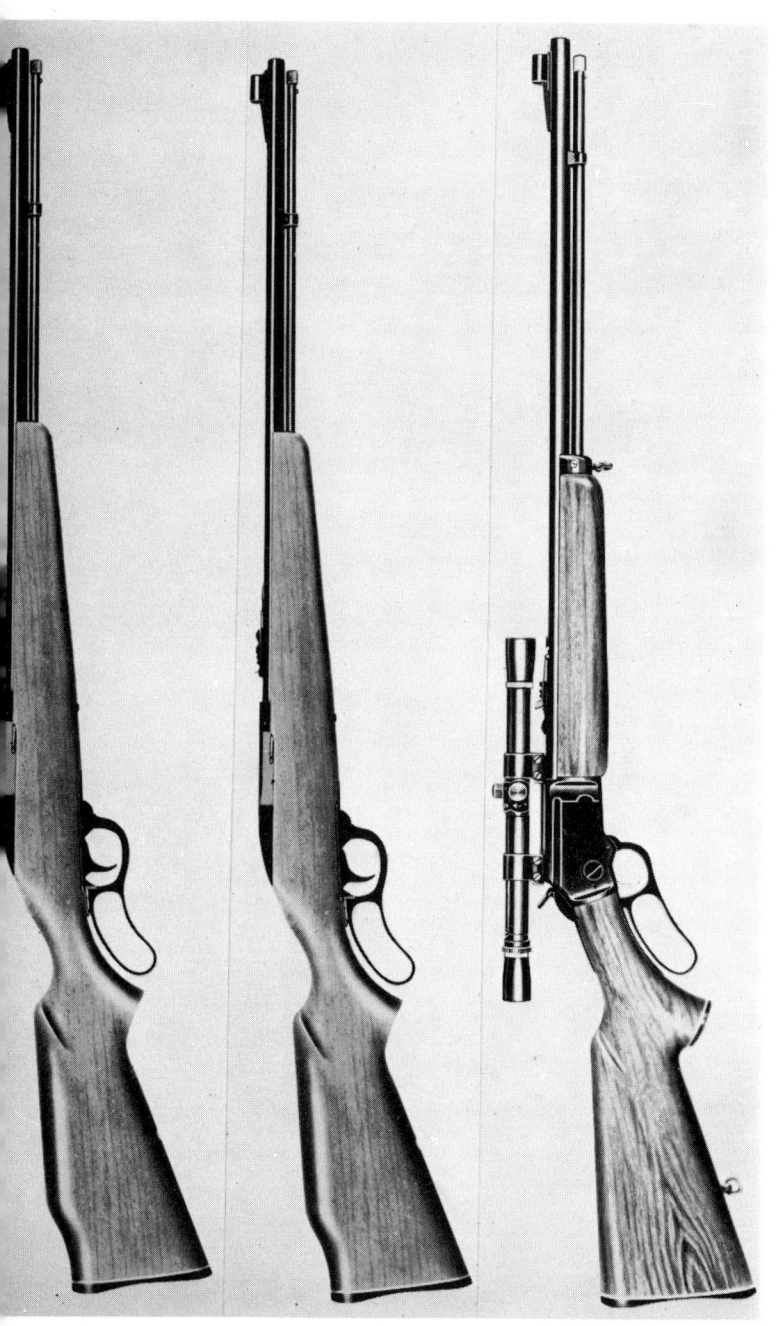

PLATE XXXIII

Top—Marlin ·22 Magnum Model 57-M. *Centre*—Marlin 'Levermatic' Model 57. *Bottom*—Marlin 'Golden 39-A' with telescope sight

PLATE XXXIV

Top—Marlin 'Golden 39-A Mountie' with straight grip for scabbard carrying and with telescope sight. *Second*—Marlin Model 56-L with 4× 'scope. *Third*—Marlin 39-A 'Mountie' with iron sights. *Bottom*—Marlin 'Golden 39-A' micro-grooved 25-shot lever-action repeater

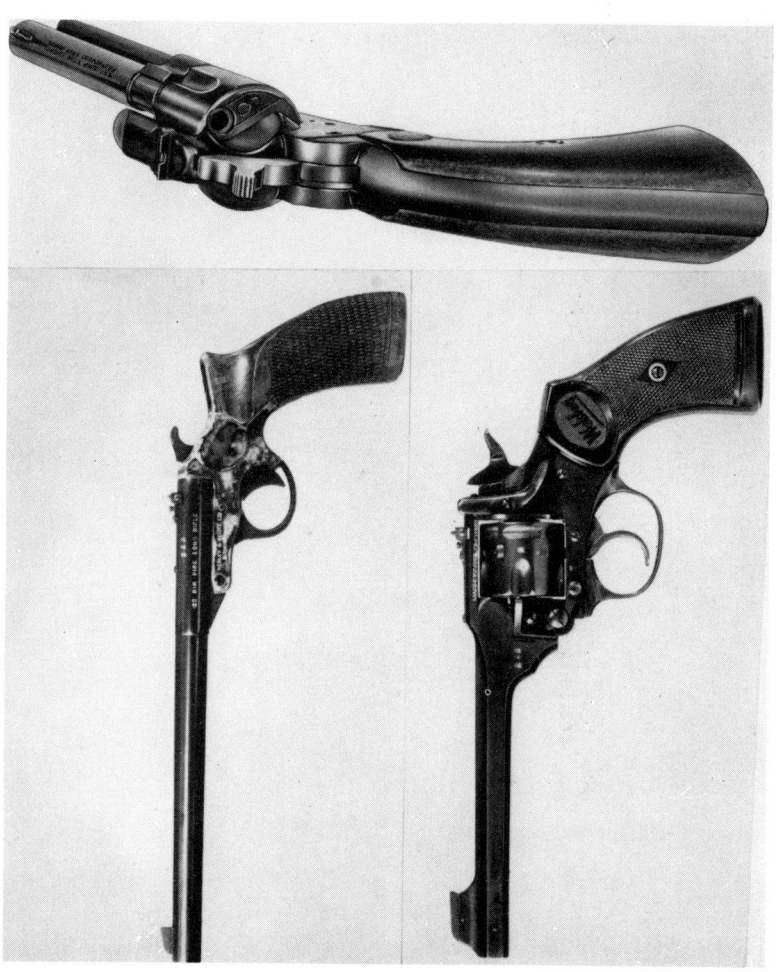

PLATE XXXV

Top left—Webley & Scott ·22 single-shot target pistol. *Bottom left*—·22 target revolver by the famous British manufacturers, Webley & Scott Ltd. *Right*—Savage Model 101 single-shot pistol

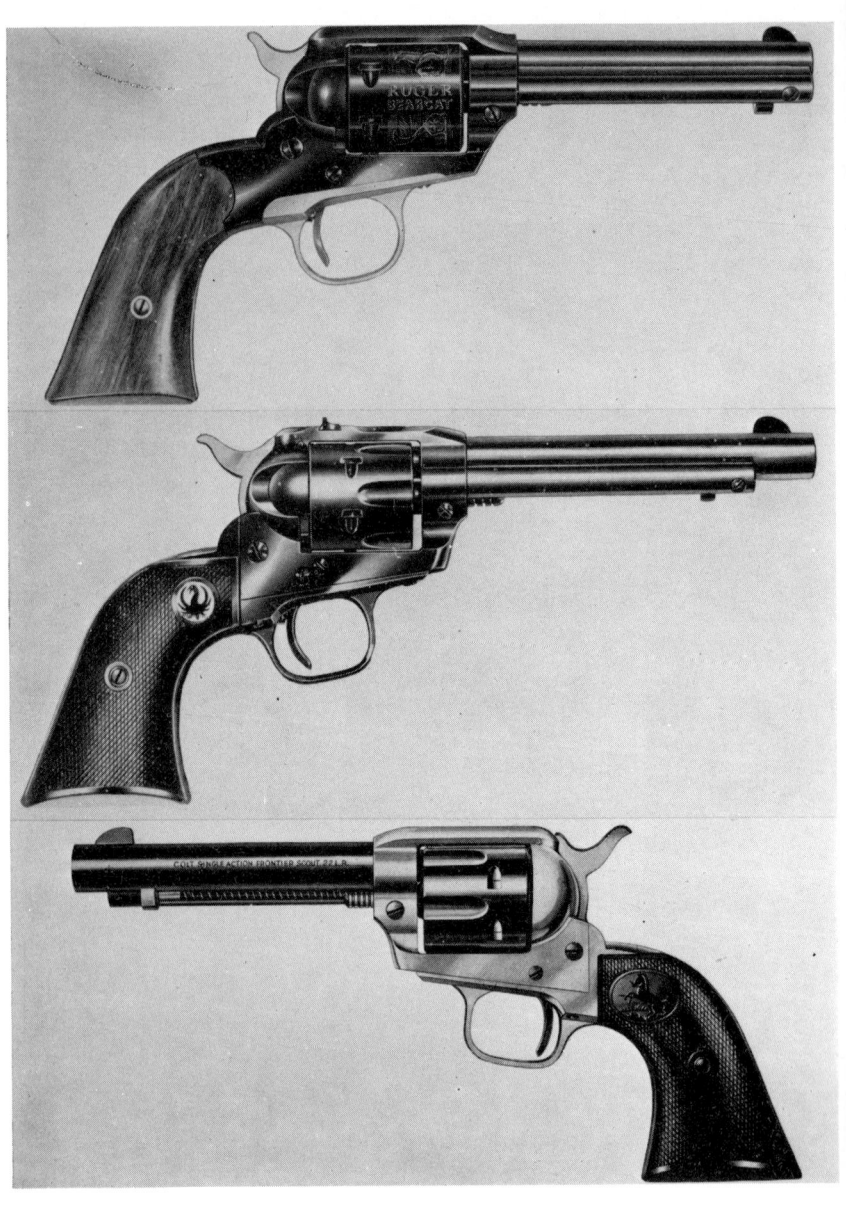

PLATE XXXVI

Top—Ruger 'Bearcat' Model BC-4, ·22 revolver with 4 in. barrel. *Centre*—Ruger 'Single Six' with 5½ in. barrel. *Bottom*—Colt single-action ·22 L.R. 'Frontier Scout'

THE ·22 PISTOL

200 Pistol Clubs and Clubs with Pistol sections under its aegis, but pistol shooting is nothing new in England so far as competitive shooting is concerned.

In 1885, upon the urgent insistence of Major Charles Ford, revolver competitions were instituted by the N.R.A. at their meetings, and a special range was constructed for this purpose. Today, many would consider that self-loading or semi-automatic pistols are comparatively modern, but it was in 1898 that self-loading pistols were allowed for the first time in N.R.A. matches.

The National Pistol Meeting, of the N.S.R.A., was first held in September 1948 at Bisley and was supported by only 100 competitors. Since then it has steadily grown, progressively, encouragingly, though not spectacularly.

Competition pistol shooting is entirely different from rifle shooting.

In Great Britain we are continually beset upon by moaners and groaners, critics who have nothing or very little good to say about target shooting with the rifle. These critics *never* appear on various club ranges, but, though they find nothing to interest them in target rifle shooting, they would probably find much to interest them in match pistoleering.

Pistol shooting is very much a personal matter and it depends far more on the individual's temperament than rifle shooting. Furthermore, it demands a lot of practice in holding, sighting, and trigger release. But match shooting will not appeal to the types who fancy doing Wyatt Earp or Bill Cody tricks with revolvers. Fancy ideas, principally 'leather slapping' contests and so forth, picked up from American magazines and television about handgun shooting, should be forgotten. Target shooting with the pistol is hard, painstaking, yet very rewarding. It is also unspectacular.

There are two kinds of target shooting. There is rapid-fire work, which sounds, and is, extremely attractive. There is slow-fire, which is not a matter of speed, but of accurate and precise shooting. In the rapid-fire competitions revolvers or self-loaders are necessary: in the slow-fire matches, single-loaders, with long barrels and accurate sights, are required.

Rapid fire *means* rapid fire. A typical competition consists of thirty shots at twenty-five metres at silhouette targets. The thirty shots are divided into six series of five, probably two series of eight seconds each, in which the five shots have to be fired, two of six seconds and two of *four* seconds.

Silhouette targets, which are black with white scoring rings, are shaped like a human figure. When the pistoleer is ready to fire, the targets, which are electrically operated, appear at full front to him, and turn sideways immediately the time limit is reached. The slow-fire competitions take place against the more normal type of target, with black-aiming ring and bull.

Free match pistols appear monstrosities to the novice. They have peculiar handgrips, long barrels, systems of adjustable weights to combat recoil, and all types and kinds of sights. But, as I have stressed earlier, a pistol or handgun is a personal weapon and must be built to suit the person using it. The old duellists realized this, and when they had pistols made in pairs they were tailored to suit them. When the opponent was offered the case and told to choose his weapon he was really at a great disadvantage!

It is in International and Olympic Matches that pistol shooting in competition really comes into its own and it is a surprising fact that though the British do not build anything like the Hammerli or Russian match pistol, nor do they build any semi-automatic match pistols, British pistol ammunition in ·22 calibre has the reputation of being the finest in the field.

Pistol shooting appears not only in straight pistol matches but is included in the very rigorous Pentathlon event. Though standards of International Match shooting are extremely high, so far as Olympic shooting is concerned, British pistoleers are capable of holding their own against the world's best. But this demands much practice and great devotion to the sport.

Let us take a typical example of the devotion required.

Mr F. Cooper, with Mr A. Steele, represented Britain in the 1956 Olympics at Melbourne and he finished in eighth place. His score was actually eight points better than the previous British record which was established by Wing Commander R. F. Guy in the Finnish Olympics in 1952. I cannot do better than quote from

THE ·22 PISTOL

the official report of the N.S.R.A., which, after commenting upon the very difficult conditions under which Mr Cooper fired, added:

'Undoubtedly Cooper's success was due to the long hours of practice that he put in prior to the match. During the nine days available for practice, he averaged eight hours a day, and his standard rapidly improved as a result.'

This is true, not only of champions, but of all enthusiastic shooters.

Practice, practice, and still more practice, coupled with a willingness and readiness to acknowledge mistakes and rectify them, is the answer. The difference between the average shot and the champion lies in the fact that the champion is never too big to acknowledge that he requires continual practice: he is never satisfied.

In order to encourage marksmanship in pistol shooting the N.S.R.A. inaugurated Pistol Rating Competitions, the top rating of which is the Master Shot: other ratings being Marksman, Class 'A', Class 'B', and Class 'C'.

Slow-fire competitions are fired at ranges of 10 yards, 20 yards and upwards to 50 metres. The International Slow-fire Match is fired at 50 metres, and at this range the targets look *very* small. The international course consists of 60 shots, in 10-shot strings, with a maximum time-limit of twenty minutes per string, that is an average of two minutes per shot! Above this there is a sighting period, to begin with, of twenty minutes, a five-minute break between strings and half-an-hour's rest after 30 shots. In consequence slow-fire is hardly spectacular!

The shooting must be absolutely deliberate, and this requires not only a steady hold, and accurate trigger release, but a complete single-mindedness of purpose by the pistoleer.

The rapid-fire, or silhouette match, is quite different. In this the five all-black targets are shaped to represent the human figure, and there are scoring rings in the silhouette. The targets are placed thirty inches apart and turn on an axis so that they may be presented either edge-on or face-on to the shooter. When the pistoleer takes up his position opposite the silhouettes, which are 25 metres away, the targets look almost impossible to miss. Presented edge on, when the pistoleer, with pistol 'down', calls 'Ready', the targets are turned to face him. When the targets are facing him he has to raise his arm, sight the weapon and fire one shot at each target. At the end of the allotted period the targets suddenly turn edge-on again and do this so quickly that any shot which is fired while they are turning is automatically a miss. In actual fact there is a tolerance of only plus ·2 seconds during the targets' return to their side-on position!

The time-limit varies according to the string of shots. International Match Rapid Fire competitions have five shots in eight seconds for the first string, five shots in six seconds for the second string, and five shots in four seconds for the final string. This last is less than one second per shot which includes raising the arm, aiming, and firing at five different targets. Consequently pistols and ammunition which have a heavy recoil operate to the detriment of the shooter, likewise a heavy trigger pull, and great concentration has been given to manufacturing weapons to overcome these obstacles.

All this match shooting is a very far cry from the pistol shooting taught for military or police purposes, and vastly different from the Wild West stuff so often lauded undeservedly. Pistol match shooting and pistol shooting in combat are two different matters: just as target rifle shooting is almost entirely divorced from military shooting in a theatre of war. It is easy to learn how to shoot a handgun, fairly accurately and quickly, in wartime manner: it is extremely difficult to learn how to handle a single-shot pistol with precision for slow-fire shooting. But when it comes to the rapid-fire match, the requirements are probably even greater. The match is scored primarily by hits, and then by numerical score, and an expert's tip is to try and shoot for tens in the eight-second strings, and try for hits in the four-second ones.

There is great scope for the enthusiastic pistol shooter in Great Britain and the National Small-bore Rifle Association is doing its praiseworthy utmost to encourage it. Unfortunately, however, not all club ranges are suitable for pistol shooting, as pistol ranges have to be specially approved by the War Office. These difficulties are, however, not insurmountable, and the N.S.R.A. will give every assistance to genuine enquiries.

Britain has some of the best pistol shots in the world, and there is no reason why their numbers should not increase substantially.

THE ·22 PISTOL

There is plenty of material available in the personnel of the various rifle clubs who have, perhaps, hung back because they were uncertain about the reception they would get if they proposed a pistol section. The real enthusiast who is not just attracted to a sport from its spectator appeal, but who genuinely wishes to see how things are run, and what the possibilities are, is urged to attend one of the N.S.R.A. National Pistol Meetings at Bisley, or make enquiry to the N.S.R.A. itself. But the person attracted to pistol shooting because he wishes to try out some Wild West stunts will find that his presence is not required and, in any case, he would lack the strength of character to get down to serious practising and accept the constructive criticism which would be so freely given by others who have worked hard to achieve a high standard.

Match Shooting

THE pistoleer who wishes to enter into competition shooting will find that the N.S.R.A., and the I.S.U., have laid down certain rules concerning the pistols to be used and various other matters attending thereto.

The barrel length of a pistol under N.S.R.A. rules must not exceed 10 inches, and this includes the cylinder of a revolver. Open sights are the rule, but these may be adjustable and must not be more than 10 inches apart. The trigger pull is not less than 2 lb.

Aperture, peep or telescope sights are not allowed but the shooter is allowed to use normal or tinted shooting spectacles. These rules as to sights apply also to 'free' pistol shooting. For free shooting there are no restrictions as to length of barrel, distance between sights, or trigger pull. There are restrictions in 'standard' pistol shooting competitions regarding the permitted type of grip in that no extension or attachment is allowed which extends beyond the junction of hand and wrist, nor is it permissible to give any support via the grip to the wrist or forearm.

The I.S.U. regulations provide that any type of ·22-inch (5·6 mm. calibre) pistol or revolver may be used provided it has been examined and approved by the arms controller. As in N.S.R.A. competitions, optical lenses are prohibited and no prolongation of the butt is allowed which could be used as a support. There is a limitation as to weight of the pistol in that it must not exceed 1,260 gm. Whilst there is no limitation as to barrel length, there are limitations to the size of the pistol in that it must be such as to go into a rectangular box with interior measurements of 30 × 15 × 5 cm., though there is a permitted tolerance up to 5 per cent in any one dimension. There is a limitation as to the height of the weapon which must not exceed 40 mm. inclusive of all accessories. One important rule is that which lays down that the centre of the bore must pass *above* the upper part of the hand in normal firing position.

The firing position is 'standing' and the shooter must not receive any support. Only one hand is permitted to hold the pistol and wrist protectors are not permitted. The test is—is the hold such that the wrist may move freely? If so, the position is legitimate—otherwise the shooter is violating the rules.

Incidentally, it is important to realize that shooting kits are to be of such a size that, when taken to the firing points, they will not interfere with other competitors, nor must the kit be used to provide a wind break.

Field Shooting

THE ·22 pistol is an excellent hunting weapon. It is often used as an ancillary arm by hunters, trappers, and the like but quite a growing number of devotees use it as a specialist hunting arm.

East of the Mississippi in the United States a number of pistoleers use the ·22 for dealing with small pests and game, and throughout the United States there are various enactments relating to the use of both ·22 in general and handguns in particular in the field.

For knocking off marauding crows, the grey squirrel, rats and the like a ·22 pistol can be a useful little tool. But field shooting with a pistol bears no resemblance whatsoever to target shooting with the small arm.

The field shooter, for instance, is not beset with the shooting laws regulating the position of the targeteer. He may, and should, choose any position which is both comfortable and steady regardless of whether or not it is conventional or otherwise. Lying in the prone position and holding the weapon with both hands, lying half-prone in the back position with the pistol hand supported by the knee, sitting and holding the pistol with both hands, or resting the pistol in the elbow of the free arm, may all be used, with infinite variations by the field hunter.

In field shooting the long rifle cartridge should be used and it is essential that the shooter put in a lot of practice on animal-shaped targets.

Incidentally, a recent innovation has been the appearance in America of telescope sights for handguns, and this combination of pistol and 'scope sight makes an excellent one for the handgun hunter.

General Hints

WHEN choosing an automatic pistol there is one very important point to consider, and that is the *angle* at which the butt and the barrel are joined. This is not anything like so important in the case of a revolver, as the grip can be varied to suit the shooter, but in the case of an automatic pistol this grip variation is not possible.

To ascertain whether or not the butt/barrel angle is suitable for you, point the pistol at a target, but don't aim the barrel! Do not hold the shooting position with the forefinger over the trigger, but lay the finger alongside the barrel (not necessarily level with it). Simply lift the pistol to shoulder height and aim with your forefinger, not the pistol sights. The butt/barrel angle will reveal itself because, if the angle between barrel and grip is too small, the barrel will point downwards and not at the point where the outstretched forefinger is pointing. If, on the other hand, the angle between barrel and butt is too great, then the sights of the pistol will point upwards. To try to get a correction of aim means that in the former case the wrist has to be bent upwards, and in the latter bent downwards. This imposes a considerable unnatural strain on the wrist and, of course, detracts from accurate shooting. Because relaxation is the golden rule in shooting, it is therefore of paramount importance that the shooting wrist must be held naturally and thoroughly relaxed. Do not, therefore, purchase a pistol in which the angle between butt and barrel means that the wrist must be bent from a natural pointing position in order to sight onto the target.

As the pistol is very much a personal weapon, it follows that individuals prefer to adopt different methods or shooting styles. But, basically, the principles are the same throughout.

No one can hold a pistol perfectly steady—that is a very fundamental truth—and it is only by constant practice, and yet again more practice, that the amount of movement at the muzzle end can be reduced.

There is an additional difficulty in that, unlike the rifle, the distance between sights on a handgun is fairly short, and this tends to increase errors in aiming. But, unfortunately, many beginners expect too much accuracy from a pistol, find that they are apparently not performing to their own expectations, and, in disgust throw the whole job up. But, in good hands, with constant practice, the handgun will perform almost wonderful shooting.

There are three cardinal rules in pistol shooting.

1. *Maintainance of a firm and even grip.*
2. *The maintainance of a constant sight picture, and*
3. *A smooth, steady trigger squeeze.*

Let us take the grip first because this is of extreme importance. It will be appreciated that the little ·22 does not have anything like the recoil of the larger bores and, in consequence, a little carelessness in the hold will not bring the same disastrous results, but bad habits beget bad habits and in no time the grouping will become poorer, the shooter lose confidence in first his pistol and then in himself, and finally give up handgun popping.

Hold, if you are right-handed, the palm of the right hand well up on the grip. In the case of a revolver or single-shot hammer pistol, make sure that you do not interfere with the cocking of the hammer, but get the hand as high up on the grip as possible. Now curl the fingers round the front of the grip and support, as nearly as possible, the weight of the pistol by the second finger. The thumb should rest lightly along the side of the frame without any pressure. In this position the heaviest pressure is applied between the palm and the middle fingers from front to rear. The first finger, the trigger finger, should meet the trigger at the bend of the first joint but if, however, the shooter has a small hand, it is quite in order to rest the ball of the trigger finger against the trigger.

Naturally, the physical peculiarities of the individual, size of hand, and fingers, as well as the size and shape of the pistol, do cause a few complexities. As a result it is impossible to lay down any fixed and definite rules as to the *position* of the grip.

Once the basic position has been taken up, the grip should be adjusted until it feels comfortable, but there must be no crooking or undue bending of wrist—the holding of the weapon, and also the squeezing of the trigger, must be in a straight line with barrel, wrist and forearm.

Recoil has to be taken directly through the line of the forearm, and any pistoleer who shoots with a heavy big-bore handgun will realize the importance of this after his first shot.

Whatever grip is adopted it is of vital importance that it is not gripped in such a manner that either muscle fatigue or muscle tremors set in. Practice in gripping the gun should be taken time and again until the necessary muscles have become attuned to this work. At all times pressure should be in a forward-to-rearward motion and *never* from the sides. Undue pressure by the thumb is responsible for a lot of shots being thrown wide to one side of the target.

At this stage it should be appreciated that whereas the thumb, palm and three lower fingers are filling the role of gripping the gun, the trigger finger must be absolutely independent. Its sole function is to let off the trigger, and movement of muscles in the trigger finger should have no effect on the grip whatever.

Now with regard to alignment and maintainance of a constant sight picture, absolute precision is required here. The top of the front sight should be level with the top of the sides of the notch in the rear-sight and an equal distance between the two rear-sight notches.

Both eyes should be open throughout the shooting process but it will be found that no matter how one tries, the sights will waver and waggle in all directions over the target. No one, not even the world champion shots, can prevent this happening though they can minimize it to a certain extent.

With a comfortable and positive grip, and with the sights aligned properly, although weaving about, it will now be appreciated how important a correct trigger squeeze is. The trigger must be let off at that instant in time when the sights come closest to correct position on the target, and this is only achieved by plenty of practice and a proper co-ordination to time that moment.

The secret of good trigger let-off lies in gradually increasing pressure—there is no sudden pull as the sights line up—and, above all, there must be no flinching. An excellent method of sorting out the personal problem of flinching, which is due to anticipation of recoil coupled with tenseness, is, in the case of a revolver, to ask a companion to load it for you. He must, without telling you the number or order, put some practice cartridges (snap cartridges) into the chamber. You then take the handgun and commence shooting at the target. You will not know which is going to be a live round and which a 'snap' round, so that if you have a tendency to flinch it will be well and truly revealed. If you are flinching-prone, when you let off the weapon and the hammer falls onto a 'snap' round the muzzle will be pulled down out of aim due to flinching. The procedure I suggest here should enable you to overcome this very bad habit.

The same cure can be applied with an automatic weapon, but dummy rounds must be used otherwise they will not feed correctly from the magazine.

As with the rifle, breathing is very important. The shooter must also be relaxed and confident. When the pistol is about to be lined on the target, take a breath, expel it, take another, let out a portion and hold the exhalation of the rest until after the shot has been fired. Above all, don't emulate our 'Switzer' rifleman of 100 years ago and hold your breath puffed up like a bull frog. If one finds that one cannot get off the shot in time, relax, take the arm down out of aim, have a little rest, and then try again. But, above all, put in a lot of practice, and then more practice, both dry shooting and with live ammunition; that it is the only road to success—dull, hard, wearying though it often may be.

CHAPTER SIX

OF GROUPS AND GROUPING

IN the world of sporting shooting it must be recorded, albeit with many blushes, that the average hunter does not put in anything like the practice hours which his target shooting counterpart does. In Great Britain one can anticipate one answer to this question, an answer which is continually made time and time again: 'We are limited by the police in the amount of ammunition we can purchase, hold and use, so that by the time we have sighted in a rifle, and put in a decent amount of practice we have little or no ammunition left for sporting purposes.'

This is not an unusual complaint, in fact whilst this book was being written a customer approached me for a sporting rifle. Examination of his firearms certificate, issued by a police office in Wales, showed that he was allowed to hold at any one time 50 rounds of ·22 ammunition, and to have or acquire in three years 300 rounds. This firearms holder was a farmer! And though it was rather an extreme example, none the less I do find that in many districts, though not all, in Great Britain, there is an unnecessarily tight restriction on ammunition permits.

If a sportsman is handicapped by lack of sufficient ammunition through restriction on his firearms certificate, he can of course go to his local police office and apply for a further amount. It is rare for the police not to meet his request. On the other hand he may, and this seems to be general practice by sporting shooters, accept the certificate as issued and carefully husband his ammunition for sporting shooting and expend as little as possible on practice.

Very few ·22 sporting rifles will shoot as accurately as the target rifle; first because of their lower weight, 5 to 6 lb. against 10 to 12 lb., which allows more 'wobble' or barrel deviation through movements of the shooter, and second, because the barrels are subject to great barrel vibrations or flip.

Nevertheless, excellent results are obtained by these weapons used properly, in the right hands and at the proper ranges. However, it is a little perplexing at times to hear sporting shooters proudly proclaim that their weapon is capable of giving a group so small, so definite, that at upwards of 30 yards the whole string of shots will centre inside a sixpence. When one hears such things, unless the weapons concerned are subjected to a practical test, the immediate reaction is: why don't the manufacturers concentrate on this one supreme model to the exclusion of all others? In actual fact, of course, these wonderful groups and grouping potentialities are bracketed with the extremely long ranges carried out by superbly hard-hitting weapons wielded by certain members of the shotgun fraternity. In other words, the statements are made rather loosely, combined with the dickens of a lot of wishful thinking. In fact one is inclined to wonder why, in light of these shooting claims, the sportsman concerned and his type, does not oust the traditional angler from the position of chief sporting Ananias.

Of course, the true meaning of the word 'group' as applied to the shooting of firearms, is not entirely understood by the sportsmen concerned who make these absolutely fantastic claims.

At ranges of 25 yards it may be stated without contradiction that the best rifles and ·22 ammunition are almost perfect and even if the shooter should aim a little imperfectly a bull should not be impossible. But before going into the implications of this statement one has to consider what the standard grouping is. So far as target shooting is concerned the target is so designed that, allowing for angular deviation of the cone of fire within certain definite limits, a possible at 25 yards would also be a possible at both 50 yards and 100 yards. Theoretically, assuming wind and weather and ballistic conditions of rifle and ammunition to be constant and perfect, it should be equally as easy to score a possible at the longer ranges as at the 25 yards range.

In practice, of course, theory is routed and an analysis of shooting scores and records will reveal that the greatest number of possibles are scored at 25 yards, and equally so a greater number at 50 yards than at 100 yards.

The permissible angular deviation of the cone of fire is slightly over one minute of angle from the centre of the cone. For the non-technical reader a minute of angle may be defined as that subtended by a deviation of one inch at 100 yards, and coupled with this should be the additional deviation of half the diameter of the ·22 bullet, thereby introducing what is known as the allowable deviation.

Thus, when a manufacturer claims that his products group in a 2-inch or 1½-inch ring he is claiming that the rifle (using a certain type of ammunition), will place ten consecutive shots in a group which may be circumscribed by a ring of 2-inch or 1½-inch diameter.

This 'group'-claiming by a manufacturer points to a most important factor in rifle shooting, a factor which must be thoroughly assimilated and understood by the rifleman. This factor is that the rifle will not place every shot inside the same bullet hole on the target, as some sportsmen and most non-shooting members of the public believe, but that the accuracy of the rifle, and the correctness of it centres upon its groupings. In other words, the rifleman must everlastingly think in terms of groups, and never consider the effect of single shots.

Unfortunately Services training is sometimes at fault here. It is a common practice, or was, in the Services for a soldier to be taken on to the range, after basic instruction had been given, and instructed to fire at certain targets at fixed ranges. One shot is generally allowed to 'clear the barrel' of oil, or as a 'sighter' and thereafter the recruit is expected to go on and score for the bull. This is wrong, utterly wrong, because the unfortunate shooter—and this also happens in civilian life to those sporting shooters who have not had the benefit of club experience or other tutorial benefits—aims and observes the effect of his shot. If he hits the bull, probably by a fluke, confusion ensues because he takes the same aim and, not being group conscious, is dismayed to find his bullet hole signalled as either off the bull, or in a different position from where he expected it to be. He could have been centring his shots with the extreme left-hand or right-hand shot of the group in the bull; the net result is that the circle or group would have its centre off the bull.

Should he find his shot, say, high and to the left, again having no knowledge of groups, he corrects his aim, lower and to the right—with again, dire consequences. And so he goes on and on, chasing his errors, magnifying them, and coming to the conclusion that the weapon he is using is useless or arriving at the same conclusion as his officer or N.C.O. in charge that he could not hit a barn door at five paces.

It is utterly and absolutely impossible to centre your group by firing single shots and then adjusting either sights or aim because *nothing*, positively nothing, can alter the potential grouping of a series of shots from a given weapon. Mind you, the grouping of a rifle may vary with different brands, or even different batches, of ammunition: the condition of the barrel, wear, fouling, and so forth, will also affect the grouping.

The first thing to do with your rifle is to find how it groups.

Unless you do this you are only wasting your own time and your money.

Having made your aim on the target and noted where the first shot went, do not adjust your aim or the sights. Fire another shot and observe its position on the target. And so on until you have fired at least ten shots. Assuming your sights to be correct for range, it may be that the resulting ten holes in the target are $1\frac{1}{2}$ inches to the right of the bull and 1 inch above it, so far as the centre of the group is concerned. The whole of the shots should be within the guaranteed circle at 100 yards.

But it is important to remember that it is not the sights you are testing, it is the group of shots which is under trial—and the position of the group on the target is only material to testing of the sights, something entirely different.

Still without adjusting the sights or aim, fire a second string of ten shots, and observe the position and grouping of the bullet holes on another target at the same range. Identical grouping, providing there have been no imperfections in aim, should have resulted. Now find the centre of the group. There is nothing difficult about this.

Draw a vertical line on one side of the group and ascertain the average distance of this line from the centre of the bullet holes. Draw another vertical line at this distance from the first one and it will be seen that the centre of the group is cut by this line. Now draw a horizontal line at the correct distance with the centre of the group lying on it. The intersection of the horizontal and vertical line will show the true centre of the group.

Having now found the centre of your group, and this cannot be found until all your ten shots have been fired, the next step is to adjust your sights so that the centre of your group should coincide with the centre of the bull. If this is done properly the rifleman does not then proceed to try to get each individual shot into the centre of the bull—*he aims the centre of his group into the centre of the bull* and, provided he is shooting properly, the bullets should then fill it, though in due course.

Ignoring the human factors in shooting, assuming that a rifle has a good barrel and action and that the ammunition is 'in tune' with it, the greatest factor affecting the good grouping of the weapon is the bedding of the barrel and action in the stock.

Most shooting men know that when a rifle is fired, a shock wave travels up the barrel towards the muzzle at a greater speed than that of the projectile up the bore. The shock wave reaches the muzzle first and the direction in which the muzzle is pointing, as a result of this shock wave and not as a result of aiming, at the moment the bullet leaves the muzzle has an effect upon the direction of flight of the projectile towards the target, and thus upon the group, or potential group, of the rifle in question.

This jump, muzzle flip, or barrel vibration, can be compensated by adjustment of sights or cartridge loads, but if the barrel and stock should be bedded poorly, groups will become erratic and poor shooting will result.

Just what then is accurate bedding of a rifle barrel and how is it achieved?

First, if the barrel is fixed rigidly in a full-length stock, the barrel must be properly bedded throughout its full length most carefully and accurately. If the bedding is carried out carelessly it may be possible for the steel barrel to be bent to the groove in the stock or it may prevent the natural vibrations of the barrel. A wooden stock, in a cheap weapon, may warp with dampness, or loosen with age. Warping, swelling, or looseness brings different pressures to bear on parts of the barrel, so that the free vibration of the barrel is deflected.

To overcome the problem of barrel bedding, some weapons incorporate the 'free-floating' barrel. In these arms the 'floating' fore-end is attached to the barrel only at the breech-end and there is no contact between barrel and fore-end forward of the breech. This leaves the barrel free to vibrate in a natural manner, but, if the floating fore-end should be insecurely fastened, or allowed in any way to come into contact with the barrel, groups and accuracy will suffer immediately. The free-floating barrel would appear at first sight to be the obvious solution to the barrel-stock-bedding problem; but, in practice it has been found that damping pressure applied through the floating fore-end can improve accuracy.

Screw tension, band tension, fore-end packing, even the pull of a sling, can affect the barrel vibrations, and if a rifle is consistently giving poor 'groups' though other factors *may* enter into it, the solution to the problem will probably lie in the fact that the barrel is improperly bedded.

To overcome this, manufacturers are bringing out mechanical adjusters built into the weapons, electrical bedding devices, and so forth, as well as a change-over in material from which stocks are manufactured. The warping of wood, or swelling, is the chief cause of bedding failure. But this is now being overcome by the introduction of metal stocks, light alloy of course, and plastic components and glass fibre.

Carving a stock so that the barrel is inlet properly is a tedious job: packing with plastic or rubber material is, at best, a poor substitute; furthermore, permanent accuracy under all climatic conditions cannot be assured by these methods. Every time a rifle is fired the barrel and action move backwards under recoil, compressing the stock in the recoil areas and gradually loosening themselves in the stock. One method I used with a ·303-inch sporting rifle was to hollow out the fore-end, fill it with plastic wood and then press the barrel into it, so that I got an almost perfect fitting of barrel to stock. The weapon shot well, but was,

PLATE XXXVII

Top left—Smith & Wesson 'Airweight' Model 22/32 Kit Gun. *Top right*—Smith & Wesson ·22 'Combat Masterpiece'. *Centre*—The 1953 Model 22/32 Smith & Wesson Kit Gun. *Bottom left*—Smith & Wesson K-22 'Masterpiece'. *Bottom right* —Smith & Wesson 1953 22/32 target model

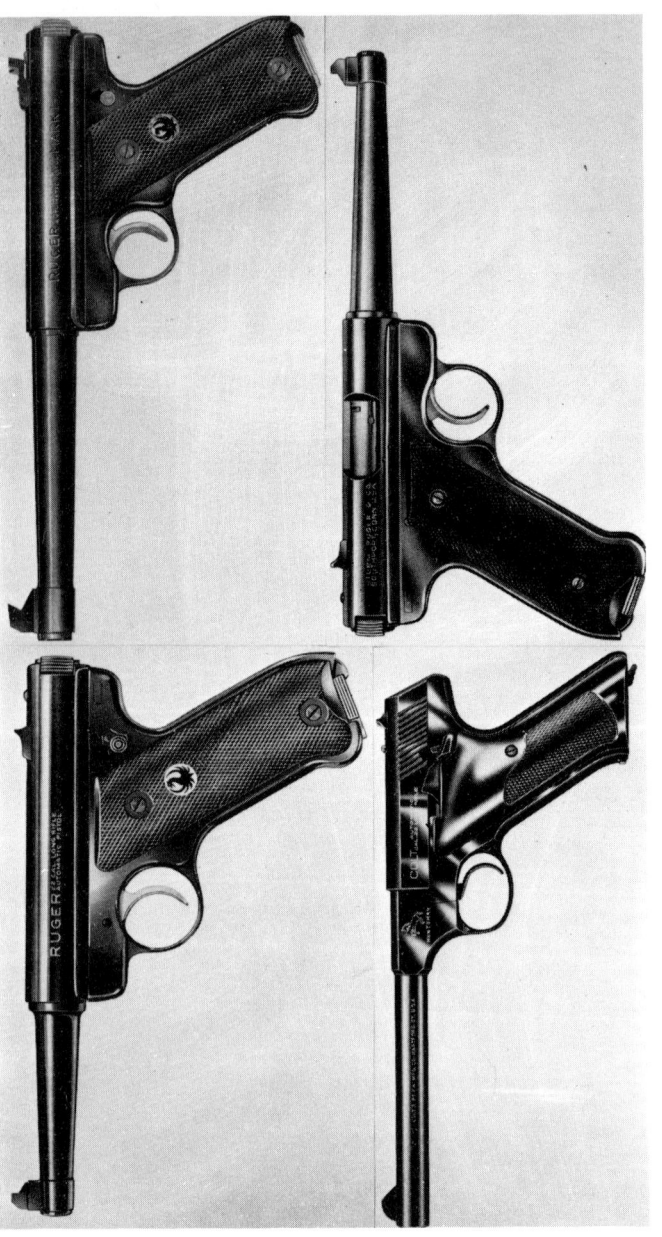

PLATE XXXXVIII

Top left—Ruger (RST-4) Standard ·22 L.R. autoloading pistol with 4¾ in. barrel. *Top right*—Ruger Mark I ·22 L.R. Target pistol with 6⅞ in. barrel. *Bottom left*—Colt 'Huntsman' ·22 L.R. *Bottom right*—Ruger Standard automatic ·22 with 6 in. barrel

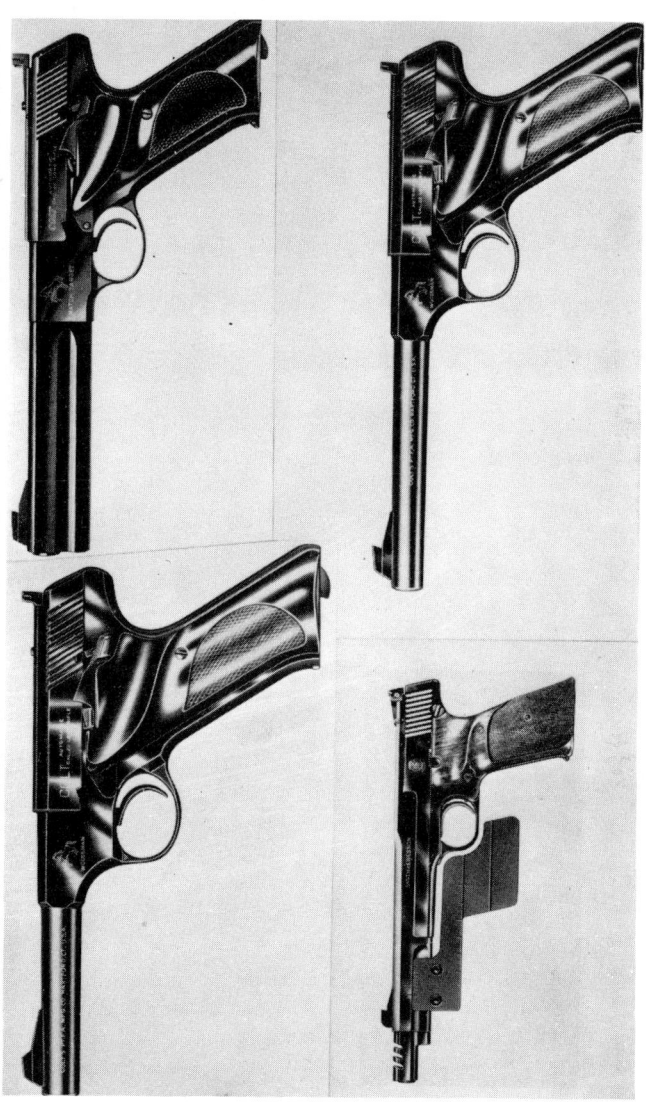

PLATE XXXIX

Top left—Colt 'Woodsman'—short barrel (sport model). *Top right*—Colt automatic ·22 L.R. 'Match Target'. *Bottom left*—Smith & Wesson Match model with muzzle brakes and adjustable weights. *Bottom right*—The Colt 'Woodsman' long barrel (sport model)

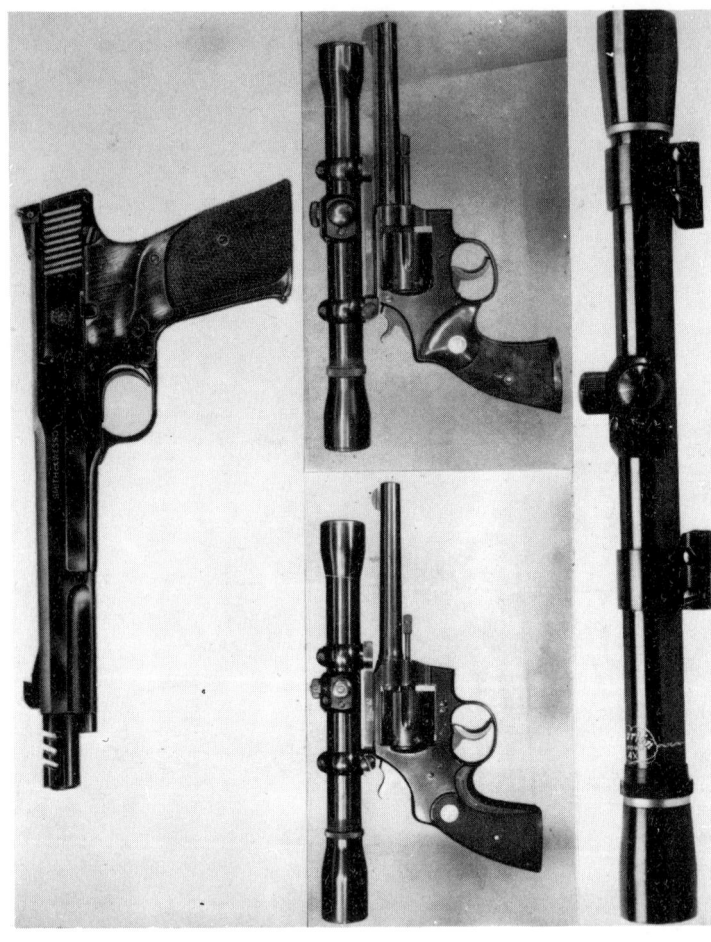

PLATE XL

Top—Smith & Wesson ·22 Match pistol with recoil reducer. *Left centre*—4× Weaverscope mounted on ·22 Colt O.P. with Buehler pistol mounts. *Right centre*—4× Weaverscope on Buehler pistol mounts with Smith & Wesson K22 pistol. *Bottom*—Marlin Micro-vue 4× telescope sight

unfortunately, a little on the light side for comfortable shooting. If fairly fast shooting is required, the expansion of a metal barrel takes place at a different rate from a wooden fore-end, and as a result, there is a temporary misfitting of barrel and stock, resulting in a falling off of accuracy, and a tendency to throw 'wild' groups.

In the United States there is a growing practice for field sportsmen to cut down the weight of their rifles as much as possible, especially for mountain hunting. The addition of compensators and recoil-eliminators to muzzles assists greatly to this end, but excessive reduction in stocking can result in tendencies for the barrel to shake loose. From the United States, therefore, we can expect developments to overcome this problem, probably the most important being the Remington 'Nylon 66' mentioned in an earlier chapter. However, there have been other steps taken in this direction. For instance, Herter's of Waseca introduced what they call the 'Herter-Glass Process' for bedding rifle barrels. Though the process is best carried out by a competent gunsmith, nevertheless Herter's retail a special kit enabling the home guncraftsmen to carry out accurate and strong rifle bedding. 'Do it yourself' has always been with the home-loaders, and it is only to be expected that the tendency will spread amongst amateur guncraftsmen.

The Herter kit consists of a silica compound which can be cut or sanded and which is filled into a gun stock and then the rifle action and barrel are forced down into it whilst it is still unhardened and in paste form. The glass compound strengthens the stock and beds the barrel accurately and permanently and is unaffected by heat or moisture.

Anglers, of course, have their fibre-glass rods and dinghies, wildfowlers their fibre-glass punts, now riflemen may use fibre-glass to bed their barrels for accurate shooting, and one does not need to be an over-bold prophet to suggest that sometime, in the not too distant future, fibre-glass or other similar tough compound will oust the traditional wooden stock. It would certainly simplify accurate bedding, would reduce production costs, and could still be pleasing aesthetically. Inaccurate shooting *may* be due to poor *inletting* of barrel and action into the stock. Perhaps the future **rifleman** will not have this trouble as his barrel and action will be *moulded* into the stock, so that poor shooting can, more than ever, be blamed on the human element.

Electrical Bedding

EARLIER in this chapter I made mention of the system known as 'electrical bedding'. This provides a very accurate method of accurately bedding a rifle fore-end.

There are several different methods of electrically bedding a rifle but the following is, perhaps, the simplest and easiest to undertake by the 'do it yourself' brigade.

First of all remove the barrel and action from the stock. Almost at the tip of the fore-end drill a couple of holes through the fore-end body into the barrel groove at an angle of 45 degrees through the centre of the stock. This means that a line in prolongation of the holes should intersect in the centre of the rifle bore. Now insert two bushes with flanged heads into the holes. These bushes should be tapped to take a *fine* threaded screw. Pin the bushes to prevent their turning when the screws are inserted and tightened. The screws inserted into the bushing are your contacts for the electrical bedding process. After screwing the screws home, unscrew them until they are clear of the barrel groove and then replace the barrel and action. Make sure that neither screw is touching the barrel.

The electrical work is very simple. A torch battery is connected at one terminal by wire to a screwdriver and the other terminal connected to one contact of a flashlamp bulb. The other contact of the bulb is then connected by wire to the barrel itself.

To operate the electrical bedder—carefully screw up each screw in turn with the wired screwdriver until the bulb lights. This means that the screw is just making contact with the barrel. Then adjust the other screw similarly. Thereafter, by screwing in the screws, each an exact number of turns, it is possible to bed the barrel with any desired tension.

Thus, from the foregoing it should be appreciated just how important it is that a rifleman should know precisely what grouping is and how his particular rifle groups with a particular brand or batch of ammunition. Furthermore it will be seen that though match rifles, in particular, are built to very tight specifications, nevertheless there is a variation in each which brings its own peculiar bedding and grouping problem.

Finally, though there are different methods of measuring the group, from centre to centre measurement, or from inner edge of the bullet holes, by mean radius or extreme spread, in actual fact the spread is, for the serious target shooter, much more important than the mean radius figure.

It is only after grouping has been determined that the rifleman can go further into questions appertaining to his own performances with the weapon and such other subjects as sights and sighting.

CHAPTER SEVEN

SIGHTS

A SHOOTING acquaintance, many years my senior, and to whom I owe a great debt for the hints, tips, and invaluable knowledge he passed on to me, once told me that whereas a chain had only the strength of its weakest link, a rifle, no matter how expensive it might be, was no better than the sights with which it was equipped.

And how very true this is.

Generally speaking there are two types of sights: metallic and optical. But just to make the matter a little more complicated, metallic sights are subdivided into open sights and aperture or 'peep' sights. Aperture sights might again be re-classified into two other groups, disc aperture sights and metallic tube sights.

The metallic open sights are again divided into fixed, adjustable and folding leaf rear sights, whilst the metallic front sights may be divided into posts and beads. Aperture sights are again divided into hooded or non-hooded front sights, whilst aperture rear sights are again subdivided into receiver, tang, and receiver extension models, and the whole field of sights are classified as to whether they are target sights, or hunting sights.

Telescope sights are generally subdivided into two main groups: target sights and hunting sights, though the Americans usually add a third group, the 'varmint' sight, and even a fourth group for plinking. Target 'scopes, where very high accuracy is required, principally in bench rest shooting, have a power of anything from $8\times$ to $24\times$, whereas hunting telescope sights usually run from $2\times$ to $4\times$. The American varmint 'scope is usually $6\times$ but may go as high as $10\times$, whilst the plinking sights are usually about $2\times$.

Returning to the question of a rifle only being as good as its sights, I am afraid that experience confirms this with me, and when I am contemplating the purchase of a rifle or examining one with

SIGHTS

1. LYMAN 'All-American' telescope sights
   (A) 2·5 × model, (B) 4 × model, (C) 6 × model, (D) 10 × model,
   (E) 'Super-Targetspot' high magnification model

a view to trade, quite often the first impression made on me is that of the sights. No matter how attractive a rifle may be, if the sights are poor, or of a cheap quality, I am no longer interested in it.

Metallic Sights
Open Sights

THE open sight is the type usually found on cheap rifles, though expensive open sights are to be found on better grade weapons. Certainly, by and large, the open sights are the commonest type provided by manufacturers of rifles. Open sights consist, in general, of a blade or bead fore sight, which may be ramp mounted or not, and a back sight which consists of a thick metal plate with a U- or V-shaped notch in the centre. On cheap rifles the factory generally installs a mass-produced type of rear sight and front sight and these, with all respect, are merely put on as a gesture and are only placed there because it is the conventional thing to do. The manufacturer of cheap rifles wishes to keep his costs down and enter into a very competitive market and costs are all important to him.

It would be a very fine thing if manufacturers produced rifles for sale without any sights on them so that the purchaser could choose and select his own.

One type of sight I hate to see on any rifle is the leaf sight with a sliding notched arm for elevation adjustments. It is common enough—too common, and the keen rifleman should replace this at the first opportunity. In the first place there is no proper adjustment possible for elevation, secondly there is every possibility that the sight can be shifted out of position, tilted or pushed sideways by the slightest accidental knock. Far better is the leaf-type rear sight, or the tangent style. Another monstrosity which seems to be popular in the United States of America is the buckhorn or semi-buckhorn iron sight. The wide ears of this model without doubt give good visibility, but that is all that can be said for it: its accuracy is almost non-existent.

When one considers that the function of a set of sights is to provide the shooter with the medium whereby he may align his

SIGHTS

A

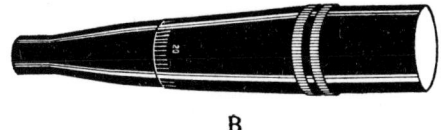

B

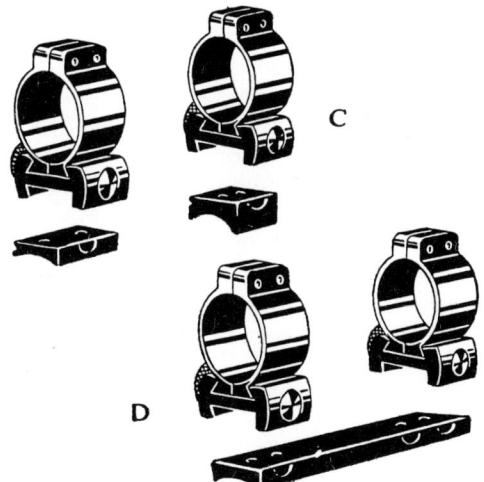

2. LYMAN 3-point mount for 'Super-Targetspot'
    (B) Sunshade for target 'scope sight
    (C) and (D) 'All-American Tru-Lock' 'scope sight mounts

rifle on the target in such a manner as to exploit its grouping potentialities to the full, it should be realized how important the function of the sight is, and why shoddy, cheap sights are the indictment of the cheap rifle-maker.

For quick, off-hand shooting at vermin and small game at comparatively short distances, very expensive sights are not necessary, and for this type of shooting open iron sights are perfectly adequate.

A bead sight is preferable to a post sight for hunting, especially if an ivory or gold bead is used, though even better in my view is something on the lines of Ithaca's 'Raybar' shotgun sight with its wonderful light gathering power. For the rear sight, it is up to the sportsman concerned to decide on whether he prefers a V or a U notch but whatever combination of front and rear sights is chosen it must balance. The front sight must not be of such a size that it obscures the target, and the notch in the rear sight must not be so small that the front sight cannot be seen clearly, nor must it be so large that the front sight is 'lost'.

For shooting at running game the open sights, in the hands of an experienced shot, cannot be bettered. It aids considerably if the rear sight is absolutely flat on the top, without any notch, and has a white line in the centre. A bead front sight is used in combination with this rear sight and centred by means of the white line. The value of this combination is that it gives an unobstructed picture of the target and for moving game is hard to beat.

A V notch should always be used with a bead front sight. But the V notch can again assume different forms, being for instance, a wide shallow V for snap-shooting, or a deep narrow V for shooting at stationary targets.

But there is a disadvantage in the use of open sights. The eye has to line up three things—the target, the front sight, and the rear sight. The rear sight must take a correct picture of the front sight, centrally and to the right height. When this has been obtained the coupled sights have to be aligned correctly on the target.

As the eye has to continually take in these pictures, focusing back and forth, it is easy to see that the muscles may tire, the

SIGHTS

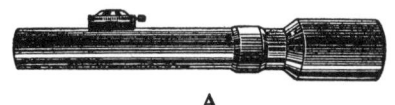

A

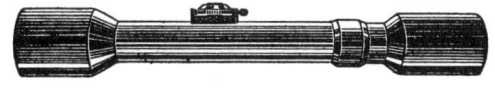

B

C

D

E

3. Telescope sights—(A) 'Ajack' 2·5 × 70, (B) 4 × 90, (C) 'Ruediger' 2·5 ×, (D) Nickel 'Supralyte' 2·5 × 52, (E) Nickel 'Supra E' 4 × 81

images seen may be incorrect, and inaccuracies will inevitably creep in. But this defect can be overcome by abandoning the open rear sight and installing a receiver peep or aperture sight.

Aperture Sights

THE aperture sight is now in almost universal use, even being adopted by the forces on the infantry rifle and called a 'battle' sight. It would be true to state that the open rear sight has virtually disappeared from ·22 target work, the fine micrometer-adjusted peep or aperture sight having taken its place. But there is no such thing as a universal aperture to a peep sight—bright lighting conditions demand or require a smaller aperture than in darker conditions and a lot depends, too, upon the eyesight of the shooter, particularly if he has to wear spectacles.

On the question as to why one should choose a peep sight as opposed to open sights I do not think I can do better than quote the dictum of Mr Harvey Williams who founded the famous Williams Gun Sight Company in Davison, U.S.A. To the question —why use a receiver or peep sight? Mr Williams says:

'The answer is simple. You shoot better. The guy doing the most hitting in the woods and winning rifle shoots always uses something besides the conventional factory open sights. In fact, we can't remember any match in modern times ever being won with open sights. With open sights, the rear sight is mounted in the centre of the barrel, cutting down the sighting distance or radius. With the peep sight, the distance between front and rear sights is much greater—and hence much more accurate shooting results. Even with the very best of flat-top open sights—you see only half of your target, and with the semi or full buckhorn you black out just that much more. With anything but the best light, the top of the open sight appears "fuzzy". In a hurry, a shooter is very apt to shoot high with an open sight, while the proper receiver sight is self-centring and clear.

'Some shooters become discouraged with receiver sights because, knowingly or not, they are supplied with the wrong type of aperture. Most sights are sold with an aperture suited

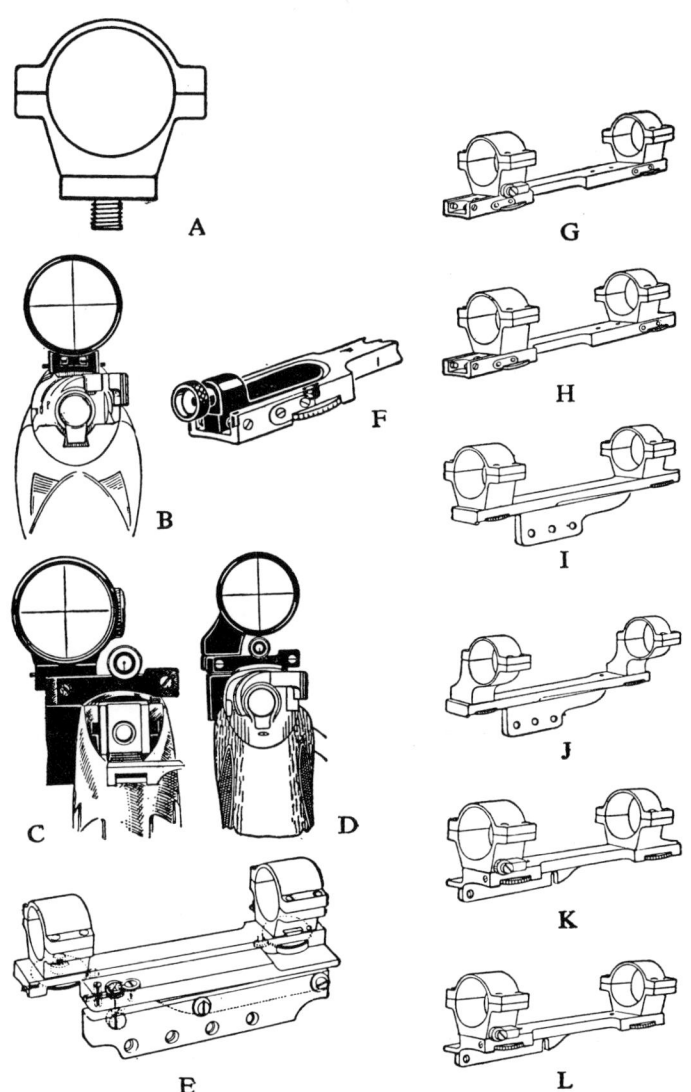

4. WILLIAMS 'On-The Range' telescope sight mounts
(A) (B) 'Quick-Convertible' top mount—low central overbore with (F) 'Ace-in-the-Hole' peepsight. (G) Micrometer windage and split ring. (H) Split and extension ring. (C)(D) 'QC' side mount—offset or overbore. (I) Split and extension ring. (J) Central overbore rings. (E) Micrometer mount—low central overbore. (K) Micrometer windage and extension ring. (L) Micrometer windage and split ring

for target work only and are highly impracticable for hunting.'

Mr Williams, after a careful study of hunting sighting conditions found that the eye will take up centre naturally with a large inner hole and for that reason 'it is best to use an aperture that covers up as little as possible and lets a lot of light through so that the shooter can aim quickly'.

Finally, Mr Williams comes across with some really sound advice—'To get the most out of your receiver or peep sight, you should have at least three or four discs. They are inexpensive, and an assortment pays off in more game and higher scores.'

Mr Williams ought to know, for he and his family have been manufacturing sights for all types of firearms since 1926, including aperture sights for shotguns. They have also managed to put some very cheap though reliable sights on to the market.

The famous Lyman Gun Sight Corporation manufacture a fabulous number of sights, open and rear, as well as telescope models, especially for target work with very fine mocrometer adjustments. In the same field are Marble-Goss, Redfield and Vaver in the United States.

In Great Britain excellent sights are built by Messrs Parker-Hale Ltd, of Birmingham, for both sporting and target work. Their 'Sportarget' aperture sight is world-renowned for its neatness and quality. They also manufacture aperture back sights for match rifles with quarter-minute click adjustments and ingenious 'Iris' eyepieces for aperture sights which, working on the same principle as a camera shutter, afford any size of aperture from ·02 to ·14 inches. A more de-luxe model incorporates a diaphragm with rotary filter unit, giving green, blue, yellow, polaroid or clear vision at choice of the shooter.

Front aperture sights are frequently used by the target rifleman, but, unless the aperture is large enough it can be rather a disadvantage to use. In fact it is a common fault with the novice to try to use too small an aperture front sight.

What the shooter must take into account when selecting a ring or aperture fore sight is the effect of bending of light rays. If the aperture is too small the edge of the disc will be too near the aiming mark and consequently it is not easy to spot when the sight is off centre. A fairly wide aperture or disc overcomes this

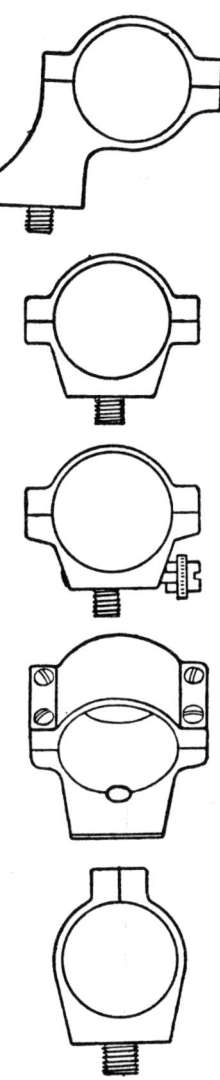

5. **WILLIAMS** mount rings, providing these sighting combinations:
    HCO.   Central overbore ring. Sizes 1 in. and 26 mm.
    SPLIT.   Sizes 1 in. and 26 mm.
    MICROMETER WINDAGE.   Sizes 1 in. and 26 mm.
    EXTENSION.   Sizes 1 in. and 26 mm.
    SOLID.   Sizes $\frac{7}{8}$ in. and $\frac{2}{3}$ in.

disadvantage. In sporting shooting, however, a disc front sight is neither necessary nor desirable.

In recent years, however, there has been an increased interest in the 'tube' sight. At first glance this appears to be a telescope sight, but in actual fact it is a metallic sight, aperture variety, built in the form of a tube.

Metallic Tube Sights

BASICALLY, a metallic tube sight consists of a metal tube with an aperture at the rear. There are no magnifying lenses of any description incorporated into its construction. It does have to be mounted on to a rifle, however, in a similar manner to a telescope sight and probably this has given rise to misconceptions concerning it.

Although only now arousing interest in Great Britain, the tube sight is a fairly old device and was marketed in the United States as far back as 1925. In the main, though different patterns are on the market by Lyman, Freeland and Unertl, and others, they consist basically of a metal tube about eighteen inches in length, the rear end of which is fitted with a threaded cap accepting standard sighting discs for rear aperture sights. Polaroid systems for light control are incorporated into the Lyman tube sights, but the Unertl models incorporate a series of diaphragms in the tube to eliminate light reflection from its inner surface.

But one thing is very important—there must be correct lining up with the tube sight and the front sight and great care has to be taken in selecting a proper combination.

Advantages claimed for the tube sight, which, by the way not every shooter can use, is the elimination of errors by moving the eye out of the centre of the rear aperture. Owing to the very narrow field of vision of the tube sight a blurring of the picture when the eye gets out of centre gives adequate indication that an incorrect sight picture is being obtained. It is also claimed that a tube sight permits adjustments as fine as one-eighth of a minute of angle, but against the advantages is one very real disadvantage. Owing to the narrow field of view it is possible for a competitor to cross-fire on to another rifleman's target, and furthermore,

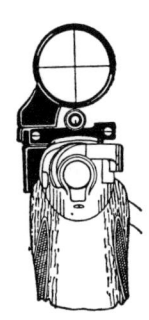

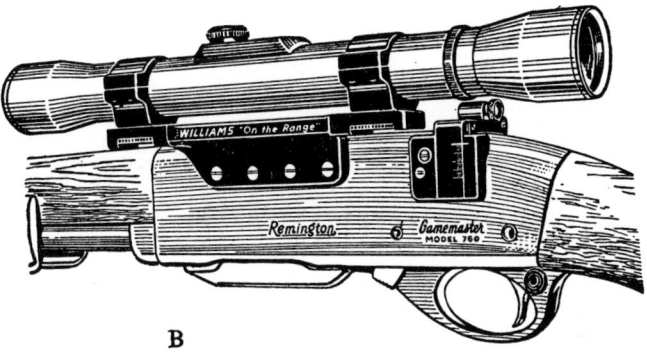

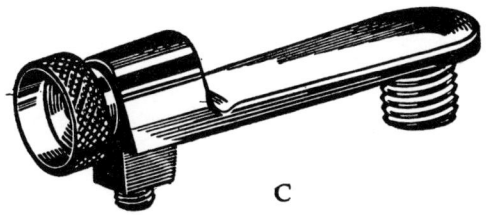

6. WILLIAMS (A) 'Quick-Convertible' telescope sight mounts
    (B) Side mount in combination with 'Foolproof' receiver sight on Remington 'Gamemaster'
    (C) 'Ace-in-the-Hole' peepsight

poor lighting conditions operate most effectively against this type of sight.

In actual practice it has been found that the tube sight is best reserved for prone positional shooting only, though a very *short* tube may be used for off-hand shooting.

Telescope Sights

THESE are gaining in popularity and provide many real advantages over iron sights, particularly for sporting or hunting shooting. In the United States it has been found that the use of telescope sights on sporting rifles is a major factor in the prevention of shooting accidents, those accidents in which, with iron sights, human beings might be mistakenly identified as vermin or game, with dire consequences.

A telescope sight is really a telescope with the addition of an extra lens which corrects the image to the right position. By means of a telescope sight the human eye is automatically centred on the target and the difficulty in trying to keep, with conventional sights, the target, front sight and back sight in focus is eliminated.

Telescope sights are manufactured in various 'powers'—or degrees of magnification. Thus a 4-power, or $4\times$ telescope means one with four degrees of magnification. But in actual practice, ignoring bench-rest shooting, or high power rifle shooting at long ranges, for a ·22 rifle a magnification of $2\frac{1}{2}$ to $4\times$ is adequate. For off-hand shooting any greater magnification would be a grave disadvantage. For prone shooting or longer range shooting from a rest, up to $6\times$ may be permissible.

A telescope sight is a compromise. The higher the power or magnification of the telescope, the smaller will be the field of vision, also the higher the power the greater, or more apparent, will be the unsteadiness in aim, or inadvertent movements of the shooter. In fact, though a telescope sight does make for cleaner kills, nevertheless it also ensures clearer misses. What would be, say, a miss by one inch with iron sights, may well be as much as six inches off target with a telescope sight! But a telescope sight does not magnify errors, the sights show the *actual* aim but seem to accelerate the movements of the barrel over the target.

SIGHTS

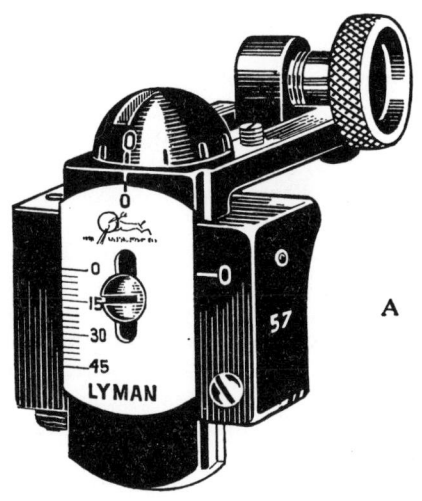

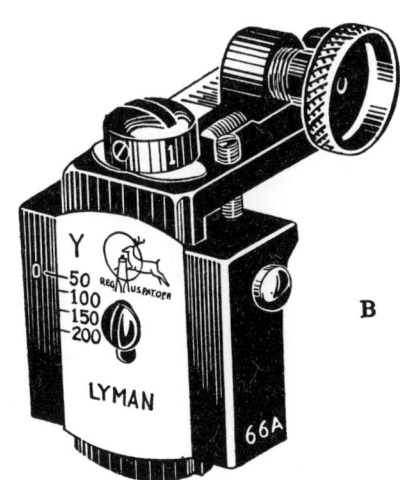

7. LYMAN (A) Model 57 receiver sight. (B) Model 66

A telescope sight is not a short cut to successful shooting as so many people realize. In fact, until one becomes experienced, a telescope sight can be a very disappointing piece of apparatus.

The sighting elements in a telescope sight generally consist of cross-hairs, a post, or a combination of cross-hairs and a dot. The centring of the reticle on the target if the 'scope has been correctly adjusted for range and windage should result in hits.

There are several excellent 'scope sights on the market. Before World War II, German sights were popular in Great Britain, but today the swing has been towards the United States. The W.R. Weaver Company, of El Paso, Texas, were the pioneers of telescope sighting in the United States and today more Weaver-scopes are in use than any other. Furthermore they cater for all purses and tastes. But there are other excellent makes, Leupold, with 'fog-proof' models, which completely eliminate internal fogging; Lyman, Mossberg and even Colt have entered the game. Of Continental telescope sights, the Italian 'Jaeger' is worth mentioning. There is, of course, an excellent American 'Jaeger' 'scope as well. Telescope sights mounts are highly important, varying from tip-off or slide-on mounts for dove-tailed receivers and barrels, to detachable side mounts, low-swing models, and others as built by Packmayr, Lyman, Weaver, Griffin & Howe and others.

The cheaper 'scopes generally have their adjustments for windage and elevation internally; the more expensive models have external adjustments.

A rather striking reticle is that known as the 'T. K. Lee Dot'. This has the cross-hair manufactured from pure silk from the Black Widow spider. In order to obtain supplies for their 'scopes the Lee concern actually have a farm where they raise, scientifically, these spiders. To obtain the silk the spider is fastened down on its back and then prodded into spinning his silk on to a U-shaped frame. Proper care and diet are important because if this is not done correctly, the silk will be worthless.

The Lee cross-hair is only ·00008 to ·0001 inches in diameter and has the property of expanding and contracting under different weather conditions.

I have referred to Pachmayr Lo-swing mounts—in this type of

telescope sight mount the mount is fixed to the receiver top and swings to the side.

I append below details of the principal telescope sights and mounts on the American market. I specify the American market because they have much greater experience than we have in Europe of such shooting accessories.

TABLE 1

Sporting Telescope Sights (U.S.A.)

Make and Model	Power	Field at 100 yds.	Eye relief (in.)	Adjustments
Bausch & Lomb				
Balvar . . .	2·5	34 ft	4	External
Balvar . . .	4·0	26 ft 2 in.	4	,,
Balfor . . .	4·0	26 ft 2 in.	4	,,
Baltur . . .	2·5	34 ft	4	,,
Bushnell Scopemaster .	2·5	40 ft	3¼–5	Internal
	4·0	33 ft	3¼–4½	,,
	6·0	20 ft	3¼–4	,,
Leupold Riflescope .	2·25	40 ft	2½–5	,,
Pioneer . .	4·0	35 ft	2½–4½	External
Lyman All American .	4·0	30 ft	3¼–5	Internal
Alaskan . .	2·5	40 ft	3–5	,,
Challenger .	4·0	30 ft	3–5	,,
Wolverine .	6·0	19 ft	3½	,,
Mossberg 2M4 . .	4·0	20 ft	2¼	,,
Unertl Falcon . .	2·75	40 ft	4	,,
Weaver K2·5 . .	2·5	43 ft	3–6	,,
K4 . .	4·0	31 ft	3–5½	,,
K6 . .	6·0	20 ft	3–5	,,
B4 . . .	4·0	30 ft	2	,,
B6 . . .	6·0	20 ft	2	,,
J2·5 . .	2·5	37 ft	3–5½	,,

Tables 1 and 2 are by no means exhaustive but are merely representative of telescopes manufactured in the United States.

On reference to the figures shown under the heading of 'Eye Relief' and given in inches, this means the distance between the

TABLE 2

Target Telescope Sights (U.S.A.)

Maker and Model	Power	Field at 100 yds.	Eye relief (in.)	Adjustments
Fecker Commando	6, 8, 10, 12	13–7 ft	$2\frac{3}{4}$	External
Champion	10–30	8–3 ft	$2\frac{3}{4}$	,,
Litschert Spot Shot	8–25	10–7 ft	—	,,
Lyman Junior				
Targetspot $\frac{3}{4}$ in.	6, 8, 10	16–12 ft	2	,,
Super Targetspot $1\frac{1}{4}$ in.	10–25	12–6 ft	2	,,
Unertl 1 in.	6, 8, 10	16–10 ft	$2\frac{1}{4}$	,,
$1\frac{1}{4}$ in.	8, 10, 12, 14	12–6 ft	$2\frac{1}{4}$	,,
2 in.	10, 15, 18, 20, 24	10–4 ft 8 in.	$3–1\frac{3}{4}$	,,
Weaver K–8	8	14 ft	3–5	Internal
K–10	10	12 ft	3–5	,,

rear end of the telescope sight and the eye. The ·22 rifle has sufficient eye relief, in its rim-fire form, with 2 inches but for higher power calibres, including centre-fire ·22 rifles, where there is more recoil, a little more eye relief is necessary.

A good quality telescope sight has the advantage that it gives a fine clear image even in poor light, such as twilight shooting, and if the lenses are bloomed, sunlight glare and dazzle are eliminated.

Parker-Hale of Birmingham manufacture some excellent quality 'Roll-Off' telescope sight mounts. In these mounts one side of the dovetail is hinged which enables the mount to be positioned without sliding it endwise on to the dovetail. This allows of a concealed recoil stop to be located in a plain drilled hole.

Finally, lest one should think that telescope sights are the prerogative of the rifleman alone, it must be pointed out that they are now available to the handgun enthusiast, though, owing to the sharp recoil given by high-powered handguns, they are best fitted to ·22 models.

Originally, though others have followed him in the field, Maynard P. Buehler of Orinda, California, introduced such a sight on a Smith & Wesson revolver. So quickly has the idea

SIGHTS

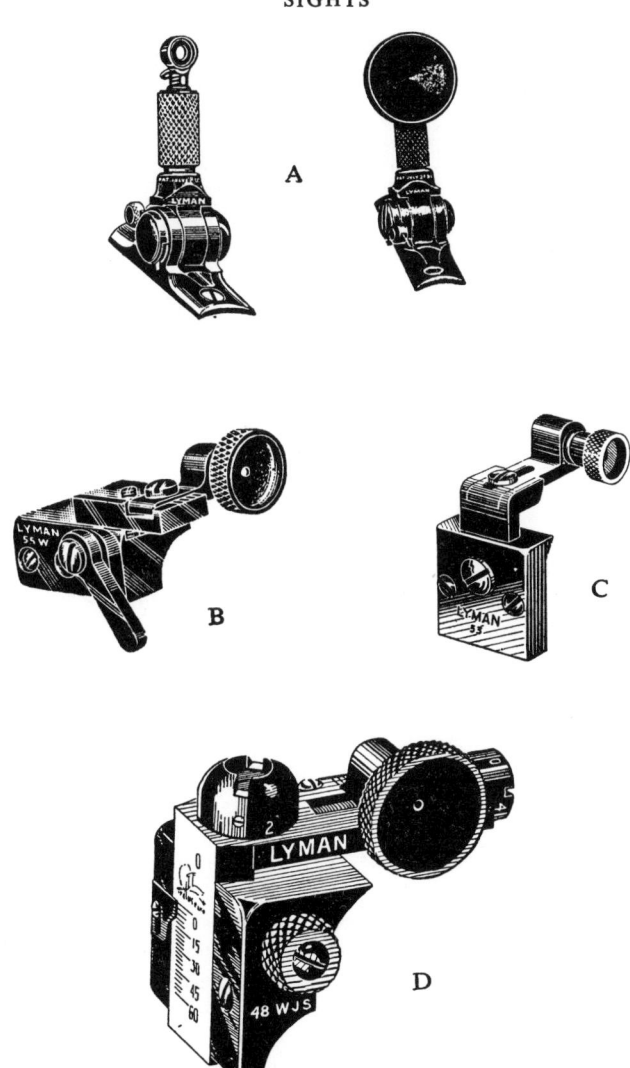

8. LYMAN (A) 'Tang' sights 1a and 2a. (B) Model 55 receiver sight. (C) Model 53. (D) Model 48

caught on, however, that they have designed special mounts for pistol telescope sights.

In addition to the normal telescope sight there is a variation known as the half-scope. This is a modification of a standard hooded front sight and is achieved by the placing of a converging lens in the hood. This has the effect of magnifying the target. This half-scope or front-sight lens is used in conjunction with a normal peep or aperture sight, but it is advisable to increase the size of the aperture. One particular model of the half-scope was on the British market prior to World War II, but appears to have disappeared from the scene. This was clamped on to the rifle barrel and was manufactured by Parker-Hale. There was also, about the same period, an American half-scope sight on the market known as the 'Semi-Scope', manufactured by the Semi-Scope Company of St Louis, Missouri. This consisted of an adaptor, a combination tube and eyeshade, and, of course, a lens.

A semi-scope sight has no real advantage over a conventional telescope model. It has to be built in low power and may, perhaps, score on cheapness but against that one advantage the semi-scope has very low magnification, and in dull conditions does not give as clear a picture of the target. A shooter using a half-scope or semi-scope also suffers from the disadvantage that he cannot spot the shots through this type of sight and readily hold off for wind.

Half-scope sights are not permitted in shooting matches under N.S.R.A. rules, but can, of course, be used in the *any sight* competitions. As, under these conditions, they would be matched against telescope sights proper, it will be appreciated that there is not much point in using them.

Briefly, then, telescope sights are divided into two categories, (*a*) target and, in America, 'varmint' shooting scopes and (*b*) hunting scopes. Those in the former class require a high degree of magnification and the field of view must be comparatively restricted. Adjustments are carried out externally for windage and elevation, and they are generally very expensive. Telescope sights in the latter class are usually only low-powered, require a fairly wide field of view (in order to assist the hunter in picking up his

SIGHTS

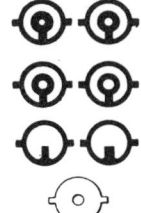

A B

C D

E

9. LYMAN (A) Model 17a front sight: with interchangeable inserts
(B) Middle sight No. 16. (C) No. 77 front sight. (D) 'Bead front sight No. 26/32. (E) 'Dovetail' and 'Blade' front sights

target), have internal adjustments (though external adjustments are also popular), and must be capable of being easily removed from the rifle in order to allow iron sights to be used if necessary.

Finally, on purchasing a telescope sight it is advisable for the buyer to carefully examine it and where price is a consideration to settle on low powered models. It is also important to ensure that the model be tested for parallax.

Parallax is the bugbear of cheap sights. If the reticle of a telescope sight does not lie in the focal plane of the objective lens neither object nor reticle will be in focus simultaneously. This results in inaccurate sighting and is easily discovered by moving the eye from one side to the other—if this reveals an apparent movement of the reticle relative to the target, then the reticle and target are not focused correctly and the result is parallax.

The beginner will hear experts, in conversation, referring to movement of adjustment on sights, particularly in target shooting, by 'so many clicks'. In fact, this is a very simple and effective way in which adjustments in elevation and windage can be made. Modern target sights all have 1/4 or 1/8 minute clicks for sighting adjustments. One minute of angle is, for all practical purposes in sight adjustment, equal to 1 inch at 100 yards. Thus, a 1/4 click adjustment would be 1/4 of an inch at 100 yards, and it would require 4 clicks to make an alteration of 1 inch. At fifty yards the one minute of adjustment would be equivalent to 1/2 inch; and at 200 yards, 2 inches.

Conclusion

CONVENTION seems to have decreed that iron sights should be mounted on top of the rifle barrel. But in the Olympic Games at Melbourne in 1956 the Iron Curtain Countries caused a minor sensation by using offset iron sights.

In the free rifle match held at Malmo on the occasion of the 1952 Olympic Games, it was noticed, although the Russians did their best to prevent other competitors and interested spectators from inspecting their rifles, that their sights were offset to the left instead of being centred over the barrel. One reason suggested for this was that it enabled the rifleman to hold his head straighter. This could very well be a good reason, but there is probably a stronger one.

Many match rifles are equipped with a broad black fabric band along the top of the barrel, extending from the base of the fore sight to the rear sight. The reason for this band is to prevent heat waves rising from the barrel obscuring the sights. The reason for offset iron sights on Iron Curtain target rifles is probably to avoid 'mirage' caused by heat waves rising from the barrel itself and interfering with the sighting.

Whilst this book was being written I had the opportunity of inspecting and trying the Russian match rifles which have the offset iron sights, and certainly they provide a very comfortable shooting position, especially in the off-hand position, and I was very impressed by them.

The historian is continually coming across devices which, brought out in an earlier age, are rediscovered in his own times and brought into use again, albeit perhaps for different reasons.

Offset iron sights are not unknown. Perhaps the most popular example is that of the Hall Rifle, designed and patented by John H. Hall in the United States in 1811. Hall rifles manufactured for flintlock ignition were built with fixed sights offset to one side of the barrel. The front sight was carried on an offset bayonet lug. The reason for this was perfectly sound; it was to avoid the 'flash' from the burning priming powder. When the percussion system was introduced, the sights were then placed in the conventional position on top of the barrel.

In the United States there is what is known as the 'custom' gun trade. This means the building of a rifle to a customer's special requirements; and as a result all sorts of unusual, even freak, stocks, receivers, and sights, some first-class, some good, others useless, are constantly appearing. Some custom-built rifles have been built with offset sights to suit riflemen with a master left-eye but who are unwilling, particularly with a bolt-action, to shoot from the left shoulder.

A typical case springs to mind in the example of a rifleman who lost his right eye but still wanted to shoot from the right shoulder.

As the weapon was a self-loader with the magazine in the butt, it was not possible to adopt shotgun practice. The answer was simple, to offset the sights to the left. This brings obvious difficulties in manufacture as the sights must be hinged, and they are extremely prone to damage, more so than on the conventional rifle. It needs little imagination to see what could happen if the rifle were laid down on its left side!

It is not, of course, unusual for telescopic sights to be mounted to the side of a barrel; but for iron sights the occasions are rare enough to excite comment. For the serious matchman, the Russian practice would appear to have a lot in its favour and certainly the performances of their shooters in international and Olympic matches seem to justify this unusual placing of iron sights. Experimenting in this direction may well pay dividends, though for sporting purposes the practice would not have as much value as for match work.

Technically, of course, though sights are mounted in a central position on the top rib of a side-by-side double rifle, they are offset in relation to the individual barrel.

In the case of automatic arms, where the magazine is placed on top of the action, thus interfering with the normal position of sights, it becomes necessary to mount the sights on one side, generally to the left. Typical examples were the French 7·5-millimetre Chatellerault light machine-gun of the middle 1920s, and the Bren light machine-gun with which most of us are so familiar.

I am sure that many readers will recall the sights mounted on the side of the S.M.L.E. Rifle Mark III, the No. 1 rifle of the full-bore target men. Normal sights of this model were up to 1,800 yards, but special long-range sights were attached to the side for shooting from 1,600 to 2,800 yards. The rear sight was a simple aperture back sight, hinged on a pin at the rear of the receiver, and on the left-hand side of it. This sight was placed conveniently for the eye and could not be adjusted for elevation, nor could allowance be made laterally. The fore sight was attached to the furniture just behind the lower band. It consisted of a flat pointer terminating in a small bead, which, itself, was offset to the left of the pointer. Immediately behind the pointer, which could be

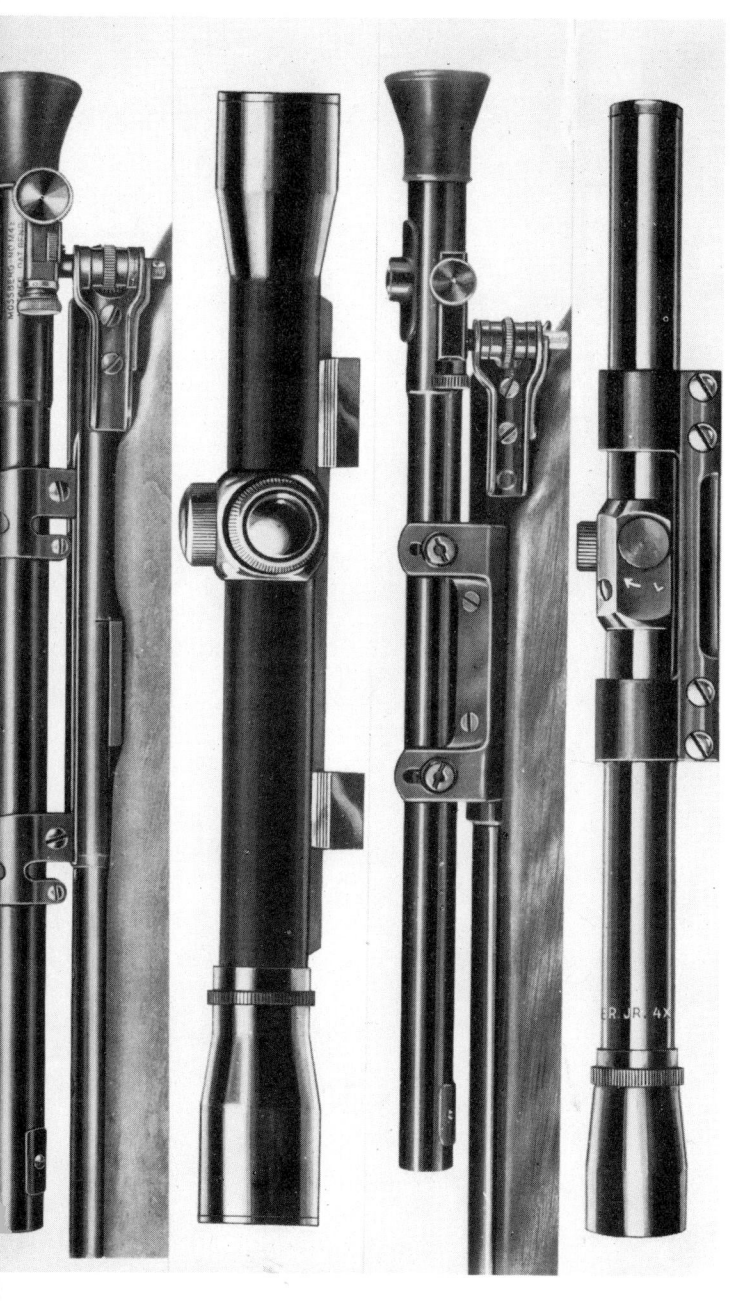

PLATE XLI

Top—Mossberg Model 4M4 telescope sight. *Second*—Coltmaster 2·5 × telescope sight. *Third*—Mossberg Model 2M4 telescope sight. *Bottom*—Coltmaster Junior 4 × 'scope sight

PLATE XLII

Top—Rimfire bullets are made from lead alloy wire, extruded in this hydraulic press. *Bottom*—The lead alloy wire is fed from a rotating drum into the bullet-making machine, which produces large runs of identical bullets

PLATE XLIII
—ICI rolls its own high-quality brass for the cartridge case. Here cups pressed out of blanks are entering a drawing machine. *Bottom*—Priming. The wet explosive mixture d onto the charge plate. The pegged plate is brought down, knocking the priming ition into the cases underneath

PLATE XLIV

Top—Putting the 'fire' into the 'rim'. The machine bed rotates slowly, positioning the cases under a punch. The punch, revolving rapidly, spins the priming mixture into the rim cavity. *Bottom*—Under a special light an operator inspects primed cases to make sure that the composition completely fills the rim recess

PLATE XLV

Top—The primed cases, thoroughly dried, pass to the automatic loading machine, which feeds them with minute, accurately measured charges of propellent. *Bottom*—Charged cases and bullets get together in the bulleting machine. Cases not containing the exact quantity of propellant have been automatically rejected

PLATE XLVI

Top—The canneluring machine turns in the case onto the bullet and makes the final adjustment to bullet dimensions. A most critical operation in the manufacture of a ·22 cartridge. *Bottom*—Final inspection with the aid of mirrors, where all aspects of the cartridges are studied. Perfect cartridges are allowed to drop through the opening

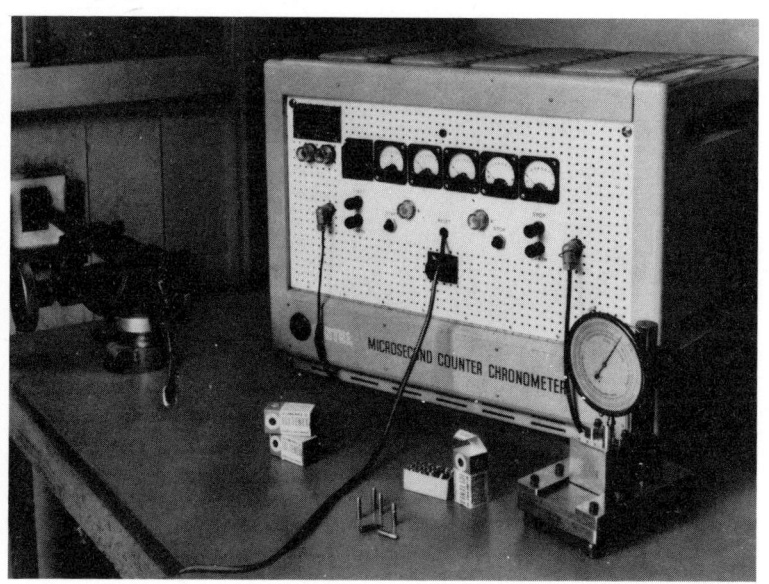

PLATE XLVII

Top—A counter chronometer, capable of recording time intervals as small as one-millionth of a second, measures the bullet's velocity. Samples are checked from every batch of ammunition. *Bottom*—Every batch of target ammunition is accuracy tested by firing from target rifles

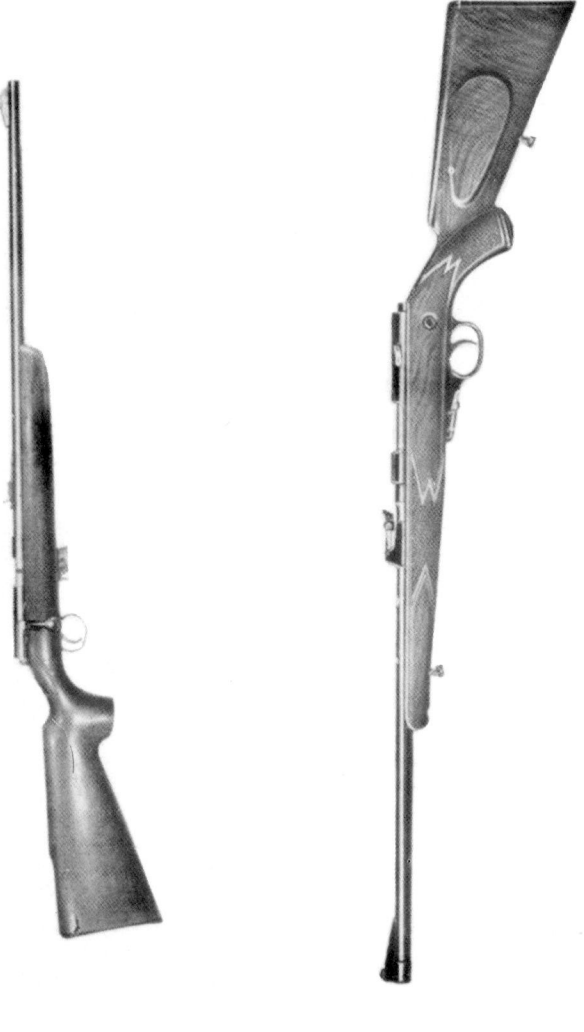

PLATE XLVIII
Top—B.S.A. Supersport rifle. *Bottom*—German Walther KKJ ·22 L.R. sporting carbine

SIGHTS

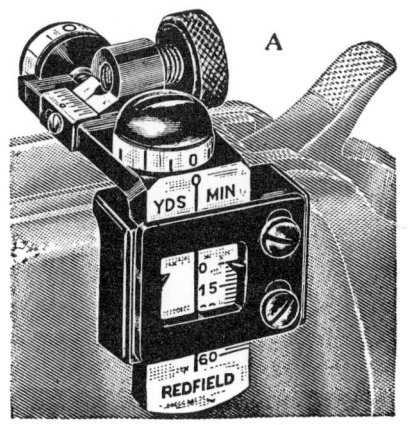

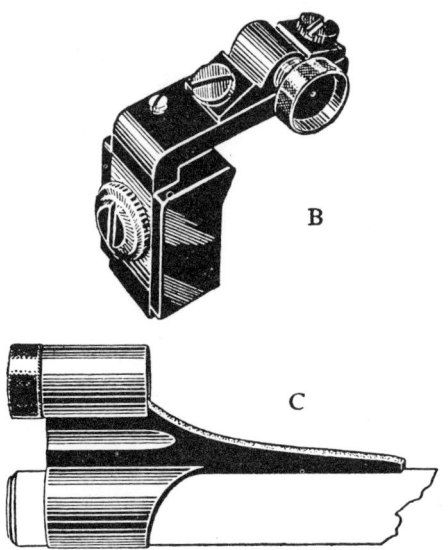

10. REDFIELD SERIES (A) 70 receiver sight. (B) Hunting sight. (C) Ramp

moved in a semi-circle, was a metal dial, on which were marked the various ranges from 1,600 to 2,800 yards (graduated at intervals of 100 yards). *All adjustments for elevation were made by moving the fore sight*, so that the pointer, at the opposite end of the arm carrying the sight bead, was set to the range required. Thus, for shooting at 1,600 yards the bead was at its highest position, while for shooting at the extreme range of 2,800 yards the bead was *below* the woodwork of the rifle, practically level with the bottom band.

This sight was not, in the nature of things, a precision job, but only a rough and ready type: nevertheless it proved itself useful for long-range shooting under climatic conditions, as in South Africa, giving clarity of objects at much greater ranges than in Europe.

Offset sights have also been applied to shotguns! Probably the most successful was the 'Monopeian' gun which, as seems usual in the history of firearms, was invented by a clergyman, the Rev. E. Elmhirst. This was designed to eliminate the ugliness inherent in stocks bent for cross-eyed shooting. The gun had two sights attached to the barrel, one at the tip of the fore-end, the other near to the muzzle. These sights, which were flat triangles in shape, were attached to the side of the left-hand barrel by short arms, about one-inch long. Both sights were about half-an-inch above the tops of the barrels. Thus the shooter aligned his offset sights instead of looking over the top rib at the target.

The introduction of recoil-less weapons in World War II, familiarly known as 'Bazookas', in which the weapon is fired from a position over the top of the shoulder, has necessitated the placing of the sights, optical and iron, to the left of the barrel, a typical example being the American 57-millimetre recoil-less rifle M18, which was used so devastatingly in the Pacific campaign.

There seems to be no reason why the offset iron sight should not become popular in the ·22-calibre target and match shooting field. It could certainly assist the shooter with the master left eye who wishes to shoot from the right shoulder and allow him to shoot with both eyes open, thus being able to dope his wind conditions better. Probably we stick to conventional positions of the sights because the cross-bow had its sights so mounted, just as we stick to the engine in the front of a car because a horse once occupied the shafts of earlier type vehicles.

Incidentally, if the subject of sights seems to have received undue importance, why not try shooting your rifle, at 25 yards, at the whole target but with the sights removed? The results will be very enlightening.

CHAPTER EIGHT

TARGET SHOOTING

TO many enthusiasts target shooting is the most important aspect of the sport. Today, in Great Britain, there is increasing enthusiasm for match or target shooting and nearly all papers, national and provincial, find a little space for it, even if it is merely reporting results of competitions. Of course, the more sensational type of papers, the papers which exploit sex and politics, pander to the anti-sports brigade and generally behave in a pretty low fashion all round, do report rifle shooting too. But whereas they are quick off the mark to report shooting accidents, the only times they report target shooting is to give space to a picture of a pretty girl holding a rifle. But maybe this is better than nothing.

In Great Britain target shooting may well assume even greater importance than ever before. The 'anti's' are at work to try and stop shooting in many forms and, unfortunately, many selfish and self-opinionated shooters themselves are apt to play into their hands and endorse their complaints. 'Plinking' is a sore point with some of them, and many of the restrictionists, not content with present legislation, are out to include even airguns and shotguns in the firearms laws.

It is possible that the various shooting bodies, such as the N.S.R.A., for example, may assume even greater importance in the training of beginners, as it has been mooted, and probably quite rightly so, that no one shall own or possess a firearm without having first undergone a course and obtained a certificate of proficiency. Something similar to the British Road Driving Tests. Unfortunately, even if tests are passed there is nothing to prevent a person, apparently successful and safe, from lapsing into bad habits thereafter.

Target shooting is not without its critics.

Too many of the critics, writing in the shooting press, are prone

TARGET SHOOTING

to shout about the following matters, which, for convenience, I will compress under headings:

1. 'Target shooting is dull, it lacks spectator appeal.'
2. 'It is artificial and bears no resemblance to field shooting.'
3. 'It's too easy.'
4. 'Shooting matches and club meetings are often conducted in dreary buildings and premises.'

First of all, let's get this straight: ninety-nine point nine recurring per cent of these critics do not indulge in club target shooting! Secondly, if they did, they certainly have never shone! Thirdly, why don't they try to do something about it?

Superficially, of course, these various criticisms may have the *appearance* of accuracy, but let's face up to it and acknowledge that the standard of marksmanship in present-day clubs, particularly the ·22 clubs, is very high indeed. In fact, I doubt very much if the combination of rifle, ammunition and the person using them has ever been higher.

One hears suggestions that the fairground enthusiasts who shoot at celluloid balls on jets of water can show the club prone position shooter just what rifle shooting is. Even if the fairground enthusiast has mastered the very simple art of knocking celluloid balls off jets of water at three paces, and should then set about using a highly accurate match rifle, with modern, reliable ammunition, on a club range in the prone position, he would have the shock of his life, because the unmoving bull would remain unperforated.

The simple truth of the matter is that rifle shooting is primarily a recreation. The majority of enthusiasts do not embark on a club career with the idea of being trained as potential battle fodder. It has been suggested that a military type of training or course be included in the target shooter's repertoire—by someone, of course, who has no intention of indulging in this fun! Just as the club shooter does not regard his shooting as a prelude to warfare, neither does the foil, épée or sabre enthusiast (of which I am one), regard the game as a prelude to blood-letting. Both have their origins either in hunting to live, or fighting either for conquest or in defence—today they are harmless, healthy recreations.

As for spectator appeal . . . that may be all very well for the exhibitionist type who likes to shoot at coins or balls thrown into the air and hit them before an admiring gallery of *innocents*. But such tricks are mere tricks and not feats at all and I can do no better than quote the late Wyatt Earp who denounced 'fancy and trick shooters as being quite incapable in *real* action'. Target practice for such a man as he, and countless others, who depended upon their shooting skill to live, was at targets which had no similarity to a living being. The capable shooter in action had to be able to place his shots instinctively, and coolly, and above all, *unhurriedly* in the right place.

Against the criticism of lack of spectator appeal a further criticism is often made—'Look at Bisley,' the critics say, 'with a line of targets and flags flying in the wind—what a circus!' What's wrong with a line of targets? As for the wind flags, they have a useful purpose and it requires skill and experience to interpret them correctly.

One of the charges made against Bisley, and other meetings is that all the spectator sees is 'a line of backsides and bootsoles'. Personally, I have always understood that when on the firing point shooters should only show their rears!

The simple truth of the matter is that the average rifleman who has become experienced makes the whole thing seem unbelievably easy. The fly-fisher who drops his lure gently on the water, effortlessly and easily is not half as spectacular (from the spectator appeal angle) as he who clumsily splashes his fly down, or hooks himself in the ear. The expert skater practising edges and simple threes or brackets, is not half so full of spectator appeal as the average youngster trying out his first clumsy Paulsen—and I have yet to meet the genuine marksman or target shooter who could really enjoy shooting before a gallery of spectators. Are we to develop a new system of getting into the sling, coupled with all the tricks of the stage conjurer or weight-lifter? Or, before getting into the prone position, should we adopt a pose worthy of a male ballet dancer? Besides, how could one reconcile military training with spectator appeal—that is, spectator appeal to induce them to *want* to take part in the sport?

Let us admit it freely—an influx of sporting shots into the ranks of target shooters would be a good thing—but equally a vast

TARGET SHOOTING

number of sporting shooters would benefit from good, hard, conscientious practice on a proper club range. Critics have condemned the prone position as stultifying shooting: but this is the safest way in which to teach beginners: it also provides the novice with the best exercises in correct exhalation of breath before letting off the shot. In any case, the criticism is not valid because that there are competitions for standing (or off-hand) shooting, as well as sitting and kneeling.

Nor is the prone position a ridiculous one when it comes to combat shooting! Speaking from experience as an infantryman in World War II, apart from street and house-to-house fighting, which is a very nasty business, I found that both my comrades and myself preferred to get as prone and inconspicuous as possible when engaging the rather dangerous game in *feld-grau* which we met. In any case, to deal with range shooting from a purely military standpoint is not realistic because it would be necessary to introduce the battle-school technique in which the rifleman not only engaged, or tried to engage moving and disappearing targets, whilst on the move, but was also subjected to machine-gun fire, 68 grenades, smoke and tear-gas. I can hardly see the average recreational shooting wishing to undergo this, and most certainly I feel that the majority of critics who advocate this would be rather conspicuous by their absence. On the other hand, though, this would have a definite spectator appeal!

Furthermore, rifle shooting at the target caters for all ages, from mere boys and girls to nonagenarians. I could hardly hope to see the latter in the class of military riflemen these critics would hope to produce. But the idea that a nation of firearms experts is dependent on realistic shooting rather founders because although there is a close affinity between Swiss rifle clubs and the militia, the conventional, unnatural bull with the chance shots nearest the centre is still the most coveted target.

As for club ranges and premises which have been described as barns, Nazi torture-chambers, and the like, not all clubs are fortunate enough to afford lush premises. In these modern days of acute housing, industrial and commercial buildings shortage, the club is fortunate that can obtain an old mill, disused warehouse or garage, in which to set up a range under the strict safety regulations which are imposed. But it says a lot for the club enthusiasm and fascination of the sport that today, in Great Britain, there are over 4,000 small-bore clubs enjoying the sport under the dismal conditions which the reformers and critics envisage. It would, therefore, appear that the surroundings are not so very important after all. The main essentials are rifles, ammunition, good fellowship in the sport, and a desire to learn.

One popular criticism is that the ·22 rifleman, in the main accustomed to prone position shooting, would be lost if he ever encountered dangerous game. What a stupid argument! Frankly, the great majority, not only of ·22 target men but of all shooting men, will, in the nature of things never have an opportunity to shoot dangerous game. Also a considerable proportion of target shoots are interested in shooting as a skill and would not consider, without being anti-sports in any way, shooting at live targets whether game or vermin, large or small. They find their pleasure on the range. But though many of the riflemen will never face dangerous game it is stupid to suggest that they would hunt such targets without having first undergone some practice and instruction for that purpose. Some of us have had to face dangerous game *armed* for our destruction, whether in World War II, Korea or elsewhere, and sometimes (as I can well recall on a couple of very desperate occasions) that dangerous human game was well and truly after our blood. In such a situation the practice we had put in on unnatural targets, the bull and aiming mark, was of far greater importance than the expenditure of a hundred times as much energy and ammunition on shooting fountain balls in front of a gallery of girl friends.

The only way in which target shooting can become of military value is when it is incorporated with fieldcraft—and fieldcraft has no part in recreational competition shooting. There is a vital point which all these critics of target shooting overlook. When an enemy is engaged at small-arms range—as opposed to close-quarter street fighting and cover fighting with 'burp' guns—it is very rarely directly identifiable: sometimes only a dim portion of the landscape which no target can simulate. The trained man on the target range knows how to centre his group accurately on that tiny aiming mark and I would much prefer to go into rifle action

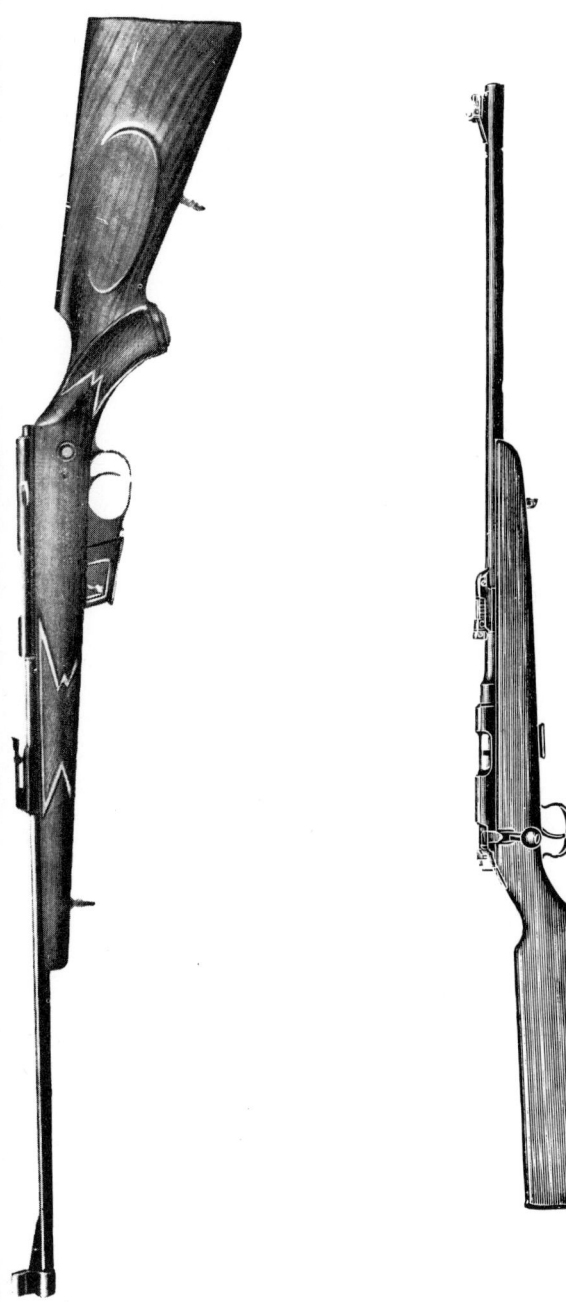

PLATE XLIX

Top—German Walther KKJ-H ·22 Hornet sporting rifle, also available in ·22 L.R. as Model KKJ. *Bottom*—BRNO (Czech) bolt action

PLATE L

Top—German 'Krico'. *Bottom*—Finnish 'Sako' in ·22 Hornet calibre

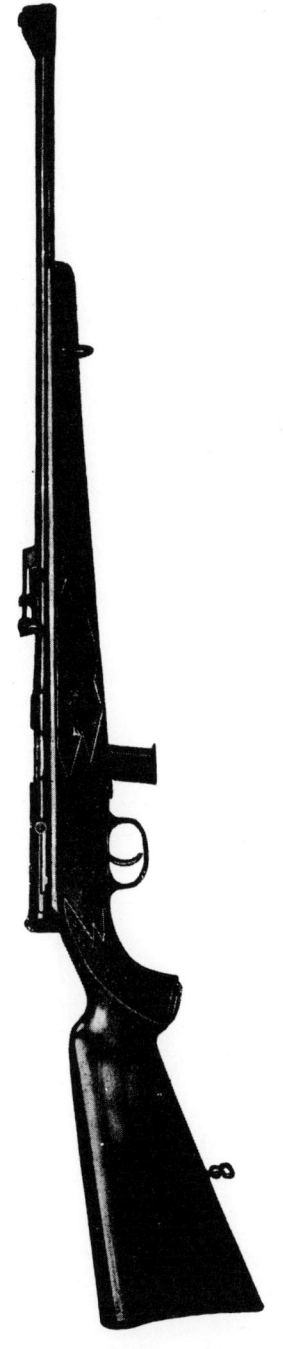

PLATE LI

Top—Austrian Tyrol Model

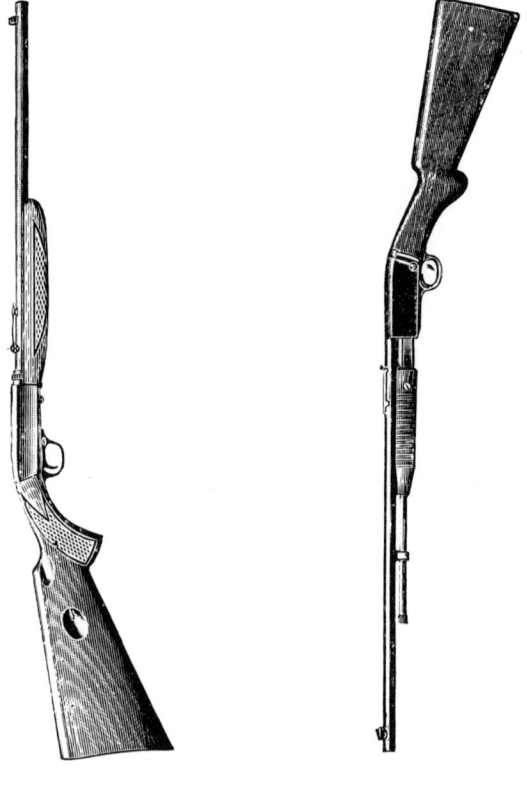

PLATE LII

Top—Browning self-loader, Model 'B' standard. *Bottom*—Browning slide-action repeater

with three or four first-rate target marksmen as my companions than be accompanied by a whole platoon of fairground shooters.

Consider this. In the American Civil War many muskets were found on the battlefields loaded with several charges of ball and powder: in World War II it was established that almost 30 per cent of infantry personnel engaged in direct action did not discharge their weapons for some emotional or psychological reason, and it appeared that the majority of these men were those who had undergone military training only and had never done any target or club range work in civilian life.

In short, target shooting is all right. It does not require spectator appeal to increase its membership: it does not need to have military style training incorporated in its curriculum: and in spite of dreary premises, backsides and bootsoles will continue to flourish.

But on the whole these criticisms stem from the publicity which rifle shooting has had, of recent years, in the Press. In actual fact the non-shooting public are led to think that this is the latest sport.

Which poses the question—how old is rifle target shooting?

Many, casting an eye back to the first Wimbledon Meeting of 1860, will state that target shooting in Great Britain started with the birth of the National Rifle Association in 1859: others will say that it originated in the training of skirmishers and the Rifle Brigade (forgetting that military training does not enter the orbit of recreational target shooting), whilst the wiseacres will assert that target shooting must have been practised as a sport from time immemorial because men love to pit and test their skills against each other.

The wiseacres are right, of course, because target shooting as a sport has been practised almost since the invention of gunpowder, merely carrying on the traditions of archery and cross-bow shooting, competitions for which were held regularly in towns, villages, and in districts throughout Europe.

The earliest mention of rifle shooting at the target as a recreation was an edict, issued by the Swiss Government at Berne in 1563; though target shooting with the smooth-bore arquebus was organized at Geneva from 1474 onwards with the equivalent of the modern Queen's Prize under the title of King of the Arquebus as the coveted award. Ironically enough the edict is in the nature of a penalty against riflemen!

'For the last few years,' it declared, 'the art of cutting grooves in the chamber of guns has been introduced with the object of increasing the accuracy of fire; the disadvantage resulting therefrom to the common marksmen has sown discord amongst them. In ordinary shooting matches marksmen are therefore forbidden under a penalty of £10 to provide themselves with rifled arms. Everyone is nevertheless permitted to rifle his military weapon and to compete with marksmen armed with similar weapons for special prizes.'

It was only natural that as the firearm gradually ousted the bow from the sporting and military scene, it should also take over its place in competition shooting.

As long ago as 1525 the Swiss held regular rifle shooting competitions, in spite of the later edict, as well as competitions for the ordinary arquebusiers. The targets were based on the old archery targets, and there was a system of marking in vogue which seems peculiarly modern. The marker, who (after the manner of modern American hunters) was clad in red as a safety precaution so that he was clearly visible to the competitors, hid in a substantial shelter in line with the targets, emerging to cover the bullet mark on the target with a disc on the end of a long pole. When a bull was scored he performed an amusing ritual jig ending with a somersault!

Every man in a Swiss district, except the very poorest peasant, had a firearm and 'shoots' took place at regular periods. There was no range in our sense of the word, and in some cases the markers took shelter in trenches in front of the targets, instead of the traditional hut, though the marking disc was used to signal where the ball had struck the target.

Competition shooting was also a feature amongst the early American pioneers, but, strangely enough, whilst popular on the Continent was not in vogue in Britain. True enough, shooting matches were sometimes entered into between the gentry, generally for substantial wagers, but there was no general 'club' shooting. In truth, on the Continent and in America the general public were encouraged to become good shots and were encouraged to have

TARGET SHOOTING

their own firearms, but in England, with its long tradition of feudalism, there was a distinct prejudice against allowing the 'lower orders' to possess such things. A feeling, I regret to write, which is still extant in certain quarters to this day. When one considers the various rebellions which have torn the history of Britain, particularly the Civil War, the Monmouth Rebellion and the Jacobite Risings, there may have been just cause for such fears on the part of the rulers concerned, and so it was not until the threat of French invasion that the public were encouraged to take up precision shooting.

For the last hundred years, however, rifle shooting in Great Britain has gone from strength to strength and never in all its history has it had so many efficient target shooters, reaching standards almost unbelievable even fifty years ago.

From time to time efforts have been made to depart from the usual run of target shooting. Attempts have been made to introduce novelty into the sport, aimed at amusing the shooters, and perhaps even inducing a little 'spectator appeal' in order to promote the sport.

For example, at Wimbledon in 1863 pool shooting at ordinary crockery was introduced. It was amusing, but soon died a natural death. In 1877 we had the 'torpedo target'. This consisted of an ordinary target, shot at 200 yards, with a six-inch bull. In front of the bull's-eye was a circular piece of wood which, when struck, discharged a loaded Snider rifle concealed behind it. This again provided amusement and novelty for a short time, but, like all novelties, was short-lived. A night shooting competition was introduced in 1864 under the title of an 'Owl Shoot', in which competitors scored 'owl's-eyes', shooting in the dark against small discs of light. But this competition was not repeated a second time.

In his book *Modern American Rifles* published in 1892, A. G. Gould described a competition in which the target consisted of a double eagle from which the heraldic devices of crown, orb, and so on had to be shot away by successive shots. The whole was finally exploded by a well-directed shot into a small hole, only three-quarters of an inch in diameter, in an iron plate in the centre of the bird's body behind which was a small dynamite charge. This too seems to have died out after only a few competitions.

Shooting at clay discs has, of course, remained and is a popular form of shooting: whilst the moving targets are also popular. But the basic Swiss, 1474, type of competition target shooting has stood the test of almost five centuries. The unrealistic circular targets, in which shots nearest the centre are the most prized, has outlasted all attempts to bring novelty and 'spectator appeal' into the sport. The only changes have been improvements in rifles and ammunition. The shooters themselves pursue their sport with the same enthusiasm and keenness as their ancestors.

It is interesting, therefore, to note that in contrast to the requests, by the non-target-shooting fraternity, for more 'interesting' shooting, the movement has been towards the other extreme. In the United States, groups of enthusiasts, chasing after the ultimate in accuracy, have evolved a very highly skilled form of shooting known as 'Bench-rest' shooting. Here the object is to place the group in as small a space as possible and to that end specially built rifles, with hand-loaded ammunition, fired from a rest are brought into play. In Great Britain, the review and introduction of new-style targets, guaranteed to defeat Mr Average Shot, have been brought about in an effort to divide and still further sub-divide the top-flight marksmen and make possibles more difficult.

This chasing after perfection is innate in the target shooter—he wants to get the best out of rifle, ammunition, and himself. But the chase after perfection sometimes brings new answers to old problems. For instance, 'How did you get on at Bisley?' I greeted one small-bore acquaintance. The reply I got was unexpected. 'The new target is impossible.' This shooter went on to say that the average rifle was not good enough to enable a first-class shot *to score as he should*. He thought that the new targets would not lead to an improvement in shooters, but to improvements in rifles. He added further that rifles were available, but the cost was too high.

This is an interesting point, and somehow I have a feeling that my friend is right. Perhaps the tools are not good enough for the job—or are they?

'Firing from a beautifully-contrived rest, at 500 yards he can put any number of consecutive balls within a space less

TARGET SHOOTING

than that occupied by a five-shilling piece; and it is said that he will not be contented until he can throw a bullet from the barrel of one rifle into the barrel of another placed at 500 yards' distance. His ordinary rifles are guaranteed, in the hands of a good marksman, to be true at the same distance within eight inches.'

The writer—Major H. A. Leveson, was referring to experiments carried out by Sir Joseph Whitworth over a hundred years ago, when the hexagonal bored rifle, with mechanically fitting bullets, was introduced. The Whitworth rifle, of course, was used for many years by the National Rifle Association, for the second and final stages of the Queen's Prize, and it was a Whitworth rifle which, on that memorable 2nd of July, 1860, was fired by Queen Victoria to open the first Prize Meeting at Wimbledon. This rifle was fixed in a mechanical rest and the bullet struck within a quarter of an inch of the absolute centre of the target, which was 400 yards distant.

The enthusiast, however, who is anxious to try and achieve Sir Joseph Whitworth's goal, and place all his shots within the same bullet hole, must enlist the aid of mechanical rests from which to shoot, because a human being, even at his most skilled, is comparatively unreliable. One cannot make comparisons between normal shooting from the shoulder at 100 yards and getting the average group with a rifle fired at the same distance and obtaining a group as small as ·17-inch, centre to centre, when a rest is used. The two styles of shooting are poles apart.

Bench-rest shooting covers all calibres; covers all style of weapons, including muzzle-loaders, capping breech-loaders, and black powder arms. But, in the main, with the passage of time, American enthusiasts for this form of shooting have found that the ·22-calibre rifle is the one likeliest to win, or be placed, in a fair proportion of matches. Popular cartridges are the ·222 Remington, ·219 Donaldson, ·219 Zipper and miscellaneous ·22 'wildcats'. The most successful rifles are bolt actions, generally modified Mausers, whilst extremely heavy and long barrels are the rule rather than the exception. Furthermore, a significant feature of the bench-rest rifles is the fact that the majority of the stocks are built specially for the shooter concerned, and are rather massive, often ugly-looking, pieces of furniture.

But surely, such a form of shooting cannot be skilled—one can hear the conservative shot criticize. On the contrary, shots at ranges of up to 200 yards, mirage and/or wind, can test the skill of the competitors severely. But what about marking and scoring? It is bad enough with ordinary competitions, hence the necessity for a backing card: how does one score accurately if the group is from ·143 to ·345 centre to centre?

Mr J. B. Sweany, of California, devised a measuring instrument, known as a 'Reticle Rule', and this consists of a six-inch precision scale which is read with a 4× magnifying glass, and which also views a circular reticle set concentrically with the bullet holes of the group. Repeated readings on clean-cut holes can be made, with this instrument, within an acceptable plus-or-minus error of ·001-inch. Telescope sights are essential for this style of shooting, and the dot reticle is by far the most popular. There is no preference, however, for any special degree of magnification which varies from 12× up to 36×, though an average would indicate around 20×.

The lessons taught by precision shooting from the rest or bench, lessons learned as far back as 1854 by Whitworth and his assistant Westley-Richards, are still being learned today. The new target, the acceptance of frailty of the human element, the possibility that the average rifle is 'not good enough' for consistently higher scorings (assuming the human factor to be constant) may assist in bringing about new developments, new improvements in rifles and ammunition. The precision shooters, whether from the shoulder or bench, will meet and conquer the new problem, and perhaps in due course Whitworths' ambition, the ultimate in accuracy, will be obtained.

On 5 October 1957, the National Small-bore Rifle Association approved five new target designs for prone position shooting and four new designs for the standing and kneeling matches. This was largely brought about as a result of suggestions by many marksmen that a large aiming mark was necessary, and also by organizers of matches that a more difficult target had become necessary to differentiate between first places in top-flight marksmen. As a result it can be stated that the new targets are much more difficult, nearly twice as hard as the decimal target so far as the long-range matches are concerned.

The immediate result of the issue of the new targets was seen to advantage in that the 100 yard and 50 yard targets are identical in scoring difficulty—formerly the discrepancy was greater—and also the new targets are identical in so far as sighting appearance is concerned. Incidentally, the manner in which possibles were scored in an almost monotonous manner on the old targets has virtually disappeared. Possibles are possible—but not in the same frequency.

Personally, and this suggestion is put forward in all sincerity, I feel that it should be possible to introduce another class into target shooting. To try to encourage the hunter and field sportsman, and also to satisfy the critics, shooting matches should be arranged in which the weight of the rifle is limited to, say, 6 or $6\frac{1}{2}$ lb., sights to be fixed iron 'open' type and the shooter to shoot from any position. The use of elbow pads, and special clothing should be banned from this type of competition, also the use of a spotting telescope. Additionally, a time limit should be imposed for a string of shots inclusive of getting into position. This might bring a little more of the 'sporting' or 'hunting' element into target shooting, but, and this should be borne in mind, it is only a suggestion for an *additional* shooting class and not meant in any way to modify existing target shooting conditions, rules, or regulations.

In Great Britain target shooting with the ·22 rifle and pistol comes under the control of the National Small-bore Rifle Association. This really magnificent body, and the phrase is in no way an overstatement but really does describe it, commenced life as a Society of Miniature Rifle Clubs in 1901 when the British Rifle League joined forces with the Society of Working Men's Rifle Clubs. The S.M.R.C., as it was affectionately known, changed its title to the present one in 1947. Its objects are to promote skill in shooting by British subjects, and, note this very important phrase, 'more particularly by working men'. It promotes and controls club shooting, gives prizes, promotes marksmanship grades, gives clubs and members the opportunity to acquire firearms and accessories, and also publishes a quarterly journal, *The Rifleman*.

The National Small-bore Rifle Association has not confined its activities merely to Great Britain, but has fostered international competitions and was the prime mover in formation of the Joint Shooting Committee of Great Britain, and is, in consequence, a member of the International Shooting Union (I.S.U.) and the British Olympic Association.

In addition to clubs, the N.S.R.A. looks after small-bore shooting activities at county level through the county rifle associations and local leagues, and has been instrumental in bringing to near-perfection the postal competitions in which clubs fire matches on their own ranges against opponents elsewhere. It also gives invaluable assistance in the formation of clubs, inspection of premises, the obtaining of certificates of exemption from gun licence dues, and insurance of a collective nature at nominal premiums.

Meetings are shot under the control of a range committee and a range officer, who is empowered to test rifles at any time during the meeting and can refuse to allow any weapon to be used which fails the test. Needless to add, competitors *must* conform to his orders and directions. There are hard penalties for certain offences, even leading to suspension from taking part in any other N.S.R.A. activities and such offences as dangerous conduct, in particular, or dishonest dealings (for example, falsely marking cards) can lead to expulsion. In general the Chief Officer of Police in the offender's district is also notified so that appropriate action *may* be taken in respect of his firearms certificate.

To meet handicapped sportsmen who through physical defect are unable to comply with the strict rules appertaining to shooting positions, the N.S.R.A. issue special dispensations to allow them to compete on equal terms with their fellows.

The N.S.R.A. also lay down certain regulations, not only as to conduct on the ranges, method of witnessing for postal shoots and dozens of other matters, but also prescribe how external paddings, such as elbow-pads, may be worn, of what materials they may consist, and their size.

The Association organizes a national classification scheme, an

TARGET SHOOTING

annual championship, and club team matches.

In the United States there is also a National Rifle Association and this covers both full-bore and small-bore rifle shooting. It came into being in 1871 and the famous Creedmoor Matches will be for ever associated with its name. Its activities extend not only to rifle shooting, but also cover such matters as affect the gun collector, the hand loader, and primary instruction to the beginner in the field. It publishes an extremely fine monthly journal, *The American Rifleman*, which, in addition to news of association activities, gives information on shotgun sport, collecting, military matters, law enforcement, ballistics, and news from other lands. Its chief concern at the moment is carrying out the aims according to which it was founded, namely to fight restrictive legislation and to pursue a nation-wide gun safety campaign.

By and large, it covers the field which is at present covered in Great Britain by the National Rifle Association, The National Small-bore Rifle Association, and the Clay Pigeon Shooting Association.

There are, of course, rifle associations and shooting bodies in practically every country throughout the world, each of which operates very much on the same lines as our own N.S.R.A.

Buck Fever and Target Shooting

IN all forms of shooting, target shooting and field shooting there is a phenomenon called 'buck fever' which attacks without warning, though often it is the sign of the novice, particularly in his first open meeting.

Most shooting men understand the term where the anxious hunter, about to take a shot, is unable to control the wavering barrel of his rifle. However, though the association would seem to be applicable to field shooting solely, it is the target rifleman who encounters buck fever in a big way!

Many target shooters, especially the beginner, remember those all too familiar days when 'clean' targets seem about to be realized. As each shot scores the maximum, feverish excitement, coupled with anxiety, mounts in the shooter—often there is a pounding in the chest, the fore sight wavers all over the target, and the next shot results in a spoiled score. On the other hand, consider the occasions when, after a bad first shot, the next rounds fired have all been bulls—a fairly common occurrence. Clay pigeon shooters also experience this phenomenon. For some reason it is harder to break the 100th clay than the 99 that led up to it—yet if 101 birds were thrown and the first missed, it is fair odds that the sportsman will break the ensuing 100.

In warfare, until a soldier becomes experienced, the first shots fired in action are hopelessly off target—the tight belly muscles, dry throat, and the noise and din of battle induce tensions in the physical muscles of the shooter which prevent him shooting accurately.

Team shooting can be an ordeal to the shooter who has been nominated to shoot for his club. No matter how well he has shot individually, no matter what his record is as an independent shot, the first time he shoots with a team can try his nerves severely. Indeed, many a brilliant individual shot has failed hopelessly when introduced into a team. The essence of a good team man is complete self-control, and this is only achieved by experience. Besides, the nervous shot included in a team may well induce restlessness and lack of confidence in the other members. Indeed, the most troublesome emotion which the target shooter can suffer from is the tension which arises from a strong desire to win, and if this is coupled with an 'anxiety lest the team be let down', the results can be disastrous.

The trouble is not merely a mental one: the tension also has physical causes, and these centre round the heart. Under stress of emotion the heart beats more forcefully, and this results in a shaking of the whole body: presence of food in the stomach, as after a recent meal, also increases the work which the heart has to do. It follows, therefore, that better shooting is done before rather than after a meal. Indeed, the ideal situation really demands a slight feeling of hunger!

If the sportsman is going to participate in a competition for the first time the worst thing he can do is to hang about watching other competitors. Using as many practice cards as possible is the answer, and shooting without being in a hurry when it comes to the competition itself. If a competitor puts up a fairly good score early on, it is surprising how hard it is for a subsequent

TARGET SHOOTING

opponent to beat it. If the scores are fairly level when the last few shots are coming on, buck fever, or its target equivalent, can well determine the contest in favour of the first shooter.

It is in such circumstances, particularly in the shooting-off of ties, that the cool sportsman really asserts his superiority—nervous tension, not accuracy of fire, is the deciding factor, and the one whose emotions get the better of him is the loser.

Assuming that the target shooter, a beginner, is doing well and he looks like handing in a 'possible' (provided there is no time-limit, which he is finding all too short), the moment he feels the pounding in his chest, the moment the aim becomes unsteady, he should *stop shooting for a few moments and try to relax*. A careful aim, not too long, and a very slow trigger-squeeze should then give him full marks, and any following shots which may be necessary will probably follow, easily and naturally, to complete a 'possible' or near enough to it as matters to the particular shooter.

This all boils down to the fundamental rule of shooting relaxed—all muscular tension should be avoided and a *comfortable* shooting position adopted. Thoughts of 'possibles', of letting the team down, should be pushed ruthlessly out of mind, and the job in hand, getting off the next shot, concentrated on.

The field shooter will find, often enough, that a long stalk, or a scramble over rough country, will result in an exhausted physical state which renders accurate shooting impossible. Under such circumstances the wise hunter will relax for a few minutes before putting his sights on to his quarry: it is better to let that animal escape unsaluted than to shoot hurriedly, in a state of nervous or physical exhaustion or tension, which may well result in a wounding shot.

I cannot say that I have never experienced buck fever in the field with the rifle, but I have encountered this much more on the range, whilst the most outstanding occasion occurred when, after a long stalk with a gun punt, I missed my first shot at wildfowl with the big weapon solely on account of buck fever—I simply could not control the bootjack! My very first punt gun shot went yards *over* the fowl.

A very interesting experience in regard to buck fever was published in the *Remington Rifle News* in 1949. A famous

American rifle instructor often noticed that in extreme cases of buck fever the first shot was often wide at two o'clock. His remedy was simple. He often shot in two-man matches and when he observed that his shooting partner was entering a phase of buck fever, he would tell him to reduce elevation and take several clicks left windage for the first shot. That shot successfully fired, he would then tell the sportsman concerned that conditions had changed and get him to adjust his sights to their original setting while never indicating to the shooter the true reason for these instructions.

Buck fever may arise from several causes—but the effect is the same—bad scores. It may be defeated by adopting a comfortable shooting position, ignoring the scores turned in by others, avoiding heavy meals immediately prior to shooting, not holding on too long between shots. Above all else, by avoiding fussiness.

The beginner should remember that the object of target shooting is to get *all* the shots into the bull: practice, skill will get them there: concentration on the job in hand, will also get them there: worry and speculation, dithers and fussiness, will certainly ensure that they won't. If you can get nine shots in, there *should* be nothing easier than the tenth! Which reminds me ... there are lots and lots of excuses apart from buck fever for accounting for that final, damning shot ... but buck fever is never admitted to, openly, because it is associated with tenderfeet, yet I'll be willing to wager that buck fever is the real cause in almost every case.

CHAPTER NINE

SPORTING SHOOTING

SPORTING shooting with the ·22 is divided into two categories, shooting the rim-fire cartridge and shooting with the centre-fire cartridge. Popular associations of ·22 shooting are with the ubiquitous rim-fire cartridge and, truth to tell, the centre-fire cartridges are only ·22 in name—being really powerful large-bore ammunition necked down to take a ·22-calibre bullet.

Most sporting shooting with the ·22, not only in Great Britain but throughout the world, including the United States where so much is made of ·22 centre-fire cartridges, is done with the long rifle ·22 rim-fire ammunition.

On modern ·22 long-rifle cartridge boxes there is the legend imprinted DANGEROUS WITHIN ONE MILE. Time and time again shooting men discuss this and various viewpoints are expressed: can it kill at a mile? Is this just a gimmick?

After the 1914–18 War had ended the Ordnance Department in the United States conducted a series of experiments with various calibres in order to ascertain their *extreme* range. Included in these tests, which were conducted at Daytona Beach, was the ·22 long-rifle ammunition and it is interesting to note that the ammunition of that day, at an elevation of 8·8° had a range of 1,050 yards; with an elevation of 17·8° the range was increased to 1,252 yards, and at the same degree of elevation an extreme range of 1,324 yards was also recorded.

Today the ammunition is much more powerful, and with wind conditions favourable there is no reason why a ·22 rim-fire bullet should not carry 1,760 yards. For safety's sake, therefore, all ammunition boxes using this type of ammunition are labelled DANGEROUS WITHIN ONE MILE. The centre-fire cartridges will go a little further, but whether they would travel further than a mile is debatable.

It is with this factor in mind that the sporting shooter should approach his sport—careless shooting might well bring, injury, disfigurement, blindness or even death to some innocent third party at a fantastic distance away. The word fantastic is used because most ·22 rim-fire shooting is conducted at ranges of between 30 to 60 yards.

Whether one agrees with bull-fighting or not, the fact remains that the fatal sword-thrust executed by the matador is a most highly skilled procedure. To kill cleanly the sword must be thrust into exactly the right place, to the right depth. Bungling, or failure to observe the fundamentals, brings the displeasure of the crowd upon the unfortunate bull-fighter; on the other hand, a clean kill, executed with full artistry, brings a full complement of *Olés* and the hero-worship of ecstatic supporters.

But there is an invisible element behind the skill of the matador, the death of the bull, and the plaudits of the crowd, which binds up the three essentials into one homogeneous whole. That invisible element is the duty of the matador towards his adversary, the bull: the duty to kill cleanly, and with respect. The shooting man owes a similar duty to his quarry, be it grey squirrel, crow, rabbit or larger game. True, there is no crowd to praise his skill, to hurl scorn and derision upon him if he bungles the job, but he should take a similar pride in his chosen weapon. He should place his bullet in exactly the right spot, at the right moment, from the right range. The quarry must die quickly, painlessly, cleanly. He should feel as humiliated and outraged, when placing a bad shot, as the unskilled or nervous matador.

In fact, the true shooter who enters into rifle sporting shooting never loses respect for his quarry: and, if he should, by ill chance, wound and not kill, the thought will haunt him for no little time.

There are many sportsmen who acquire a ·22 rim-fire rifle with the object of doing a little pest control, vermin shooting, or even small-game shooting. The light weight of the arm, its lack of report and recoil, the cheapness of ammunition, have a special appeal. But all too often he has an exaggerated idea of its ranging powers. He considers he should be able to pick off small game or vermin at 100 yards: he also, regrettably, begins to look upon the scatter-gun shooting as slightly unsporting.

SPORTING SHOOTING

Armed with a ·22 rim-fire he thereupon sallies forth after taking a little practice and zeroing his rifle, and looks for his proper quarry. The number of misses, wounded game or vermin given a second shot or despatched in other manner, or, worse still, wounded quarry escaping, is dismally high. Lest it be thought I am painting too black a picture, let each sportsman search his own conscience honestly when he will agree that the occurrences are all too common.

Field shooting and target shooting are poles apart. The calibre of the weapons may be the same, but the weapons themselves are different. The elements of aiming may be the same, but the application is different. Finally, though one may be an expert field shot, or an expert target shot, it does not necessarily follow that one would be automatically an expert at the other branch of the sport.

Target shooting demands the best possible shooting platform, and this invariably means a heavy rifle fired from the prone position. Field shooting requires a lighter rifle, which may have to be fired from any one of a variety of positions. In target shooting the *exact* range to an inch is known and regulated, but in field shooting one cannot be certain for a few yards in either direction. In target shooting the target is well-defined, the aiming mark is unmistakable: in field shooting it is often impossible to distinguish the target from the background. Furthermore, the lethal area in field shooting is as small as the bull, even sometimes smaller, than equivalent targets on the range. There are, however, no allowances in target shooting for missing or near misses: your score is registered against you. In field shooting only the hits count—the stats officer, the backing card are absent. Yes, field shooting requires more versatility from the shooter, quicker reactions, but target shooting requires an equally high skill in other directions.

The target presented to the field sportsman is very small—the head and the neck being the principal shots, the spine and the heart falling into the next best category. It is absolutely useless for the sportsman to use the whole of a bird as his target, even a ·22 long-rifle cartridge will not necessarily kill at once if the bird is hit in the body. *The head of a bird, or a squirrel is extremely small.*

This limits the sportsman to shooting at ranges at which he can clearly identify the head, and hit it with accuracy. In the absence of telescopic sights, this means a maximum of 50 yards.

To the sportsman wishing to take up rifle shooting as a sport, as opposed to target shooting, which is a recreation, I would point out that there are several elements which make up the successful shot. In the first place, field shooting with the rifle brings with it a peculiar nervous tension, which is more intense than competition shooting on the range. This tension can be overcome through practising relaxation, through being strong-minded enough not to place the sights on the animal or bird until the last possible fraction of time before the trigger is squeezed. 'Taking a careful aim' is all very well in the realms of adventure fiction, or in target shooting. In field shooting the aim is as short as possible, but every care has been taken to identify the target, register the range, note the wind allowance, and get into a shooting position before the aim is taken. By dwelling on the aim, nervous tension is apt to build up and this results in buck fever, in which condition it becomes impossible to hold the rifle steady, the shot is hurried, the trigger wrenched, and flinching is also likely to be developed. I referred to this phenomenon in the previous chapter.

The sporting rifleman *must* be able to shoot from standing, kneeling, sitting, squatting and prone positions, even occasionally when actually moving. He must be able to shoot through all sorts of cover. There is only one way to achieve this. Get out on to the grounds where you are going to shoot, adopt the positions you are going to have to use and practise dry shooting, that is, without live ammunition. Small pieces of wood should be set up to simulate the heads of rabbits, or squirrels or crows, and from these varied positions the sportsman should calculate range, swing into the aim, and press the trigger the moment the sights are lined up with the target. Shooting in this manner with live ammunition can then follow.

Range judging is, therefore, a very important part in field shooting. The field shooter must be able to judge ranges accurately. Not roughly, but accurately. On his estimation of ranges depends the elevation to which he will set his sights and he must, in addition, know the exterior ballistics of the combination of rifle and

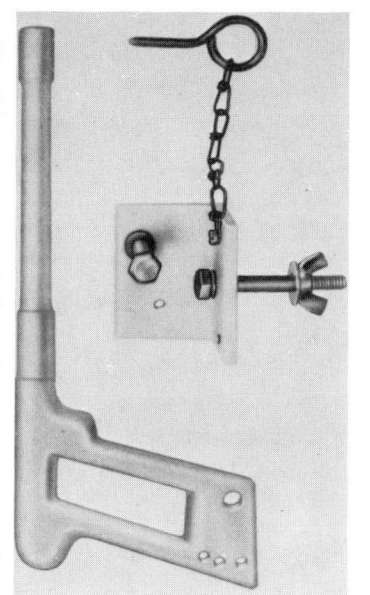

Aluminium base plate and cast aluminium, pistol-shaped frame to which spring-trap mechanism mounts for use as hand trap as shown below

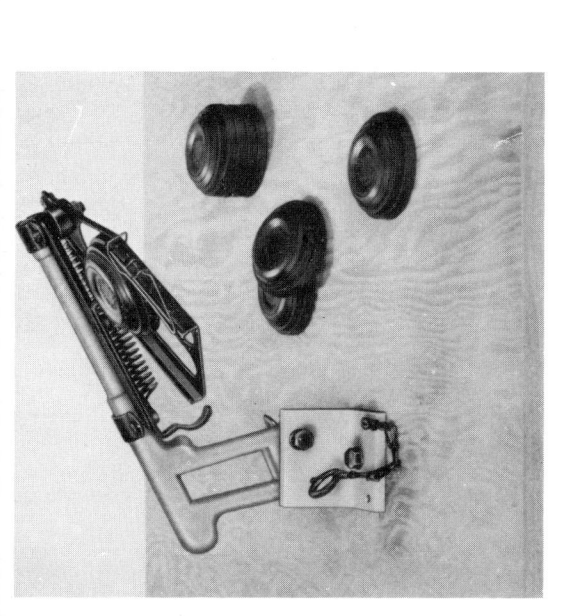

PLATE LIII
Mossberg 'Targo' spring-trap Model 1A. Complete assembly used as stationary trap

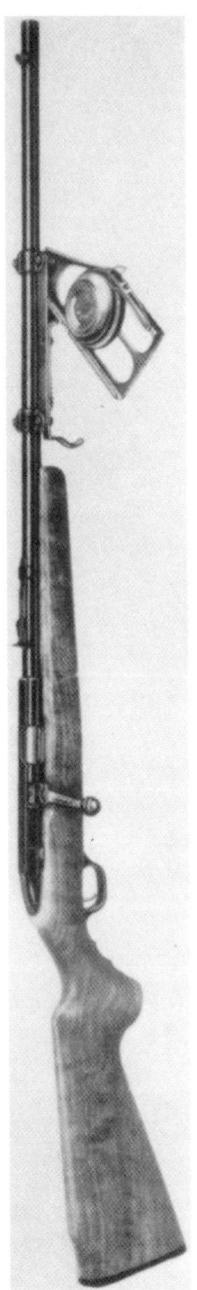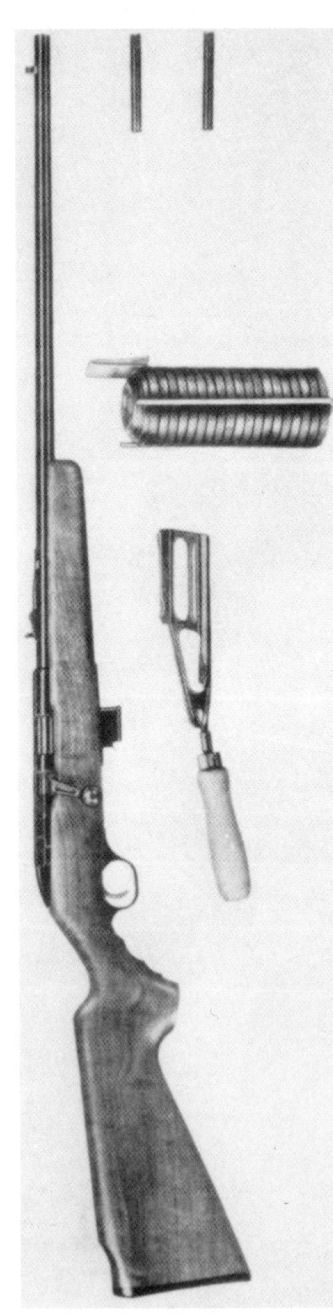

PLATE LIV

Mossberg 'Targo' shotguns. *Top*—Model 320 TR, single shot and showing spring trap mounted on barrel for 'one-man' shooting. *Bottom*—Model 340 TR, 7 shot, with which are included smooth bore and rifled adaptors ('Two guns in one') hand trap and target

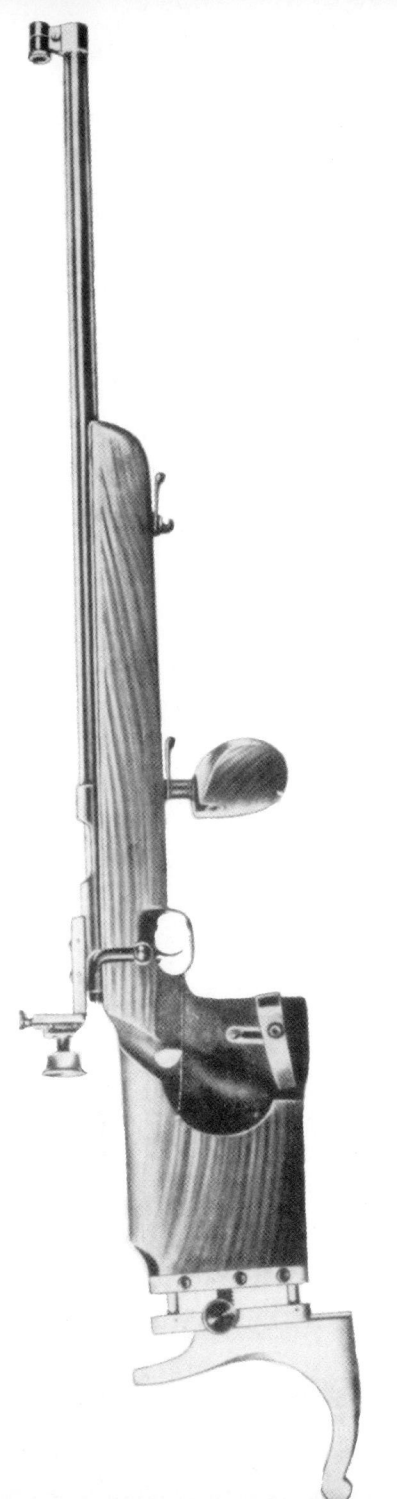

PLATE LV
Walther KKM 'Matchmaster' .22 L.R. target rifle

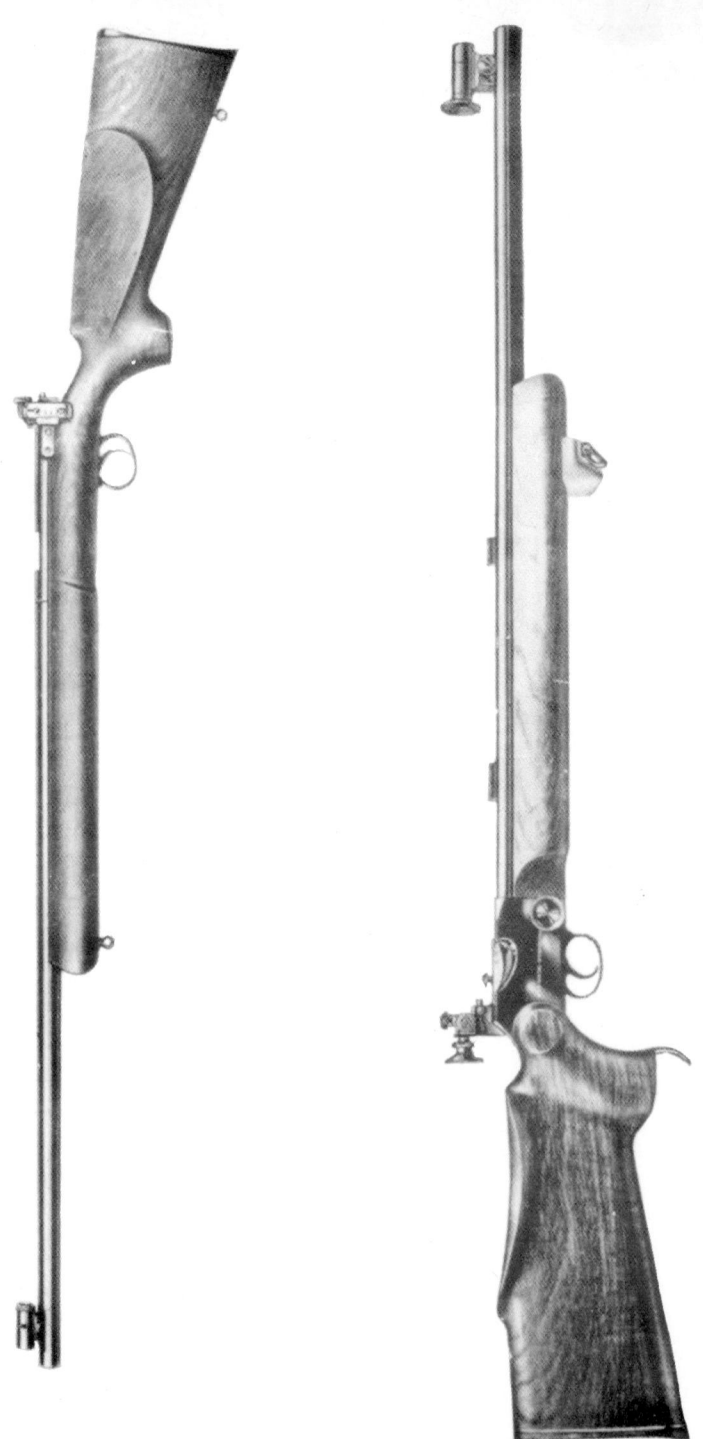

PLATE LVI

Top—B.S.A. 'Century' target rifle. *Bottom*—B.S.A. 'International' target rifle

ammunition which he is using: he should know the drop of his bullet at different ranges, because in the field there is not always time to alter sights, and once they have been set at a predetermined distance, he may aim higher or lower on the target.

The first step in learning to estimate and judge ranges is to make measurements in and about certain salient features on his own shooting grounds. For example, a certain post, or bush, may be, say, 75 yards from a certain gate. To shoot a rabbit from that gateway, against that post or bush he knows the range to an inch. Having learned the distances and ranges from spot to spot on his shoot, he must then master the fundamental of having to recognize what the target looks like at varying distances in relation to the front sight, where iron sights are used, or against the reticle if he is using a telescope sight.

There is a comparatively simple method of learning how to do this. First of all cut out some cardboard silhouettes of the game intended to be shot, for example, rabbits, rooks, or squirrels. Not only side views, but rear views, three-quarter views and so forth, and then mount these on to pieces of stick. These should be placed in the ground at distances varying from 20 to 100 yards. At each distance the sportsman must take careful note as to how large they appear. Finally, sight the rifle on each silhouette at varying distances and estimate the distance by the comparative size of the target against the front sight of the rifle. The further away the target is, the more of it will be covered by the front sight.

This does take quite a lot of time and quite a lot of practice but soon becomes almost an instinct, then, having learned how to judge distances properly, the rifleman must learn where to place his shots. An obvious enough fact, though not always so well learnt.

Having assimilated all these lessons he must then learn how to hit, correctly, moving game, which presents different problems. He must forget the rigid positions he has learnt for shooting at still targets. He must learn to use his rifle in the instinctive aiming method of the shotgunner, and in this the sights are not noticeably used. Without any doubt the best targets for this sort of work are rook and pigeons in leafless trees. On a day with a fair amount of wind, when the targets are dipping and swaying, even at a range of only thirty or so yards, the bird is by no means easy. The sights can only be aligned on the vital area for a fraction of a second. The trigger must be released the moment the sight is coming on to the target.

A special difficulty is presented with a moving target in that it is impossible to hit a moving target by aiming directly at it. There is a period of time which must ensue after the bullet has left the rifle before it can strike the target, and the greater the range the longer the period of the bullet's flight. If the shooter aims directly at the target he will miss well behind it because it won't be there by the time the bullet reaches the spot aimed at.

The directly crossing target is easier to calculate than the one travelling away, and the directly going away or approaching target is easier to hit than one travelling at a tangent. Running game or vermin travelling up or down a hillside present special problems, and if the shooter has to aim downhill, then it becomes even more complicated. I think the most difficult rifle shot of all to perform properly is at a target travelling downhill, below a shooter, at a tangent over undulating country! Yet this does occur often when shooting hill-foxes and with practice can provide a really superb thrill when a clean kill is accomplished. My most memorable shot was taken in these conditions at a fox which was traversing a boulder-strewn slope below me on a Scottish hillside, for, added to the normal complications, I could only get occasional glimpses of him, and when I did get him with my second shot I was really satisfied, except for one thing—I would rather have got him with my first!

Some shooters try to estimate a distance ahead of the target, align the weapon there and then let off the shot. This is a very unreliable method. It does bring results but the proportion of misses to hits is too large. At distances of over about fifty yards it is absolutely impossible to estimate forward allowances of say, a foot or thereabouts.

The best method of hitting a moving target is to swing or aim just in front of the nose and keep the barrel moving in the direction it is taking and whilst keeping this movement going squeeze the trigger. This 'swing', as it is termed, should be continued during and after the trigger let-off and is known as 'following through' and is the sign of the experienced shooter.

Excellent practice and training at moving targets can be done by using an air rifle in conjunction with a supply of tin cans and a fast-running stream. You should take up a stand about twenty yards from the water and have a friend release a can into the stream some yards above you. The rifle must be kept down until the moment to shoot arrives when it must be lifted into the shoulder, swung with the target and the trigger released. The position of the target in relation to the impact of the slug will be revealed by splashes in the water, or by hitting of the can. To get into shooting at moving targets from the other direction, you should shoot from either side of the stream, from above the target travelling downstream, from below it and at varying angles. Practice this way brings about results and air-rifle ammunition is cheap enough for plenty of practice.

But for real sporting shooting, as opposed to shooting in a butchering manner, the sportsman must begin to realize that the whole animal or bird must never form his target. He must centre his mind on the neck, or the spine, or the lungs, or the head, and dismiss the rest of the creature completely. It is only by concentrating in that manner that he will be able to hit his target, the bull, the vital area. Treat the whole animal as the target frame, if you must, but only the vitals, to ensure a clean kill, form your aiming mark.

To bring this point home thoroughly, take a small card target, say a twenty-five yards target, and place it over the head or behind the shoulder of a rabbit at that range. Then stand back to that distance and line up your rifle. It will then be appreciated how small the vital areas are and *how necessary it is to forget the animal picture and to concentrate on your killing area.*

I firmly believe that far too many shooting men forget this fundamental rule; even shotgunners are prone to aim ahead of the bird and not ahead of the bird's head.

For use against feathered game and vermin, the hollow pointed bullets are ideal but for fur animals, such as squirrels, if it is desired to save the pelt a solid bullet is best. If the aim is merely pest destruction and meat is not required for the table or kennel and the pelt is not wanted, then the hollow high-velocity centre-fire ·22 Hornet or ·222 Remington is the ammunition to use.

I have mentioned rabbits because there are signs that they are beginning to return and on my own shooting grounds there are indications that this sport will be possible once more. Rabbits hit in the body with high-velocity rim-fire ·22 cartridges, not the magnum, will invariably escape, only to die miserably underground.

But, by and large, the golden rules for ·22 sporting shooting may be summarized as:

1. Do not shoot beyond fifty yards, unless equipped with a telescope sight or using centre-fire ammunition.
2. Learn to shoot from a variety of positions.
3. Practise dry shooting, and still more dry shooting, and then more still.
4. Limit yourself to the vital areas such as head, spine, neck, heart or lungs.
5. Always keep your respect for your quarry. You owe a duty to the animal concerned to kill quickly and cleanly.
6. *Always shoot, even when alone, as though your own life depended upon it and that you had a critical audience around you.*

I can forgive and understand any man shooting at his target and missing it completely: even expert targetmen place their shots on the wrong target from time to time.

BUT I CAN NEVER FORGIVE THE MAN WHO PLACES HIS SHOTS WRONGLY, WOUNDING HIS QUARRY, OR WHO SHOOTS CARELESSLY, OR WHO USES THE WRONG AMMUNITION, OR BUNGLES THE JOB. He is neither rifleman nor sportsman and does a disservice to all who follow the sport and play the game according to the rules of decency and honour.

CHAPTER TEN

AMMUNITION

THE story of the ·22 ammunition has already been dealt with in the opening chapters of this book but there are many more different kinds of ·22 ammunition available than the average shooter realizes. In Great Britain the ·22 Short and ·22 Long Rifle are well known, and the ·22 Hornet is fairly widely known, as also the W.R.F. Magnum.

Unfortunately one cannot state that there is any real standardization of the ·22 rim-fire cartridges and many manufacturers vary their dimensions a little.

I am not sure, but I believe that the great American gunsmith-author Roy Dunlap declared that when he started to collect information on the ·22 Long Rifle chamber that it was so varied and there was such a disparity amongst manufacturers that any armchair amateur gunsmith could pronounce him incorrect if he gave any dimensions whatsoever!

However, all ·22 cartridges are divided into two main groups, rim-fire and centre-fire.

·22 Rim-fire Ammunition

AT the moment of writing there are available, or on the market (and this means on the world market, that is, obtainable from some source or other or still being manufactured) several different grades of ·22 rim-fire cartridges.

1. The B.B. Cap.
2. The C.B. Cap.
3. The Short.
4. The Long (now obsolete).
5. The Long Rifle.
6. Long Rifle Match.

7. Extra Long (now obsolete but still obtainable in some areas).
8. Winchester Automatic.
9. Remington Automatic.
10. W.R.F. (Rem. Special).
11. W.R.F. Magnum.
12. Dardick ·22 'tround' ammunition.

The B.B. Cap

THIS is the lowest form of ·22 ammunition and though the least powerful of all, still powerful enough to be dangerous. It was the first ancestor of the ·22 cartridge and was used chiefly for target practice. It may be used for small pest shooting, such as rats and starlings. It has a bullet weight of only 20 grains and a muzzle velocity of 780 feet per second, about the same as a modern air rifle. It delivers a muzzle energy of 24 foot-pounds.

B.B. caps will chamber and fire from standard rim-fire ·22 rifles irrespective of chamber length, but this is not to be recommended as the short case will tend to pit the chamber. In any case they cannot be used in self-loading arms, nor will they fit into the magazines of modern rifles but have to be fed, singly, manually into the chamber.

Originally the B.B. (which stands for 'Bullet Breech') cap was loaded with a round ·22 ball into the cartridge case. There was no powder charge in the case, the sole propellent being the rim-fire primer. Subsequently manufacturers did introduce a more typical bullet shape by adopting cylindrical sides and at the same time added a very light powder load to the cartridge.

This cartridge is so small that it cannot be packed in boxes in conventional fashion but is usually packed in bulk into tins or boxes, somewhat after the manner of blank cartridges.

There is little use for this cartridge today, however, and though it is still manufactured I do not think it will be long before it is finally discontinued. It is used a little on the Continent.

The C.B. Cap

THE C.B. Cap (or 'Conical Bullet' Cap) is another useless type of ·22 ammunition. This is a step between the ·22 Short and the

AMMUNITION

B.B. Cap, but though more accurate than the latter is also falling into disuse. It has been extensively used by exhibition and trick shooters on the stage and in circuses, and has had a short life in indoor gallery sport.

The original ammunition contained a small black powder charge though later a small charge of smokeless was used. A bullet weight of 29 grains became standard and some American manufacturers coated the bullet with copper alloy, principally the Western C.B. Lubaloy 'Coated'.

Energy and muzzle velocity were substantially the same as for the B.B. Cap and the only advantage it had over the former was the fact that it was more accurate.

The Short

THIS is divided into two groups (*a*) ·22 Short and (*b*) ·22 Short Disintegrating.

The ·22 Short Disintegrating was designed expressly for shooting gallery work and incorporates a bullet which is designed to break up when hitting the back stop, in order to avoid ricochets. I believe that in the United States where these are still used in shooting galleries, there are statutory enactments requiring the installation of extractor apparatus so that the employees on the range will not breathe in the minute particles which are released by these disintegrating bullets.

Manufactured principally by those two great concerns Remington and Winchester (also Peters and Western respectively), they vary in bullet weight from 24 to 30 grains. Remington and Peters bullets, which are the heavier types, are of lead, whilst the Western and Winchester are of a synthetic material.

On the other hand, the ·22 Short is a much more important cartridge than is generally realized by the great body of shooters today. This was the original ·22 rim-fire cartridge of any merit and was introduced by Smith & Wesson and must surely rate as one of the oldest cartridges still on the market. For a period it fell into disuse, in fact many shooters have never used it, but is coming back into its own in pistol matches on account of its very low recoil and excellent accuracy at the ranges at which it is fired.

As a pest cartridge it is fairly useless, though may be used against small furred or feathered vermin. It certainly should never be used against rabbits or similar game, however. The weight of the bullet is standardized at 29 grains, but there are variations in the scale, and hollow-pointed bullets fired in high-velocity shorts generally weigh 27 grains.

Velocity, on average, appears to be in the region of 990 feet per second at the muzzle for the hollow-point high-speed ammunition and about 20 feet per second less for the solid standard-velocity cartridge.

Many different kinds of bullet have been and are being used in this ammunition: for instance, plain lead, greased externally: plain lead coated with dry wax: copper-plated or cadmium plated, and the latter either dry or coated with a grease or wax lubricant.

When coated and lubricated bullets are used, the muzzle velocity of the solid bullet is stepped up to 1,130 feet per second and the hollow-point to 1,150 feet per second.

The range at which their accuracy falls off is beyond 50 yards, but at this range they can give excellent training and it was only with the introduction of match rifle shooting that the death knell of the ·22 Short, as a target round, was sounded. For plinking, small vermin shooting, initial training of boys and young shots, and of course on the fairground shooting gallery, they still hold an important position.

The Long

THIS is now obsolete. It had the same cartridge case as the Long Rifle but used the same bullet as the Short. It was an in-between cartridge and these notes are intended for the collector or for historical reading. The bullet would feed and fire in any rifle chamber for Long Rifle and Long ammunition and continued to be manufactured only after it had served its purpose to cater for rifles which had been chambered for this particular ammunition. It was fired at a muzzle velocity only slightly higher than the Short. The standard 29-grain lead bullet reached 1,030 feet per second, and the hollow-point cartridge registered 1,395. It developed approximately 100 foot-pounds of energy at the muzzle; by the time the bullet had travelled 100 yards this had dropped to 60 foot-pounds. Over 100 yards the mid-range trajectory was better than that of the Short (3·8 inches as against 4·3). The ·22 Long cartridge was also manufactured holding a small shotgun charge for firing from ·22 shotguns (a favourite ruse by stage and circus 'trick' shooters).

The Long Rifle

THIS is a very important cartridge indeed and probably more rounds of this are fired by civilian riflemen than any other.

The Long Rifle is, of course, the standard rifle for target work and the manufacturers have really gone to town on making this ammunition as accurate and as reliable as is possible and the sporting and target riflemen owe a tremendous debt to them for their painstaking work, research, and imagination.

In spite of much colourful literature on the subject, more pest and small-game shooting is done with the ·22 rim-fire long rifle than any of the other calibres and even the ·22 centre-fires fall a long way behind in total scores when number of rounds expended in pursuit of game and vermin are totted up. The bullet is usually 40 grains, though high-velocity loads with hollow-pointed bullets may use a bullet weighing 36 or 37 grains.

The hollow-pointed bullet must be used on small game or vermin, as the solid target bullets are not satisfactory for this work tending to wound rather than kill.

Modern ·22 long-rifle ammunition incorporates what is today commonplace, that is, a non-corrosive primer. This made its first appearance in 1927 when Remington introduced the 'Kleanbore' primer and in 1937 the 'Palma Kleanbore' was introduced.

The Long Rifle as loaded by I.C.I. Ltd, in High Velocity Grade, develops a muzzle energy of 1,400 feet per second: in Rifle Club grade a muzzle velocity of 1,200 feet per second, and at 100 yards the velocity of the former is still 1,036 feet per second, with a striking energy of 95 foot-pounds, as against 962 feet per second and 82 foot-pounds of the latter.

The Long Rifle is also manufactured in a special grade for

handguns, known as the 'pistol grade', and this has a reduced powder charge in order to reduce recoil, thereby improving potential accuracy.

There is also a Long Rifle ·22 shot cartridge, which contains a minute charge of shot, suitable for killing rats indoors and small birds, sparrows and so forth, up to 15 yards. I have seen, however, an expert shot with this ammunition, a professional rat catcher and vermin exterminator, shoot the tough wood pigeon at ranges of 30 feet, hit them in the head and kill them stone dead! He said he preferred to use this rather than the air rifle, which the authorities preferred for night shooting in town, because though he might wound with an air rifle, he either killed clean or (though rather rarely) missed completely with the other.

The Extra Long

THIS is almost out of production altogether, though still manufactured on the Continent. It is an in-between type of cartridge in that although the case is of the same diameter as the ·22 Long Rifle, the case is longer than standard and so cannot be used in rifles chambered for Long Rifle ammunition. Winchester built special rifles for this cartridge. Rifles built for this cartridge may use standard short, long or long rifle ·22 ammunition. The standard bullet weight is 40 grains but the muzzle velocity is (generally) somewhat lower than the standard ·22 Long Rifle ammunition.

Winchester Automatic

THIS was designed specially for the Winchester Model 1903 self-loading rifle. The standard bullet weight is 45 grains but it only has a muzzle velocity of 1,055 foot seconds. In actual fact it is almost obsolete and is inferior to the Long Rifle ammunition. A feature of this cartridge is the *inside* lubricated bullet. Rifles which have been chambered for this ammunition will not handle other ·22 ammunition, nor will they handle its counterpart the ·22 Remington Automatic.

The case diameter of the cartridge is ·2505, that is, wider than standard ·22 ammunition.

AMMUNITION

·22 Remington Automatic

THIS is another special cartridge, similar to the ·22 Winchester Automatic, but with different dimensions. The lubrication is inside and the bullet weight is 45 grains. Muzzle velocity is lower than the Winchester Automatic and is rated at 920 feet per second for solid and 940 feet per second for hollow-point bullets. Rifles chambered for this cartridge, which has a case diameter of ·2455 inches cannot use either Winchester Automatic or other ·22 ammunition.

·22 W.R.F. (Remington Special)

THIS cartridge was produced in two types: the W.R.F. with a flat-nosed bullet and the Remington Special with a round-nosed bullet. Characteristics are a slightly higher velocity than ·22 Long Rifle ammunition and a heavier bullet—45 grains. A striking feature of this ammunition is that the bullet and case are of the same diameter, that is, the cartridge case covers the bearing surface of the bullet. *Rifles chambered for these shells cannot chamber standard ·22 ammunition.* Variations on the load, including a bullet weight of 40 grains, have been tried out and it is an ideal game and 'varmint' cartridge, the heavier bullet having a much greater striking energy than standard ·22 Long Rifle ammunition —and a flatter trajectory.

·22 W.R.F. Magnum

THIS cartridge has already been dealt with in an earlier chapter but the illustration on page 216 and table of ballistics for rifles with 24-inch barrels compared to ballistics of other ·22 rim-fire calibre ammunition set out clearly the characteristics of this new cartridge.

Dardo Ammunition

THIS has been dealt with in an earlier chapter and nothing can be usefully added here.

TABLE 3

BALLISTICS OF ·22 MAGNUM RIM-FIRE CARTRIDGE FOR RIFLES WITH 24 IN. BARRELS COMPARED TO BALLISTICS OF OTHER ·22 CALIBRE CARTRIDGES

Cartridge	Velocity at Muzzle (ft per sec.)	Energy at Muzzle (ft/lb)	Energy at 100 yards (ft/lb)
·22 Magnum	2,000	355	170
·22 W.R.F.	1,450	210	123
·22 Long Rifle	1,335	158	97
·22 Long	1,240	99	60
·22 Short	1,125	81	54

·22 Centre-fire Ammunition

BROADLY speaking, ·22 centre-fire ammunition, factory loaded, is limited to ·22 Hornet, ·22 Swift, ·218 Bee, ·219 Zipper and the Remington ·222. There are innumerable varieties of ·22 centre-fire ammunition on the American scene, principally home-loaded and an infinite variety of 'wildcatters'. Of the 'wildcatters', probably the ·22/250 is the most popular. It is made by sizing down the necks of ·250/3000 Savage cases and is a well-balanced, easy-to-load cartridge. In actual fact this cartridge is quite old, being experimented with by Newton in the early part of the twentieth century, but still gives good results, even with a variety of powders and bullet weights and shapes.

Most 'wildcat' centre-fire ·22 ammunition is used by American sportsmen for 'varmint' shooting and also for that highly technical recreation, bench-rest rifle shooting. 'Wildcat' enthusiasts

AMMUNITION

have experimented with an infinite variety of cartridges and the ·303, ·30–40 Krag, 300 Holland and Holland Magnum cases, as well as several others, have all been necked down to ·22 calibre. But, for the average ·22 rifleman these cartridges, especially in Great Britain, are not of general interest or use and in subsequent pages covering ·22 centre-fire ammunition I am restricting myself to ·218 Bee, the ·219 Zipper, the ·22 Hornet and the ·22 Swift.

·219 Zipper

THIS was brought out in May 1937 by the Winchester concern and was developed from the Winchester ·25/35 cartridge which was necked down to ·22 calibre. This was designed for use in the Model 64 Winchester Deer rifle, which was of lever action. Accuracy is from 1·5 to 2·4-inch groups at 100 yards, when fired from the lever action, but this has been improved upon when fired from bolt-action models. This cartridge was not as popular as was expected and in May 1938 Winchester introduced the ·218 Bee.

·218 Winchester Bee

WHEN Winchester introduced this ammunition they chambered their Model 65 lever action rifle for this cartridge. Certainly it proved to be slightly more powerful than the ·22 Hornet but nowhere attained anything like the popularity of the latter. It has proved itself, however, to be a good cartridge but, unfortunately the Model 65 lever-action rifle was just not good enough to get the best out of it and was discontinued. Actions suitable for the Hornet are suitable for the ·218 Bee and it has found a certain amount of popularity in settled regions of the United States where the report is less disturbing to stock and human beings than the large ·22 centre-fire ammunition. Based on the ·25/20 repeater cartridge the ·218 Bee stands up to a considerable amount of repeated reloading.

·22 Hornet

THIS was one of the first of the ·22 centre-fire cartridges and its advent brought about the great interest in experimental loads and 'wildcat' cartridges in the United States which is current today.

Originally the ·22 Hornet hailed from Germany and was known as the 5·6 × 35R *Vierling*. However, though based on improvements to the ·22 W.C.F. cartridge, when it was introduced in 1930 via Springfield Armory, it was not the product of a single experimenter, but the result of first-class team work with the late Captain G. L. Wotkyns, Colonel Townsend Whelen, Captain George A. Woody and Mr A. L. Woodworth.

They experimented with the ·22 calibre Springfield rifle chambered for the ·22 W.C.F. cartridge and as a result of the excellent ballistics obtained it was introduced to Mr Pugsley, a Winchester executive. Winchester continued the development of this cartridge, altered it slightly, and in 1930 put it into commercial production as the Hornet. Incidentally, this should not be confused with the Harwood Hornet which, about 1894, was developed by the well-known experimenter, Reuben Harwood of Somerville, Massachusetts.

With its high-muzzle velocity and adequate striking energy up to 200/250 yards, this is the ideal ·22 centre-fire cartridge for small-game shooting.

Gibson, Ackley, Zoerb and other American enthusiasts experimented with the Hornet, and this ammunition undoubtedly gave birth to the Bee, Zipper, Wasp and other centre-fire ammunition as we know it today.

·220 Winchester Swift

PUT into production in 1935 by Winchester, this cartridge, the result of pioneer work by the late Captain G. L. Wotkyns, created consternation amongst the shooting fraternity. A muzzle velocity exceeding 4,000 feet per second, coupled with a flat trajectory, soon caused sportsmen to try it out against big game. It was some considerable time before it was realized that this cartridge was not suitable for deer and that it was primarily a 'varmint' cartridge. It is a very accurate load and performs well on small game up to 300 yards range. But of paramount importance is the fact that the bullets disintegrate on contact with almost anything they hit, thereby eliminating the danger of richochets. On the other hand, however, should a person be accidentally hit by one of these bullets, the effect would be most probably fatal, or at least bring about horrible wounding.

Against its advantages of super accuracy it suffers from the disadvantage that in densely settled farming areas the loud report is apt to be unpopular.

Remington ·222

THIS was announced in 1950 and has proved itself to be one of the finest all-round small game and vermin cartridges ever manufactured. Ballistically it is better than the ·22 Hornet, it has considerably less velocity than the Swift but, owing to its comparatively low report is ousting the Swift. For varminting, target shooting and at the bench rest, the Remington ·222 has proved itself as a very efficient cartridge. Groups of 1 to 1¼ inches, at 100 yards, can be consistently shot with this ammunition.

Miscellaneous ·22 Cartridges

FROM time to time variations can be met with in the ·22-calibre ammunition. Many of these are merely experimental oddities, others are of real value to the collector.

An interesting cartridge was the ·22 M1895 experimental ammunition. In 1895 the American Government experimented with a ·22 rifle and varieties of ammunition for same. The cartridge cases were rimmed and of the centre-fire variety and the bullets varied in weight from 112 to 120 grains. It is reported that during tests of this ammunition velocities of 2,500/2,600 feet per second were attained. The bullets were Cupro-nickelled steel with a lead core and overall length of the round was 3·471 inches.

·22 Rim-fire Bullets

BULLETS may be made from plain solid lead, from lead alloy wire, or hollow-pointed. Antimony or tin is generally added to lead to make it harder and it is customary to grease or wax coat the bullet for lubricating purposes. The hollow-pointed bullet is, naturally enough, lighter in weight than the solid bullet and, loaded with the same charge of powder, is propelled at a slightly higher muzzle velocity. But, conversely, muzzle energy is lower.

For hunting purposes the hollow-point is to be used, as a solid bullet will drive straight through the game without any shocking effect. This can result in escaping cripples, and crippled or wounded game or vermin is something every sportsman wishes to avoid at all costs. The hollow-point bullet is less likely to ricochet than the solid or fully jacketed bullet and is therefore the only bullet for ·22 rim-fire ammunition for sporting shooting.

The following ballistical tables dealing with leading British and American ammunition, and two of European manufacture show the velocities, striking energy, and trajectories of factory loaded ammunition. Various experimenters have been able to step up velocities, but in actual practice the commercially loaded ammunition is able to produce groups which many a 'wildcat' cartridge cannot even approach.

TABLE 4
Average Ballistics of British ·22 Rim-fire Ammunition

I. Short and Medium Ranges

Type	Bullet weight (grains)	Velocity (ft per sec.) Muzzle	25 yd.	50 yd.	75 yd.	Energy (ft/lb.) Muzzle	25 yd.	50 yd.	75 yd.
Long-Rifle—									
High Velocity	40	1,400	1,272	1,169	1,090	174	144	121	103
Rifle Club	40	1,200	1,114	1,053	1,005	128	110	98	90
Standard	40	1,025	980	938	900	93	85	78	72
Short—									
High Velocity	30	1,150	1,060	996	940	88	75	66	59
Standard	30	925	876	833	791	57	51	46	42

II. Long Ranges

Type	Bullet weight (grains)	Velocity (ft per sec.) 100 yd.	150 yd.	200 yd.	300 yd.	Energy (ft/lb.) 100 yd.	150 yd.	200 yd.	300 yd.
Long-Rifle—									
High Velocity	40	1,036	947	874	749	95	80	68	50
Rifle Club	40	962	885	820	700	82	69	60	43
Standard	40	865	801	741	629	67	57	49	35
Short—									
High Velocity	30	890	—	—	—	53	—	—	—
Standard	30	751	—	—	—	38	—	—	—

Average Ballistics of British ·22 Hornet Centre-fire Ammunition

Bullet weight	Velocity (ft per sec.) Muzzle	100 yd.	Energy (ft/lb.) Muzzle	100 yd.	Max. height of trajectory (in.) over ranges of 50 yd.	100 yd.	200 yd.
45 grains	2,500	2,080	625	430	—	0·8	4·2

AMMUNITION

TABLE 5
DROP IN INCHES—BRITISH RIM-FIRE ·22 AMMUNITION

Type	Bullet weight (grains)	25 yd.	50 yd.	75 yd.	100 yd.	150 yd.	200 yd.	300 yd.
Long-Rifle—								
High Velocity	40	0·6	2·5	6·1	11·4	28·3	55	149
Rifle Club	40	0·8	3·3	7·8	14·5	35·1	67	171
Standard	40	1·1	4·4	10·2	18·7	44·7	84	215
Short—								
High Velocity	30	0·9	3·7	8·7	16·1	—	—	—
Standard	30	1·3	5·5	12·7	23·5	—	—	—

TABLE 6
AVERAGE BALLISTICS OF WINCHESTER ·22 RIM-FIRE AMMUNITION

Cartridge	Bullet weight (grains)	Type	Velocity (ft per sec.) Muzzle	100 yd.	Energy (ft/lb.) Muzzle	100 yd.	Mid-range trajectory 100 yd.
·22 Short	29	Kopperklad	1,125	920	81	54	4·3
	27	Hollow point	1,155	920	80	51	4·2
·22 Long Rifle	40	,,	1,335	1,045	158	97	3·3
Long Rifle HP	37	,,	1,365	1,040	149	86	3·3
Long Rifle	25	No. 12 Shot	—	—	—	—	—
W.R.F. (·22 Rem. Special)	45	Kopperklad	1,450	1,110	210	123	2·7
Inside lubricated							
·22 Short	29	Lead	1,045	—	70	—	5·6
·22 Long Rifle	40	,,	1,145	975	116	84	4·0
Super Match Mark II or EZXS L.R.	40	,,	1,145	975	116	84	4·0
Short (Gallery)	29	(Disintegrating)	1,045	—	70	—	—
	15	,,	1,710	—	97	—	—
Winchester Auto. Inside lubricated	45	Kopperklad	1,055	930	111	86	4·6

Note.—The Kopperklad bullets are wax-coated, the remainder, except ·22 W.R.F. and ·22 Winchester Auto. are lubricated. Kopperklad may be furnished instead with Lubaloy Bullets.

TABLE 7
AVERAGE BALLISTICS OF WINCHESTER AND WESTERN SUPER SPEED AND SUPER X ·22 CENTRE-FIRE AMMUNITION

Cartridge	Bullet weight (grains)	Type of bullet	Velocity (ft per sec.) Muzzle	100 yd.	200 yd.	300 yd.	Energy (ft/lb.) Muzzle	100 yd.	200 yd.	300 yd.
·218 Bee	46	Hollow point	2,860	2,160	1,610	1,200	835	475	265	145
·219 Zipper	56	,, ,,	3,110	2,440	1,940	1,550	1,200	740	465	300
·22 Hornet	45	Soft point	2,690	2,030	1,510	1,150	720	410	230	130
·22 Hornet	46	Hollow point	2,690	2,030	1,150	1,150	740	420	235	135
·220 Swift	48	Pointed soft point	4,110	3,490	2,930	2,440	1,800	1,300	915	635
·222 Remington	50	Soft point	3,200	2,660	2,170	1,750	1,140	785	520	340

TABLE 8
Mid-Range Trajectory (Average) Winchester and Western ·22 Centre-fire Ammunition

Cartridge	Bullet weight (grains)	Type of bullet	Trajectory in inches (Mid-Range)		
			100 yd.	200 yd.	300 yd.
·218 Bee	46	Hollow point	0·7	3·8	11·5
·219 Zipper	56	,, ,,	0·6	2·9	8·3
·22 Hornet	45	Soft point }	0·8	4·3	13·0
·22 Hornet	46	Hollow point }			
·22 Swift	48	Pointed soft point	0·3	1·4	3·8
·222 Remington	50	Soft point	0·5	2·5	7·0

TABLE 9
Average Ballistics of Remington Rim-fire ·22 Ammunition

Cartridge	Bullet		Velocity (ft per sec.)		Energy (ft/lb.)		Mid-range trajectory in./100 yd.
	Weight (grains)	Style	Muzzle	100 yd.	Muzzle	100 yd.	
·22 Short	29	Lead	1,125	920	81	54	4·3
	27	Hollow point	1,155	920	80	51	4·2
·22 Short 'Rocket'	15	Composition	1,710	—	97	—	—
·22 Long Rifle	40	,,	1,335	1,045	158	97	3·3
	36	Hollow point	1,365	1,040	149	86	3·3
·22 W.R.F. (Remington Special)	45	Lead	1,450	1,110	210	123	2·7

Note.—All the above are 'Hi-Speed' loads.

The undermentioned ammunition have Standard Velocity loadings.

Cartridge	Weight (grains)	Style	Muzzle	100 yd.	Muzzle	100 yd.	Mid-range
•22 Short	29	Lead	1,045	810	70	—	—
·22 Short, Gallery Special Spatter-Less	29	,,	1,045	—	70	—	—
·22 Short, Spatter-Less	29	,,	1,045	—	70	—	—
·22 Short, New and Improved Spatter-Less	15	Composition	1,710	—	97	—	—
·22 Long Rifle	40	Lead	1,145	975	116	84	4·0
·22 Winchester Automatic	45	,,	1,055	930	111	86	4·6
·22 Remington Auto-loading	45	,,	920	—	84	—	5·5

TABLE 10
AVERAGE BALLISTICS OF REMINGTON CENTRE-FIRE ·22 AMMUNITION

Cartridge	Bullet Weight (grains)	Bullet Style	Velocity (ft per sec.)				Energy (ft/lb.)			
			Muzzle	100 yd.	200 yd.	300 yd.	Muzzle	100 yd.	200 yd.	300 yd.
·218 Bee Hi-Speed	46	Mushroom	2,860	2,160	1,610	1,200	835	475	265	145
·219 Zipper Hi-Speed	56	,,	3,110	2,440	1,940	1,550	1,200	740	465	300
·22 Hornet	45	,,	2,690	2,030	1,510	1,150	720	410	230	130
	45	Soft point	2,690	2,030	1,510	1,150	720	410	230	130
·220 Swift	48	,, ,,	4,110	3,490	2,930	2,440	1,800	1,300	915	635
·222 Remington Hi-Speed	50	,, ,,	3,200	2,650	2,170	1,750	1,140	780	520	340
	50	Metal cased	3,200	2,650	2,170	1,750	1,140	780	520	340

TABLE 11
AVERAGE MID-RANGE TRAJECTORY OF REMINGTON CENTRE-FIRE ·22 RIFLE AMMUNITION

Cartridge	Bullet Weight (grains)	Bullet Style	100 yd. (in.)	200 yd. (in.)	300 yd. (in.)
·218 Bee Hi-Speed	46	Mushroom	0·7	3·8	11·5
·219 Zipper Hi-Speed	56	,,	0·6	2·9	8·3
·22 Hornet Hi-Speed	45	,,	0·8	4·3	13·0
	45	Soft point	0·8	4·3	13·0
·220 Swift Hi-Speed	48	,, ,,	0·3	1·4	3·8
·222 Remington Hi-Speed	50	,, ,,	0·5	2·5	7·0
	50	Metal cased	0·5	2·5	7·0

TABLE 12
AVERAGE BALLISTICS OF GIULIO FIOCCHI (ITALIAN) ·22 RIM-FIRE AMMUNITION

Cartridge	Bullet weight (grains)	Type of bullet	Instrumental velocity ft per sec. at 10 m. (33 ft)	Energy Energy (ft/lb.)	Penetration at 16 ft in fir wood (in.)
Short 'Training'	27	Copper plated solid lead	984	58	1·732
Short 'Standard'	28	Greased solid lead	853	43	1·457
Short 'Olimpionico'	28	(For automatic competition pistols)	—	—	—
Short 'V 50'	28	Copper plated solid lead	1,230	93	2·953
Short 'Exp.'	25	Expanding hollow point	1,230	88	2·756
Long (High Vel.)	28	Copper plated solid lead	1,230	93	2·441
Long 'Z'	28	Solid (greased)	722	33	0·669
Extra Long	40	,, ,,	1,148	114	4·724
Long Rifle 'Standard'	40	,, ,,	1,082	103	4·331
L.R. 'Ultrasonic'	40	Copper plated solid lead	1,214	127	4·724
L.R. 'Expansive'	36	Hollow point, lead	1,230	123	3·543
L.R. 'Competizione'	40	Solid (greased)	1,066	99	4·330
Auto Winchester	45	Lead (greased)	984	96	2·756
L.R. 'Carb. Beretta' (for Beretta carbines)	40	Solid (greased)	1,000	87	3·937

TABLE 13
AVERAGE BALLISTICS OF NORMA CENTRE-FIRE ·22 AMMUNITION

Cartridge	Bullet weight (grains)	Type	Velocities (ft per sec.)				Energy (ft/lb.)			
			Muzzle	100 yd.	200 yd.	300 yd.	Muzzle	100 yd.	200 yd.	300 yd.
·220 Swift	48	Soft point pointed	4,112	3,610	3,130	2,680	1,870	1,450	1,090	800
·222 Remington	50	,,	3,200	2,660	2,170	1,750	1,140	785	520	340

CHAPTER ELEVEN
FIREARMS CERTIFICATES

EACH week a familiar occurrence takes place in gunsmiths' shops throughout the country. A potential customer enters, looks at a selection of ·22 rifles, generally selects a sporting model, and then is rather put out when the gunsmith enquires about his firearm certificate. Discreet questioning generally elucidates the fact that the potential customer requires the rifle for a little shooting 'at vermin'. In actual fact the weapon is generally fancied for what our American counterparts term 'plinking'. That is, for rough-and-ready shooting at odd targets such as tin cans in the countryside, generally by enthusiastic youngsters.

A lot of confusion exists about a firearms certificate. Many people, even shooting men, believe it may be obtained at a post-office, in the manner of a gun or game licence. The idea of the police authority issuing a certificate or permit appals them for they realize, in their own hearts, that their claim is in reality not fully justified, and they anticipate its refusal.

Many and various are the ruses adopted by applicants when seeking the grant of a permit for a rifle: invariably, unless the sportsman concerned actually has access to sporting shooting proper (in this connexion I am ignoring medium game shooting such as deer stalking) he thinks up that old, threadbare excuse that the rifle is required for 'vermin destruction'.

The great play made about destruction of vermin in recent years in all sections of both specialized and national press, seems the answer to his prayer.

Now let us face the fact that except in depopulated areas, the use of even a rim-fire ·22 rifle for sporting or vermin destruction can spell danger to third parties. Again we must face up to the truth that many of these would-be possessors of rifled arms are not trained riflemen, either through the medium of a recognized club, or through a good private coach; they probably lack any proper facilities for vermin destruction, even by shotguns, and we have again to realize from experience in the shooting field, that the ·22 air rifle, and the shotgun, especially the ·410-calibre, *used in combination with good fieldcraft* are just as effective (with less danger to the public) against furred and feathered vermin as the most accurate ·22 in the hands of an average shot.

The target man, member of a recognized club, is in a different position. When the time comes that he finds it necessary to abandon the club's weapons and purchase one for himself, *he will find the police co-operative*. But he will invariably find that his certificate will be issued permitting the use of the weapon on 'authorized ranges only'. This very effectively precludes him from using it for sporting shooting under the punitive provisions of the statutory enactment in force.

All too often one meets aggrieved individuals who bemoan their inability to obtain a certificate. But an analysis of their arguments generally proves the hollowness of their case.

The person who uses a firearm is subject to the provisions of the Firearms Acts, 1937 and 1965 and the Criminal Justice Act, 1968 which consolidate the provisions of the various Firearms Acts, 1930–6 relating to firearms, imitation firearms and other weapons, and ammunition.

The first and foremost principle underlying the restriction on the acquisition and carrying of firearms is that of public safety. The old argument is always advanced, with a certain amount of truth, that these restrictions cripple the gun trade, that they are liable to lay a nation at the feet of another aggressive one which encourages its citizens to bear arms. It is fallaciously believed in Great Britain that the purpose of the firearms laws is to keep rifles and pistols out of the hands of criminals. If this were true, the Acts would fail immediately, because the unlawful possession or acquisition of a firearm would never deter a criminal so minded; only the law-abiding citizen suffers. The whole essence of the Acts is summed up in two questions which the applicant for a certificate must answer honestly:

(*a*) Has he a *genuine need* for a firearm?

FIREARMS CERTIFICATES

(*b*) Assuming he has a genuine need, would its use be incompatible with public safety?

Sometimes a person who cannot fulfil the conditions for acquiring and using a sporting weapon, joins a rifle club in order to obtain a rifle. His interest lies not in the club itself, but in the possession of a firearm, a point of honour in his mind amounting almost to an obsession. His first blunder is revealed when the user, if the permit is granted, is restricted to approved ranges only. Careful vetting of an applicant by club officials can deter this kind of person from joining.

Unfortunately, in the past, certain chief officers of police in various districts have announced their intention to stop the private ownership of rifles in their areas. This is against the spirit of the Acts and against public interest. It also brings police and public into conflict, so that dictatorial edicts on the one side are met by low cunning on the other, and both sides suffer in consequence. It is only fair to state, however, that, by and large, the police attitude is most reasonable, and they will be found courteous and accommodating.

The Firearms Acts provide that certificates to acquire, hold, or use, rifled barrel weapons and/or ammunition may be issued by the chief officer of police for the area in which the applicant resides. There are certain prohibitions against types of weapons which may be held by private individuals; and there are certain personal disabilities which are a bar against obtaining a certificate.

Section I of Part I of the Firearms Act, 1937 lays down that, subject to the provisions of the Act,

> 'No person shall purchase, acquire or have in his possession any firearm or ammunition to which this part of the Act applies unless he holds a firearms certificate in force at the time.'

Such a certificate is necessary whether one wishes to purchase a firearm subject to the Acts, to borrow it, or even to receive it as a gift.

The Acts apply to any 'lethal-barrelled weapon' which is less than 24 inches in barrel length. This effectively prohibits the sale or acquisition of the deadly 'sawn-off shotgun' or smooth-bore pistol. The Acts apply to any rifle-barrelled weapon irrespective of the length of the barrel. Ammunition containing less than five shot, which must not exceed 9/25th of an inch in diameter, blank cartridges exceeding one inch in diameter are also included. Smooth-bore shotguns, with a barrel length more than 20 inches, and air guns, air rifles and air pistols not being of a type specified by the Secretary of State as being especially dangerous, are exempt from the Acts.

Automatic weapons (as distinct from semi-automatics), machine carbines and weapons capable of discharging noxious gases are prohibited under the Acts, which state:

> 'Firearm ... means any lethal barrelled weapon of any description from which any shot, bullet or other missile can be discharged and includes any prohibited weapon, whether it is such a lethal weapon as aforesaid or not, any component part of any such lethal or prohibited weapon, and any accessory to any such weapon designed or adapted to diminish the noise or flash caused by firing the weapon.'

Reduced to basic English, this provision completely prohibits anyone from fitting a silencer or sound moderator to a weapon, unless he is authorized to do so through a firearms permit. It also prevents a rifleman from obtaining a replacement part for his weapon unless he has authority for that weapon: thus without a permit, he cannot purchase or acquire a rifle barrel even, or other component parts, though the Acts do not refer to such component parts as sights, which do not require permits.

'Prohibited weapons', which really do not concern the law-abiding citizen, are described by the Acts as those, which:

> 'if pressure is applied to the trigger, missiles continue to be discharged until pressure is removed from the trigger or the magazine containing the missiles is empty; or any weapon of whatever description designed or adapted for the discharge of any noxious liquid, gas, or other thing.'

Cartridges for prohibited weapons are also banned. Briefly, tommy-guns and machine carbines, grenade throwers and such nice little weapons are the subject of this section!

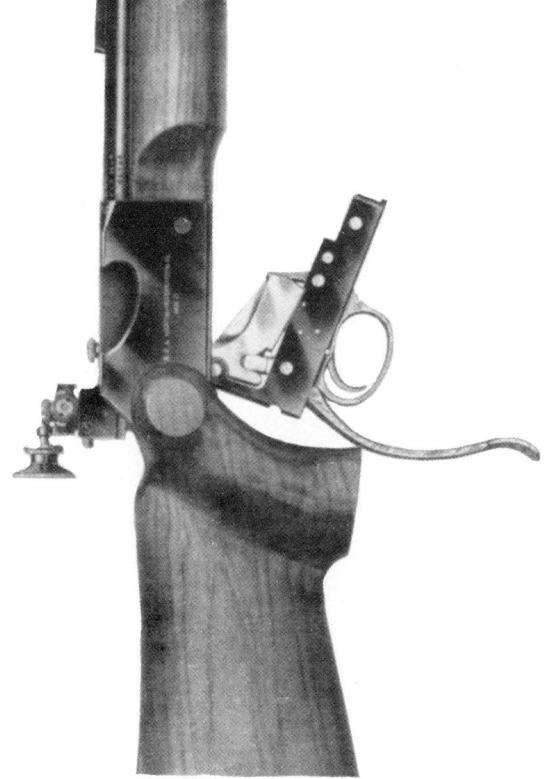

PLATE LVII
B.S.A. Martini action

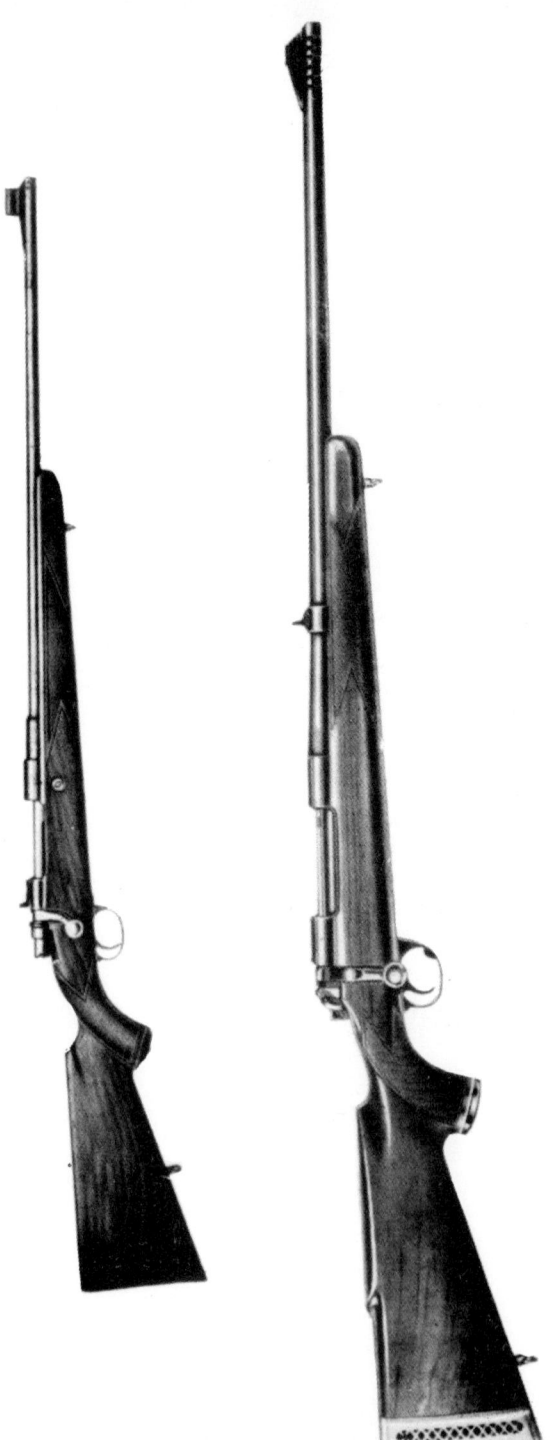

PLATE LVIII

Top—F. N. Mauser sporting rifle—·22 Swift calibre. *Bottom*—B.S.A. short-action, centre-fire ·22 rifle

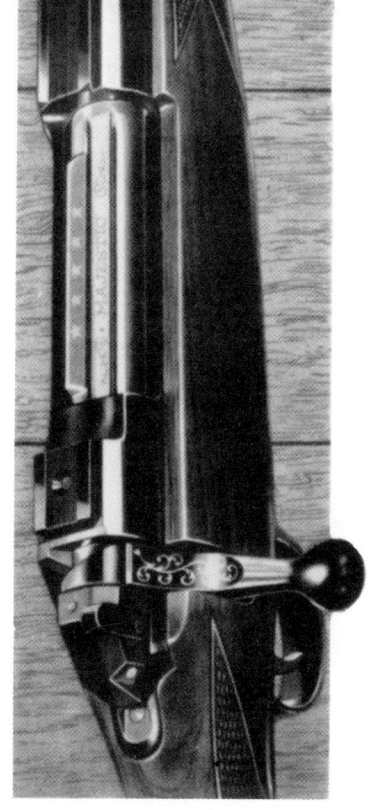

PLATE LIX
Action of B.S.A. 'Majestic' rifle

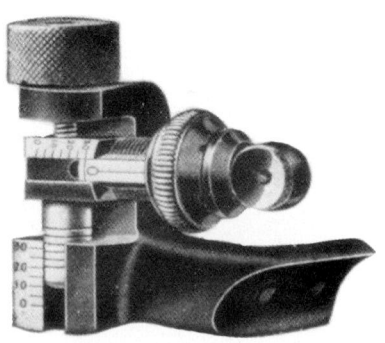

PLATE LX

Top—Parker-Hale 'International' sight.
Bottom—Parker-Hale Receiver aperture sight Model 16

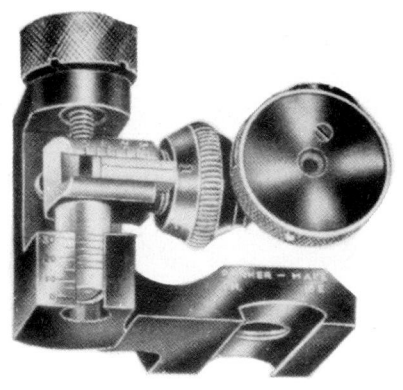

PLATE LXI

Top—Parker-Hale 'Sportarget' receiver sight.
Bottom—Parker-Hale Model 16.E

PLATE LXII

Top—Parker-Hale 18 'Neta' peepsight.
Bottom—Parker-Hale 'Quickloader'

PLATE LXIII

Top—Hammerli 'Olympia' target pistol. *Centre*—Hi-Standard 'Dura-matic' field pistol. *Bottom*—Hi-Standard 'Supermatic Tournament' 10-shot autoloader

PLATE LXIV

Top—Hi-Standard 'Double Nine' ·22 revolver. *Centre*—Hi-Standard snub-barrel 'Sentinel' revolver. *Bottom*—Iver Johnson 'Trailsman 66' ·22 revolver

FIREARMS CERTIFICATES

There are certain exceptions from the necessity of having a firearms certificate for rifles, pistols, and ammunition. The principal exception is, of course, a member of a registered rifle club or cadet corps engaged as such a member in club target practice or drill. The general public when shooting on galleries such as are generally found on fun fairs, do not need a firearms certificate. There are other exceptions concerning auctioneers, 'stalkers' when carrying a sporting weapon for an authorized possessor under instructions of that person, proprietors of slaughterhouses, officials starting races, and in theatrical and cinema filming, but these do not concern either the sportsman or target shooter.

Certain persons are under the disability of not being able to hold a valid firearms certificate for several reasons, typical instances being convicted criminals who are sentenced for a longer term than three months, who are prohibited from purchasing or possessing firearms for five years from the date of their release, or persons of unsound mind, neither of which provisions should apply to readers of this book!

There are restrictions in regard to age. A person under seventeen years of age cannot purchase or hire a firearm or ammunition, nor may a person sell, lend, or hire to such a young person any firearms if he knows or has reason to believe that the person is under seventeen. A person under fourteen cannot legally accept as a gift or loan any firearms or ammunition to which the Acts apply. I am often told by despairing retailers—'It's a heck of a job when the customer says he is seventeen.' To which I advise them, 'Don't ask him his age—that's begging the question—ask him to tell you his birthday date—if he is telling the truth he'll answer without any hesitation whatsoever; if he is lying, then you don't sell him the rifle, or any other weapon.'

It is important that the applicant for a firearms certificate should be aware of these things because, if, in an attempt to try and obtain a firearms certificate for himself or another person he should make a false statement, he becomes liable to the same penalties as those who hold firearms illegally.

Thus, if a person seeking to obtain a firearms certificate represents that he has shooting rights or permission over lands which he describes falsely, he may land in very serious trouble.

Antique firearms, rifles and pistols, are exempt from the Firearms Acts, provided the applicant does not intend to use them. If he wishes to use them and not merely hang them on the wall he has to obtain a police permit.

Penalties under the Acts are pretty tough. If one purchases, acquires or has in his possession any firearm or ammunition to which the Acts apply without having a current firearm certificate authorizing him to do so, or holds excessive ammunition over and above his certificate requirements, or fails to comply with any special conditions of the certificate, the offender will be liable, for each offence, on summary conviction to imprisonment for up to three months, or to a fine not exceeding £50, or to both the fine and the incarceration!

A firearms certificate is obtained through one's local police office. Personal attendance at the police station results in the applicant being handed a form, which he is asked to complete. The exact procedure varies from district to district, depending whether or not the local police have much experience of this sort of thing. If the application is a common one, the procedure goes through smoothly. If, however, it is 'new' to the station concerned, all sorts of little irritations crop up, but which are something and nothing really. One cannot blame the police for exercising caution, though sometimes, to the applicant, a *particular* police officer may *seem* either wooden-headed, or obstructive, or both.

On examination of the application form the applicant will find that, in addition to the usual personal details he must state:

(*a*) Arms and ammunition it is desired to acquire.

(*b*) Amount of ammunition to be purchased at any one time.

(*c*) Amount of ammunition to be held in possession at any one time; and

(*d*) The amount to be purchased in total over a period of three years.

Thus, suppose the rifleman wishes to acquire a ·22 sporting rifle, he would state that fact against (*a*). It is not necessary to state make, or chamber length. Indeed, 'a ·22 rifle' is probably a sufficient description. There is no distinction between a ·22 rim-fire rifle and a ·22 centre-fire rifle, such as the Hornet, so far as this part of the certificate is concerned.

In (*b*) he must consider the *maximum* amount of ammunition he would like to purchase at one time; for example 100 rounds, or 500 rounds.

In (*c*) it is obvious that perhaps he wishes to keep a 'float' of, say, 250 rounds: if he wishes to purchase his 500 in addition at any one time, then the maximum amount authorized to be held at any one time would be 750 rounds.

Paragraph (*d*) causes the most heart-burning because it seems to be a fairly common practice to cut down the amount the applicant suggests. Seriously, if the applicant has a genuine case for shooting, say, grey squirrels and crows, and he accounts for 300 head per annum, he would not apply for 900 or 1,000 rounds. He requires a certain number for practice, he has to allow for a percentage of misses, so that double or even treble the number of kills per annum would be a fair average. His rightful application, in this case, would be for at least 2,000 rounds over the three years.

Having completed the form and given full details of where he is going to use the rifle, he pays a small fee and awaits the result.

Presently a police officer or officers will call at the applicant's home to satisfy themselves that he has a permanent address there and that the weapon and ammunition will be stored securely and no unauthorized person has access to them. In the meantime enquiries will be made to verify his story about shooting grounds and so forth. The police will also make certain in the interests of public safety that the shooting area is not heavily built-up, that there are no roads, footpaths or other places to which the public have access, not only on the shooting ground, but within a dangerous distance of it. His character, it goes without saying, will also be checked.

In normal circumstances, however, the certificate will be delivered personally to the applicant by a police officer. It is very likely that the amount of ammunition requested has been reduced, but, having regard to this possibility the applicant will have asked for as much as possible, but not a ridiculously large amount which would render the whole application suspect.

The certificate remains in force for three years, unless revoked by the chief officer of police, or the applicant surrenders it, or suffers one of the legal disabilities referred to earlier. On expiration of the three years the certificate is renewable on payment of a further fee. If the applicant desires to have the certificate varied there is no fee payable, unless this variation increases the number of weapons which the holder possesses.

That is the simple procedure of obtaining a firearms certificate for sporting purposes. If the applicant has good reasons and a good character, and public safety is not endangered, it is almost certain that his application will be granted. Should the applicant be refused, he has a right to appeal to a court of quarter sessions against the police decision. This appeal takes the form of a notice to the clerk of the peace and to the chief officer of police who has decided against the application. The appeal must be made within twenty-one days of the refusal of the firearms certificate.

The appeal is heard before the court after an interval of at least twenty-one days has elapsed after service of the notice of appeal and at any time up to within forty-eight hours of the date of the case the appellant may abandon his appeal by giving written notice to both the clerk of the peace and the chief police officer. But he may, in these circumstances, be ordered to pay the police costs.

On hearing the appeal the court may either dismiss it, and may grant costs against the applicant: or it may allow the appeal, with such modifications as it considers expedient, and accordingly instruct the chief officer of police concerned to issue the certificate. Even if the application is successful, however, the applicant *cannot* obtain any costs against the police.

It should be remembered, however, that unless there is some outstandingly good reason for such an appeal, the sportsman concerned is advised to swallow his pride, admit the police reasons for the refusal, and avail himself of that other, excellent alternative—the modern air rifle, or take up that sport which is coming into popularity again, the cross-bow!

The club member, however, stands in a much better position than his sporting brother.

Although many shooting men complain about the provisions of

FIREARMS CERTIFICATES

the firearms laws, the club rifleman finds a great deal of pleasure in at least one of their provisions which provide that a member of a rifle club or cadet corps approved by the Secretary of State need not hold a certificate to have in his possession firearms and ammunition *when engaged as such a member in, or in connexion with, drill or target practice*, and it is this section which allows a club member to use club rifles on authorized ranges and to use club ammunition when on club premises.

The relevant passage is, of course, 'approved club'. The club has to be approved by the Secretary of State, and club ranges have to be examined and passed by the War Department before they may be used and, in the interests of public safety, they must conform to certain dimensions. The club has also to receive approval of the Home Office under the Firearms Acts whereupon it becomes entitled to purchase and hold weapons and ammunition for the use of its members.

With regard to firearms certificates for clubs, though sometimes a local police chief will prefer, probably for personal prestige reasons, to issue a free firearms certificate, the approved clubs under the aegis of the N.S.R.A. are expected to maintain in lieu of a firearms certificate and by virtue of the official recognition of their approved status a Register of Firearms and a register of members. It goes without saying that the N.S.R.A. sponsors its affiliated clubs with these applications.

If a sportsman is a member of such a club, which either has its own authorized range, or has permission to use an authorized range, he has little difficulty in obtaining a Firearms Certificate for his own private target rifle, unless he should be under a legal disability. Such a disability occurs in respect of age. Youngsters under seventeen years of age are not allowed to own firearms, but it is the policy of the N.S.R.A. to encourage juniors, provided they are physically capable of holding and handling, in safety, a rifle, and they permit them to shoot on their ranges under the personal supervision of an adult official, who remains with them on the firing point throughout the whole period of the tuition. It is possible to get the parent of the junior, or his legal guardian, to apply for a firearms certificate for the weapon, and then apply to the police for an additional certificate allowing the junior (under seventeen) to hold it 'on loan'.

Because a person is a member of an approved club he is not automatically entitled to purchase ammunition, and in the absence of a firearms certificate to take it home. This is a very serious offence and a grave breach of club rules. Possession of ammunition so obtained, if discovered, would undoubtedly lead to a prosecution, almost certainly to expulsion. A prosecution was reported where a person had properly and legally transferred a firearm to another authorized person, and *cancelled* his certificate, unfortunately he retained, albeit through an oversight, some ammunition.

There is sometimes a little confusion over the description of 'authorized' ranges. Any person in his own dwelling may construct a private range, though he would need a firearms certificate to use a rifle or pistol on it, unless the weapon were an air gun or air rifle.

To overcome any difficulties in the matter I would recommend that if any person is requiring legal information about a firearms certificate, the sportsman concerned should never approach the local police first on this point, but consult his legal adviser in the first instance. Sometimes, as we can see in matters appertaining to motor vehicles, police and magistrates in one district may have a different interpretation of matters elsewhere, and it is not profitable to save a pound or so on legal advice and end up in real trouble.

Quite recently, when this book was started, a friend of mine who had purchased an air rifle for the purposes of rook shooting, put in a little practice in his garden. The garden is high-walled and only by pointing the barrel of the rifle at an angle of more than 45 degrees could a shot be sent over it from the extreme end of the garden. Presently, after a few Sunday mornings' practice, a young police constable arrived on the scene and said: 'Are you shooting in your garden?' On being informed it was so, he said, heavily, with great *authority*, though pleasantly, 'Well, I have to advise you that you are breaking the law.'

My friend, mindful of my advice, was pleasant to him, but mentally decided to ignore the constable's dictum. His brother, however, who also used the garden for target practice, decided to

FIREARMS CERTIFICATES

seek further advice from the police station. In due course a couple of police officers arrived at the house and solemnly informed him that it would be in order to use the air rifle for shooting rats, but if he so much as shot at a paper target, he was committing an offence because the range had not been passed by the War Office!

It is this attitude which causes the rifleman to adopt subterfuges in order to obtain a firearm certificate, when all the time his rights are apparent. All in all, however, there is little complaint so far as the genuine applicant is concerned, provided he is not put off by this attitude of certain members of an otherwise excellent organization. It is in circumstances like these that I advise the rifleman to consult his lawyer: every time a retreat is made in face of wrong advice, tendered by a police officer and however well meant, the Firearms Acts have been evaded, the cause of rifle shooting has been defeated, and the individual concerned has been given just cause to cavil against 'Authority'.

In addition to other literature, the rifleman should acquire a copy of the Firearms Acts. After all, every man is presumed to know the law, ignorance thereof never being an excuse—and a perusal of its provisions may well prevent heartburning later.

Though we Britishers have the finger of scorn pointed towards us by riflemen in the U.S.A. as a horrible example of what happens when firearms are registered and control of them exercised, none the less we stand in a much better position than the American. True, he is not very restricted in the matter of acquiring rifles and handguns, but, heavens above, the multitude of laws and restrictions which bedevil him from State to State! What is legal in one is illegal in another and when you consider the position in New York under the 'Sullivan Laws', you must recognize a greater freedom in acquisition of certain types of firearms and ammunition over here. So far as the 'Sullivan Laws' are concerned, it would appear that the law-abiding person has little chance of getting a weapon unless he is able to do a little corruption first!—my American friends tell me that the only people who are able to get weapons are the cops and the crooks— and the latter often get them 'legally' after deals with crooked cops!

Of course, there are those in Great Britain, who think we have too much freedom with firearms: there is a noisy minority who want to include air guns in the Firearms Acts, they wish to add shotguns to its provisions, they want to ban rim-fire ·22 sporting rifles, and so on. We have to be on our guard against this whittling away of rights or else we may stand in a similar position to our New York cousins. Restrictions do not prevent crimes—crooks get hold of, or make, weapons without any regard to the law. As a matter of fact, restrictive laws handicap the law-abiding and assist the crooked. So far as accidents are concerned, legislation cannot prevent them, and the remedy lies in education and training. The more restrictions there are, the less education there will be, and the *ratio* of accidents to firearms must, under those circumstances increase in the long run.

As they stand, in Great Britain, properly interpreted, one cannot quarrel with the present legislation. Now and again there are 'hard cases', but, as the lawyers tell us, 'Hard cases make bad law'. By and large the present rules here, subject to one or two 'difficult' self-opinionated chief constables, whose attitude is to bend the administration of the Firearms Acts, are sensible and satisfactory. Let's keep them that way.

In the United States, throughout the various States, firearms bills are being introduced continually and the National Rifle Association out there has to be extremely vigilant. Not all legislation proposed is abolitionist, however, and some of it is well-intended. Let us take a look at the latter kind of legislation, which may well, some day come into operation over here.

In the State of Maine, in 1953, Mr Fred Wadleigh proposed under Maine House Bill No. 1083 that 'each student attending a high school or secondary school shall receive not less than two hours of instruction annually in the safe use of firearms.' The bill, as drawn, provided that such instruction should be given by teachers certified as competent by the National Rifle Association of America. Range and equipment were to be provided by the school and the ammunition used was to be supplied by the department of the Adjutant-General for the State. Its weakness lay in the fact that two hours instruction a year is barely sufficient time in which to give proper training, but it is a step on the right lines. On the other side, consider, for example, the State of

FIREARMS CERTIFICATES

Colorado seeking to introduce legislation in which licence applications for firearms would include photographs and fingerprints of the applicant!

Again, the State of California, during the same period, saw a suggested bill, Assembly Bill No. 3469, which proposed that a hunting licence would not be given to any one under eighteen who had not previously held a licence unless he produced a certificate of safe handling of firearms signed by a competent instructor. On the opposite side of the fence the State of Delaware, under Senate Bill No. 19, saw a suggestion that except in self-defence it would be an offence to discharge any type of *air gun* in any residential area of the State. This would have prohibited even indoor range work.

But these restrictionists operate on both sides of the Atlantic and are always ready to try out their pet fads and ideas. Fortunately, they have already announced their intentions in some way or another and the great body of responsible riflemen is ready to deal with them: but the restrictionists will always be with us and the sportsman must ever be ready to fight them if his recreation is to survive.

CHAPTER TWELVE

AIR RIFLES AND PISTOLS

THOUGH most people would tend to think of the ·22 calibre weapon as a firearm, the fact remains that the ·22 calibre is also popular for air rifle shooting. I will not deal with the ·177 calibre air weapon here, as, although it is the recognized target weapon for club match shooting, due to its cheaper ammunition, high muzzle velocity and flat trajectory, the subject of this book is essentially about the ·22 inch weapon.

The air weapon has a long history, and in the eighteenth and nineteenth centuries was used for sniping in warfare as well as for hunting buck and small game. The weapons were charged by means of a pump into a reservoir and they fired a large bullet or slug with considerable power. They were heavy, however, and often gave trouble with valves, whilst it was not unknown for reservoirs to burst!

Today the modern air rifle and air pistol are highly sophisticated weapons. Certainly for both short-range precision shooting and sporting shooting in the field they fill a need, for the ammunition is cheap and the 'danger area', or bullet range, is considerably reduced. However, air weapons are extremely accurate. They are smokeless and, for all practical purposes, silent, and they are easy to clean and maintain. For target shooting, only lightweight backstops are required and it is easy to convert any large room, shed or gymnasium, for example, into an air rifle or pistol shooting range in a few minutes, and equally so to remove the bullet stops etc. and to allow the area to revert to its normal usage.

Because the pellet is the sole ammunition, there are no problems of empty cartridge cases to collect; moreover, no firearm certificate is necessary for the purchase, storage or use of the ammunition.

However, there are certain legal restrictions on the acquisition and use of air weapons and in this respect I must draw attention to the provisions of the Firearms (Dangerous Air Weapons) Rules which came into effect in 1969. Under these Rules certain air weapons are now subject to Section 1 of the Firearms Act, 1968, and therefore subject to the obtainment of a firearms certificate. The Rules are restricted to air weapons which have a high power output and include air weapons of the 'pump' type, whereby through the use of a pumping action high velocity can be obtained. Air pistols with a kinetic energy in excess of 6 foot-pounds and other air weapons with kinetic energy in excess of 10 foot-pounds are considered to be dangerous within the restrictions of the Rules.

Again, there are provisions under the Firearms Acts which restrict the user and possession of air weapons. The provisions of the Air Guns and Shot Guns Act of 1962 prohibit any person under fourteen from accepting any air weapon or its ammunition as a gift, and contain an absolute prohibition against any person giving such weapons or ammunition to a child under fourteen years old.

No one under fourteen is entitled to have in his or her possession any air weapon or air weapon ammunition; no one can legally part with possession of either arm or ammunition to a person under fourteen unless that young person is under the supervision of a person of twenty-one years of age or over. No one under seventeen years of age is allowed to have an air weapon in his or her possession in any public place unless it is an air gun or rifle secured within a properly fastened gun cover so that it cannot be fired. But he is prohibited from carrying any air pistol in a public place whether or not it is secured in a proper cover.

Types of Air Weapon

THERE are three main types of air weapon: those operated through a spring, those which use a pump and reservoir, and those which use a compressed air or gas cartridge or cylinder. However, for practical use in the United Kingdom one is confined to the spring-operated type which is divided into two classes: those known as barrel-cocking types, and those classified as underlever-cocking types.

Barrel-cocking air weapons

IN these arms a powerful spring, or springs, operates a piston or plunger which is compressed manually. The compressed spring is held by a sear or trigger mechanism and when the trigger is pressed the spring is released, compressing the air ahead of it. The compressed air is directed through a small port behind the pellet and provides enough energy to drive it along the barrel and out of the muzzle at velocities of up to 600 feet per second or thereabouts. It should be noted that only the compressed air acts as a propellant and that the piston is never in contact with the pellet.

Because an air pistol uses shorter springs, which develop less power, it is less powerful than rifles and air shotguns, which latter have less power than rifles because they discharge a shot charge and not a single pellet.

In the barrel-cocking types the act of opening the barrel first exposes the breech for loading; subsequently the forcing down of the barrel on its pivot operates the levers which move the piston and compress the spring which operates it. After the spring has been compressed the sear or trigger (depending on the design of the weapon) engages the piston and holds it cocked, ready for firing. The pellet can now be inserted into the breech and seated, after which the barrel is snapped shut: the weapon is now ready for firing by pulling the trigger.

The earlier type of models using this action often suffered from loss of power through air leaks at the breech, and damaged barrels through bending when cocking were not infrequent. However, the modern barrel-cocker is strong, reliable and possesses great power.

Excellent air rifles on the barrel-cocking principle are made by B.S.A. and Webley & Scott, in this country, as are those manufactured by Millard Brothers under the trade name of 'Diana'. Europe, principally Germany and Czechoslovakia, produces some excellent barrel-cockers and I have for many years (twenty-odd in fact) regularly used a German 'Original' Model 35B for target practice and small vermin destruction. Throughout its life (and it will fire many thousands of rounds yet) it has proved strong, accurate and reliable. Indeed, of the many air weapons I have tested, I have found this to be the equal in power and accuracy of the more elaborate underlever action models.

Underlever-cocking Models

IN these models the cocking lever is contained in the forearm of the weapon, below the barrel. It is operated by pulling the cocking lever out of its seat and down against the piston spring to full cock. But the principle of barrel-cock and underlever-cock action is the same! It is in the loading procedure that the models differ. In the barrel-cocker the breech of the barrel is exposed and the pellet is inserted directly into this. This is not possible in the underlever model as, usually, the barrel and cylinder are of solid frame design which necessitates the use of a top-loading plug or tap which has a pellet cavity into which the slug is dropped. When the loading plug is closed it provides an airtight seal behind the pellet.

B.S.A., Webley & Scott, and Millard manufacture excellent and powerful air rifles in this style and from the Continent we also import very expensive underlever air rifles chiefly of the match or competition type.

Comparison of the Two Types

THE underlever scores primarily on the easier cocking it allows and the greater strength and rigidity it ensures. However, for ease of loading the barrel-cocker is way ahead of the underlever types and, from a *safety* angle, I prefer the barrel-cocker as it is easier to check whether or not the breech contains a pellet. As for accuracy, price for price, there is little or nothing to choose between the two types. However, in Great Britain the underlever models are manufactured with more power than the barrel-cocker; on the Continent, on the other hand, there is not this discrimination and German barrel-cockers are just as good (in so far as power and precision are concerned) as their equivalent underlever models. Some countries, such as Spain, offer only very low-power barrel-cockers and the United States of America concentrates on pneumatic and gas-operated guns.

Air Pistols

THE power of air pistols is considerably less than that of the air rifle, but they offer a challenge in that they demand a greater degree of skill to shoot them. In so far as the British air pistol is concerned, there is only one model, the Webley & Scott, which is produced in Junior, Mark I and Senior ranges. The Mark I and Senior are the only models which affect us as they are available in ·22 calibre and have a velocity of approximately 310–330 feet per second. These are extremely precise weapons and have a normal accurate range of 1 inch at 30 feet. They are of excellent quality and have been regarded as the 'royalty' of air pistols throughout the world. The barrel acts as a cocking lever and this has proved to be one of the most efficient systems ever invented.

The Webley is built to last a lifetime, yet not built to give excessive power. High power is not required for two reasons: firstly, it could contravene the Rules referred to earlier and secondly high power is not necessary for shooting at the short ranges at which pistol matches take place. From the Continent, however, there are very fine air pistols which handle, and look, like firearms. But, invariably, the pistols are supplied in ·177 calibre only. However, I have used a German 'Original' target pistol in ·22 calibre which is extremely accurate and a delight to use. It operates on the direct barrel cocking system and is built to a very high standard.

The U.S.A. manufactures a number of spring-operated air pistols which seem to be motivated by repeating arm ideals! but they do not cater for the high-precision match field as we do in Europe.

Shooting with Air Weapons

FIRSTLY, one must limit oneself to a maximum of 10 metres for air pistol shooting because of the limits of power and accuracy common to these models. With powerful air rifles, however, shooting can take place up to 50 metres or even more, but for really excellent target shooting the 25 yards range is first class.

However, shooting with a spring-operated air weapon is vastly different from shooting with a firearm. In the first instance, contrary to firearm shooting procedure, an air rifle should be fired

AIR RIFLES AND PISTOLS

with as little shoulder support as possible. When the trigger is released the piston springs forward to compress the air ahead of it and this means that a recoil action has commenced before the pellet has even started to move along the barrel! In fact, this is the exact opposite to what happens with firearms. Care must be exercised in shooting after the arm has been oiled, as a 'diesel' effect can be obtained which exerts considerable influence on the power and velocity of the pellet.

It is advisable to start the slug or pellet by pushing it into the breech so as to engage in the rifling (this is possible only in barrel-cockers of course), the purpose being to decrease the starting distance to the air pressure behind it.

The effect of wind on the small, light slug must be borne in mind when shooting out-of-doors, as even a light wind may move a pellet as much as 6 inches out of line over a distance of 50 yards.

When using the air weapon as a sporting arm, and there is no reason why it should not be so used, the heavier ·22 pellet should be employed and the use restricted to what are, basically, small pests such as rats, crows and so forth. The target must be the head of the animal or bird and it is advisable to keep the maximum range to about 40 yards.

I find that as a good field practice weapon the air rifle enables one to enjoy what the Americans call 'plinking'. Because of the smaller range of the pellets it is possible to practise shooting at small targets, and snap shooting etc., without being a danger to stock or folk in the hinter-range. It is surprising that the habits of loose-shoulder mounting practised with the air rifle are forgotten when one turns to the firearm, for one uses the firearm in the correct manner. But it does keep one's eye in and it is by constantly shooting whenever and as often as possible which is so important if one is going to be a safe and efficient shooting man.

No one need scorn or look down on the air-rifle or air-pistol enthusiast, for it takes a lot of skill to shoot with precision at even the shortest of indoor ranges. The air-rifle match man is to rifle shooting what the expert roach fisherman is in the world of angling because, let's face it, unless one can shoot consistently and with accuracy at the shorter ranges, how the dickens can one expect to cope with the greater distances?

In conclusion, the same rules of safe gun handling, cleaning, maintenance and consideration for others apply equally well to air weapons and firearms: the man behind the rear sight and the spirit in which he approaches it are what really matter. Every shooting man is an ambassador for his sport, a sport which is often under fire by critics in the 'sex-obsessed' popular daily and Sunday nationals, and any stupidity or selfishness or illegal act by ·22 rifleman, pistoleer or airgun enthusiast, can bring about more restrictions and less shooting. So, in the vernacular phrase—'Watch it!'

INDEX

Adaptors, 44, 45
Air weapons, 207, 246–52
Ammunition
  centre-fire, 23, 31, 35, 197, 216, 220–4
  rim-fire, 23, 25, 26, 32, 197, 216, 220–2, 224
Ammunition (types)
  1. Rim-fire
    BB cap, 23, 26, 27–9, 209–11
    CB cap, 29, 209, 211
    Short, 31, 216, 220–2, 224
    Long rifle, 61, 197, 216, 220–2, 224
    Extra long, 62
    Magnum, 60, 216
  2. Centre-fire
    ·218 Bee, 216, 217, 221–3
    ·219 Zipper, 189, 216, 217, 221–3
    ·22 Hornet, 61, 217, 220–3
    ·220 Swift, 216, 218, 221–4
    ·222 Remington, 42, 189, 219, 221–4
Anschutz rifle, 72
Aperture sights, 142, 148, 150, 173

Ballistics of ·22 ammunition, 216, 220–4
Bausch & Lomb telescope sights, 157
Beaufoy, Col., 91
Bedding of rifle barrel, 133–4
Bench-rest groups, measurement of, 190
Bench-rest shooting, 188–90
Bolt action, 33, 75
British Pistol Club, 113
BRNO rifles, 72
Browning rifles, 72
BSA rifles, 72, 73, 76, 248, 249
Buck fever, 193–6

Buehler, Maynard P., 158
Bullets, 219–20

Celanese Corporation of America, 60
Centre-fire ammunition (*see* Ammunition, centre fire)
Colt, Col. Samuel, 27
Colt rifles and handguns, 112
Critics of ·22, 70
'Custom' rifles, 76, 163

Dardick, David, 59
Dardick arms and ammunition, 58–60
Double-action handguns, 111
Double rifles, 93
Dunlap, Ray, 209
du Pont, 35, 48

Earp, Wyatt, 119
Electrical bedding, 134, 140
Eye relief, 157–8

Falling-block action, 32, 33
Farquharson action, 33
Finnish rifles, 72, 73
Firearms Acts, 42, 226–7, 238, 241, 243, 247
Firearms Certificate, 129, 225–45
Floating chamber, 44
Flobert, M., 26, 27–30
Flobert arms and ammunition, 26–9
Ford, Major Charles, 119
Free-floating barrel, 69
'Free' match pistol, 120

Gallery rifles and shooting, 30
Greener, W., 41
Grouping, 129–32
Groups, 129–32

Hale, A. T. C., 45
Half-scope sights, 160
Hall rifle, 163
Hammerli arms, 72, 112, 120
Hanger, General George, 25
Harrington & Richardson arms, 72, 73
Harwood 'Hornet', 35
Harwood, Reuben, 35
Historical outline of ·22, 23–45
Hunting pistols, 124–5

International Shooting Union (ISU), 84, 109, 123
Ithaca 'Raybar' sights, 146

Jennings system, 27

Kentucky rifle, 25
Kneeling position, 98–108

Lancaster, Charles, 36, 43
Lever action, 74
Lyman sights, 143, 145, 150, 155, 157, 159, 161

Marlin arms and ammunition, 47, 61
Martini action, 32–3, 41
Mauser action, 75
Maynard arms, 31, 35
Metallic sights, 144 *et seq.*
Micro-groove rifling, 46–7, 61
Morris tube, 32, 34, 41, 45
Mossberg arms and sights, 61, 156, 165

National Pistol Meeting, 123
National Small-bore Rifle Association, 113–14, 160, 176, 190, 192, 241
Needle-fire system, 26
Newton, Charles, 25–36, 43
Niedner, A. O., 35

Off-hand shooting, 86–93, 94–6
Offset sights, 162–76

Open-chamber system, 58
Oval rifling, 36, 43

Palm-rest, 95–6, 98
Parallex, 162
Parker-Hale, 44–5, 150, 158, 160
Pauly, M., 26
Pennsylvania rifles, 25
Police restrictions on pistol ownership, 113–14
Prone position, 79–85

Rapid fire matches, 111, 119–20, 122
Redfield sights, 150, 173
Remington arms and ammunition, 42, 48, 57–8, 213, 215, 216, 219, 222–3
Rising-block action, 76
Ruger handguns, 61, 112
Russian arms, 63, 73, 74, 110, 120

Savage Arms Co., arms and ammunition, 36, 63
Schuetzen rifle, 64
Scoffern, Dr J., 92
Semi-scope sights, 160
Shooting positions, 79–109
Sights, general, 142–75
Sitting position, 79, 108–9
Smith & Wesson arms, 27
Split-chamber system, 59
Standing position, 79, 86–93, 94
Sullivan Laws, 243

Target rifle, requirements of, 71–2
Target shooting, 176–96
Telescope sights, 142–3, 154
Thumb-hole stock, 95–7
Trigger test, 72
'Tround' ammunition, 58–60
Tube sight, 152

Walther arms, 113, 181
Weaver telescope sight, 156–8
Webley & Scott arms, 110, 112, 248, 250

INDEX

Westley Richards, 33
Whelan, Col. Townsend, 218
White, Rollin, 28
Whitworth, Sir Joseph, 189–90
'Wildcat' ammunition, 33–4, 42, 189, 220

Williams Gun Sight Co., 148–51
Williams, Marshall, 44
Winchester arms and ammunition, 30, 33, 60–2, 64, 69–70, 214–15, 217, 221–2
Wotkyns, Capt. G. L., 218